W9-ANQ-364

A-Z of Annuals, Biennials & Bulbs

Staff for Successful Gardening (U.S.A.)
Editor: Fiona Gilsenan
Senior Associate Editor: Carolyn T. Chubet
Art Editor: Evelyn Bauer
Art Associate: Martha Grossman
Editorial Assistant: Joanne M. Wosahla

Contributors
Editor: Thomas Christopher
Editorial Assistant: Tracy O'Shea
Consulting Editor: Lizzie Boyd (U.K.)
Consultant: Dora Galitzki
Copy Editor: Sue Heinemann
Art Assistant: Antonio Mora

READER'S DIGEST GENERAL BOOKS
Editor in Chief: John A. Pope, Jr.
Managing Editor: Jane Polley
Executive Editor: Susan J. Wernert
Art Director: David Trooper
Group Editors: Will Bradbury, Sally French,
Norman B. Mack, Kaari Ward
Group Art Editors: Evelyn Bauer, Robert M. Grant, Joel Musler
Chief of Research: Laurel A. Gilbride
Copy Chief: Edward W. Atkinson
Picture Editor: Richard Pasqual
Head Librarian: Jo Manning

The credits and acknowledgments that appear on page 176
are hereby made a part of this copyright page.

Originally published in partwork form.
Copyright © 1990 Eaglemoss Publications Ltd.

Based on the edition copyright © 1993
The Reader's Digest Association Limited.

Copyright © 1994 The Reader's Digest Association, Inc.
Copyright © 1994 The Reader's Digest Association (Canada) Ltd.
Copyright © 1994 Reader's Digest Association Far East Ltd.
Philippine Copyright 1994 Reader's Digest Association Far East Ltd.

All rights reserved.
Unauthorized reproduction, in any manner, is prohibited.

Library of Congress Cataloging in Publication Data

A-Z of annuals, biennials & bulbs.
        p.   cm. — (Successful gardening)
    ISBN 0-89577-584-0 — ISBN 0-89577-923-4(pbk.)
    1. Annuals (Plants) — Encyclopedias   2. Biennials (Plants) —
Encyclopedias.   3. Bulbs — Encyclopedias.   I. Reader's Digest
Association.   II. Title: A-Z of annuals, biennials, and bulbs.
    III. Title: Annuals, biennials & bulbs.   IV. Series.
SB422.A2 1994
635.9'31'03—dc20   93-37667

READER'S DIGEST and the Pegasus logo are registered trademarks of
The Reader's Digest Association, Inc.

Printed in the United States of America

Opposite: Summer colors spill from baskets of trailing nasturtiums,
lobelias, and petunias.

Overleaf: Early spring bulbs that defy the weather, these miniature
narcissi keep company with wood anemones.

Pages 6-7: Bedding tulips raise their straight-stemmed golden bowls
above a carpet of purple dark-eyed pansies.

THE READER'S DIGEST ASSOCIATION, INC.
Pleasantville, New York / Montreal

A-Z of Annuals, Biennials & Bulbs

CONTENTS

Half-hardy annuals Petunias and pelargoniums revel in sunny, sheltered spots.

A–Z of annuals and biennials

Annuals flower just once, yet their ability to grow quickly from seed and their magnificent array of bright colors have earned them an affectionate place in every gardener's heart. Many of our most popular annuals (including petunias, begonias, marigolds, and asters) originated from tropical climates and are half-hardy or even tender throughout most of the United States; they do not tolerate even a touch of frost, and the growth of truly tender species is stunted by chilly nights. The seeds of these plants are best started indoors in sterile seed-starting mix, and warmth is essential for the seeds to germinate and the seedlings to grow steadily. Your extra care is repaid, however, by long-lasting, brilliant displays of flowers.

Hardy annuals such as coreopsis, sunflowers, and sweet peas are much less trouble, sprouting readily from seed sown directly into the garden. They ask little more than decent soil, a sunny or lightly shaded site, weed-free surroundings, and an adequate supply of water.

Whether hardy or half-hardy, annuals are the faithful standbys of many gardeners, filling gaps in beds and borders, providing cut flowers for the house, and dying away without fuss at the end of the season.

Biennials develop only roots and leaves during their first year of growth, deferring their flowers until the second year. Like annuals, biennials are essential inhabitants of flower beds and borders. Wallflowers, forget-me-nots, and polyanthus primroses appear in spring. Summertime brings to bloom such all-time favorites as Canterbury bells, hollyhocks, and foxgloves.

ANNUAL EVENTS

Easy to grow from seed, annuals come in all colors and sizes, offering a chance to try new combinations every year.

There are so many annuals with so many different habits and such variation in size that their uses are limited only by imagination. Choose from true annuals, ranging from the 8 ft (240 cm) tall sunflower to the 3 in (7.5 cm) high sweet alyssum; sturdy biennials; and tender perennials treated as annuals.

Popular annuals, such as marigolds, lobelias, and ageratums, are widely used in summer beds or containers and window boxes. They can be bought in flats or packs, but seeds are much cheaper than plants and provide a far greater range of cultivars.

Dozens of annuals are suitable for the less formal mixed border. Sow them in gaps between perennials or in the spaces left by spring bulbs. Treat them as temporary features, useful until their partners have reached maturity, or resow them yearly to become part of the overall design.

Many of the old-time annual favorites — corn cockles, cornflowers, corn marigolds, and field poppies — came into horticulture as weeds in farmers' fields. They still retain much of their vigor, which means that they not only are beautiful but also require little or no care.

Annual climbers, such as sweet peas, morning glories, and canary bird vines *(Tropaeolum peregrinum),* provide quick and cheap decoration for fences and walls.

For tropical foliage color effects, sow castor-oil plants *(Ricinus),* coleuses, and kochias.

▲ **Cottage-garden favorite** The biennial Canterbury bells *(Campanula medium)* rings its bells over a pale blue sea of love-in-a-mist *(Nigella damascena).* Both are summer flowering and self-seed readily for future years.

▼ **Late-summer border** Dainty-leaved pink and white cosmos and sweet-scented nicotianas dominate a border fronted with bedding dahlias and perennial cerise-scarlet *Sedum spectabile* (syn. *Hylotelephium spectabile)* and silvery *Artemisia.*

◄ **Subtle companionship** The amiable nasturtium *(Tropaeolum majus)* is an easy annual to grow. It is a well-known fact that it bears the best and most profuse flowers in poor ground. In rich soil it tends to produce fewer blooms and more of its characteristic pale green rounded leaves — providing a good foil for bright scarlet snapdragon spikes *(Antirrhinum majus),* which can easily overwhelm a summer bed.

▼ **Summer riot** Annuals may have only one flowering season, but they more than compensate for their short life with a kaleidoscope of colors. It is impossible to ignore the impact of this carefully planned study in red, all achieved from dormant seeds in less than 4 months. Towering above the group, love-lies-bleeding *(Amaranthus caudatus)* droops its long wine-red flower tassels over spikes of carmine-pink double-flowered clarkias and clumps of scarlet flax *(Linum grandiflorum).* At their feet, nasturtiums *(Tropaeolum majus)* spread an orange-red carpet of spurred trumpet flowers.

▲ **Blue daisies** The kingfisher daisy *(Felicia bergerana)* is aptly named, for its flowers are steel-blue and borne in such profusion throughout summer that they smother the dwarf plants. South African in origin, it revels in a hot and sunny spot, spilling over the edge of a border, raised bed, or window box, perhaps combined with fragrant white-flowered sweet alyssum.

◀ **Summer brightness** The pale green feathery lushness of summer cypress (*Kochia scoparia*, now classified as *Bassia scoparia*) gives no indication of its rich fall dress of crimson-purple. In midsummer, carefully placed mounds give substance to the floating blue flowers of love-in-a-mist (*Nigella damascena*) and the sprawling golden-flowered *Mentzelia lindleyi*.

▼ **Harmony in blue** Half-hardy by nature, these two annuals revel in sun and each other's company. The multiflora petunia cultivars are more weather resistant than their larger-flowered counterparts, with elegant trumpets shielding tight clusters of lavender-blue *Ageratum houstonianum*.

▶ **Annual grasses** The misty froth of grasses such as *Agrostis nebulosa* (cloud grass) brings an aura of tranquillity to the vibrant tones of many annuals. The cloud grass also adds height to a low-growing composition. Moreover, its branched flower clusters retain their grace and charm if cut and dried for winter arrangements.

▶ **Meadows of yesteryear** Herbicides have eliminated the old wildflowers (most of them actually of European origin) that once flourished in farmers' fields and contributed to much of the charm of the American countryside. However, many blends of wildflower seeds include these nostalgic blossoms — plants such as corn marigolds *(Chrysanthemum segetum)* and delicate-looking but tough corn poppies *(Papaver rhoeas)* or blue cornflowers *(Centaurea).* If sown in a sunny corner, they provide swaths of color and a bit of old-time charm.

Adonis
pheasant's eye

Adonis aestivalis

- ❏ Height 1-1½ ft (30-45 cm)
- ❏ Planting distance 1 ft (30 cm)
- ❏ Flowers early summer to midsummer
- ❏ Sunny or partially shaded site
- ❏ Any humus-rich soil
- ❏ Hardy annual

Pheasant's eye *(Adonis aestivalis)* is the only member of this small genus grown as an annual. The cup-shaped flowers, which appear in early summer to midsummer, have deep crimson petals and near-black stamens. The plant grows 1-1½ ft (30-45 cm) high, with fine green fernlike leaves.

For best effect, plant in clusters at the front of a border with other annuals and biennials. It also grows well in containers.

Cultivation
For early flowers, sow the seeds in a seedbed in their final site in fall. After germination, thin the seedlings to 6 in (15 cm) apart and then, the following spring, to 1 ft (30 cm).

Alternatively, sow the seeds in flats indoors in spring and transplant to the final site in late spring, setting the seedlings 1 ft (30 cm) apart. You can also sow the seeds directly in the final flowering site in spring and thin out the seedlings, but flowering will be slightly later.

Pests/diseases Keep an eye out for slugs.

AFRICAN DAISY — see *Arctotis*
AFRICAN MARIGOLD —
see *Tagetes*

Ageratum
flossflower

Ageratum houstonianum 'Blue Hawaii'

- ❏ Height ½-2 ft (15-60 cm)
- ❏ Planting distance for dwarf cultivars 9 in (23 cm); for taller cultivars, 1 ft (30 cm)
- ❏ Flowers early summer to first severe frost
- ❏ Any moisture-retentive soil
- ❏ Sheltered, sunny or lightly shaded site
- ❏ Half-hardy annual

An abundance of flowers and a long season — from early summer until the first severe frost — make *Ageratum* a popular bedding plant. Its low, compact habit and its powder-puff flowers look most effective edging formal beds, filling gaps in borders of low-growing plants or brightening window boxes and containers. Some of the taller cultivars are useful for flower arranging, combining well with many other garden plants.

The original blue-flowered species, *Ageratum houstonianum,* has largely been replaced by garden cultivars. These come in blue, pink, purple, and white.

The F1 hybrids are first-generation plants obtained by crossing two cultivars known for their ability to produce consistently similar offspring. These hybrids are particularly vigorous and have the largest flower heads. You do, however, pay a little more for the seeds.

Popular species and cultivars
'Adriatic,' an F1 hybrid, has a neat, compact habit, reaching 6-8 in (15-20 cm). It bears midblue flowers.

'Blue Danube' reaches 6-8 in (15-20 cm) high and has lavender-blue blooms. It is one of the best early-flowering F1 hybrids.

'Blue Horizon' is a tall F1 hybrid, growing to 2 ft (60 cm) and good for cutting. Small purple-blue flowers are borne in clusters.

'Blue Mink' is a compact plant reaching 9-12 in (23-30 cm) high. It has powder-blue flowers.

'Blue Ribbon,' an F1 hybrid, is smothered in bright midblue flowers from early summer on. It grows 6-8 in (15-20 cm) high.

'Capri' bears rich deep blue flowers on compact plants, 8-12 in (20-30 cm) high.

'Hawaii Hybrids' are compact F1 hybrids growing to a height and spread of 6-8 in (15-20 cm). Available in white, blue, and deep lavender, they bloom strongly even in dry soil.

'North Sea,' an F1 hybrid reaching 6-8 in (15-20 cm) high, has deep blue or red flowers that continue until late fall.

'Pacific,' an F1 hybrid, grows 8 in (20 cm) high and forms a tight dome of deep purple flowers on fast-growing plants.

'Pinky Improved Selection' is

Agrostemma
corn cockle

Agrostis
cloud grass

Ageratum houstonianum 'Blue Mink'

Agrostemma githago 'Milas'

Agrostis nebulosa

a new hybrid cultivar of bushy plants. It is 6-8 in(15-20 cm) tall and has dusty pink flowers.
'Southern Cross' grows 8-12 in (20-30 cm) high and can be used for containers, cut flowers, or beds. The flower clusters are bi-colored in pale blue and white.
'Summer Snow' is an F1 hybrid, 6-8 in (15-20 cm) tall, with pure white, fluffy flower heads.
'Swing Mixed' is an F1 hybrid mixture, with flowers in soft shades of blue, purple, rose, and pink. The plants grow to 8 in (20 cm) high.

Cultivation
Sowing *Ageratum* seed directly into the garden is risky, since the plants are slow starting and may be smothered by weeds. Instead, sow indoors in early spring. Harden off in late spring, then plant out home-grown seedlings or plants from a garden center after all danger of frost is past, setting the dwarf cultivars 9 in (23 cm) apart and the taller cultivars 1 ft (30 cm) apart. They need a sheltered, sunny or lightly shaded site and a moisture-retentive soil. Deadhead regularly to prolong the flowering season.
Pests/diseases Root rots (*Pellicularia filamentosa* in the East and Midwest, and *Pythium mamillatum* in the West) may cause the plants to collapse.

❏ Height 1-4 ft (30-120 cm)
❏ Planting distance 6 in (15 cm)
❏ Flowers midsummer
❏ Ordinary or poor garden soil
❏ Open, sunny site
❏ Hardy annual

Corn cockle's delicate appearance belies its hardy constitution as a grainfield weed. 'Milas' is a superior cultivar developed from the wild *Agrostemma githago*.

Tolerating poor soil, it makes an excellent meadow flower and cottage-garden plant, with its large lilac-pink flowers on tall, slender stems. The leaves are long and narrow, so it is best to grow corn cockles en masse among other annuals and biennials. They are good for cutting, but all parts are poisonous.

Popular species and cultivars
'Milas' grows 3-4 ft (90-120 cm) high. Its delicate pink flowers, 2 in (5 cm) or more wide, deepen in color toward the edges.
'Milas Cerise' is a striking cherry-red strain of 'Milas,' reaching 2-3 ft (60-90 cm).

Cultivation
In the North, sow the seeds in their flowering site as soon as the soil can be worked in spring; sow in spring or fall in the South. Thin to 6 in (15 cm) apart when the seedlings are strong enough. Give them an open, sunny site. In the summer deadhead the flowers to prevent less vigorous self-sown seedlings from growing. Do not disturb the roots.
Pests/diseases Trouble free.

❏ Height 1-1½ ft (30-45 cm)
❏ Planting distance 6 in (15 cm)
❏ Flowers early to late summer
❏ Any well-drained soil
❏ Full sun
❏ Hardy annual

Cloud grass is a pale branched and graceful grass that serves as a good foil for brightly colored perennials and annuals in beds and borders. It belongs to the bent grass family, several species of which are used in lawn-seed mixtures. However, cloud grass itself is an ornamental grass. Its branched clusters of small white flowers have an airy charm. The blossom panicles are suitable for cutting and drying, if cut before the flowers are fully mature.

Cultivation
Sow seeds in early spring where the plants are to grow; thin the seedlings to 6 in (15 cm) apart when they are large enough to handle. Cloud grass will grow in any well-drained soil, even a poor one, and does best in full sun.
Pests/diseases Generally trouble free.

15

Alonsoa
mask flower

Althaea
hollyhock

Alonsoa warscewiczii 'Compacta'

- ❏ Height 1-3 ft (30-90 cm)
- ❏ Planting distance 15 in (38 cm)
- ❏ Flowers midsummer to midfall
- ❏ Rich, well-drained soil
- ❏ Sunny site
- ❏ Half-hardy annual

Alonsoa warscewiczii is the only species of this Peruvian genus grown in the United States, though several cultivars have been developed from it. A compact bushy plant reaching 1-3 ft (30-90 cm) high, it has glossy dark green oval leaves and red stems. The scarlet flowers with yellow centers appear from midsummer to midfall, adding color to formal beds, borders, and containers. The plants are tender perennials but flower like annuals in their first year from seed.

Popular species and cultivars
'Compacta,' 1½-2 ft (45-60 cm) high, has scarlet blooms.
'Firestone Jewels Hybrids,' to 1 ft (30 cm), come in mixes of pink, red, amber, and pure white, and are excellent for cutting.

Cultivation
Sow seeds in covered seed flats in late winter and early spring, keeping them at a temperature of 59°F (15°C). Prick out, harden off, and plant out in late spring after all danger of frost is past. Set the plants 15 in (38 cm) apart in rich, well-drained soil in a sunny spot. When the plants are 2-3 in (5-7.5 cm) high, pinch the growing tips to encourage bushy growth.
Pests/diseases Aphids may infest the stems and leaves.

Althaea rosea 'Chater's Double Hybrids'

- ❏ Height 2-8 ft (60-240 cm)
- ❏ Planting distance 9-24 in (23-60 cm)
- ❏ Flowers midsummer to fall
- ❏ Heavy, rich soil
- ❏ Sunny site
- ❏ Hardy biennial or annual

Hollyhocks *(Althaea* species, now classified as *Alcea)* are old-fashioned garden favorites. Their towering spikes of large, single or double, pink, red, dark crimson, yellow, or white flowers have a strong impact wherever they are grown. They are well suited to a cottage garden or the back of an annual or herbaceous border, ideally placed behind much shorter plants to show off their stately magnificence of up to 8 ft (240 cm). The large, light green leaves are lobed, rough, and hairy.

Popular species and cultivars
The true species hollyhock *(Althaea,* or *Alcea, rosea)* has been superseded by cultivars bearing single or double flowers in mixed or single colors.
'Chater's Double Hybrids' bear peony-shaped double flowers in a variety of colors.
'Majorette' is a dwarf cultivar reaching 2-2½ ft (60-75 cm) high with double, fringed flowers in a mixture of pastel shades.
'Nigra' has single, rich chocolate-maroon flowers and stands 5 ft (150 cm) high.
'Pinafore Hybrids' have semi-double and single, fringed flowers in pink, carmine, rose, yellow, and white. They grow up to 36-40 in (90-100 cm) high.
'Powderpuff Hybrids' have double red, pink, rose, white, and yellow flowers, and reach 6-8 ft (180-240 cm) high.
'Summer Carnival' has fully double blooms covering the entire length of its 5-6 ft (150-180 cm) high stems. The flowers come in

Alyssum
sweet alyssum

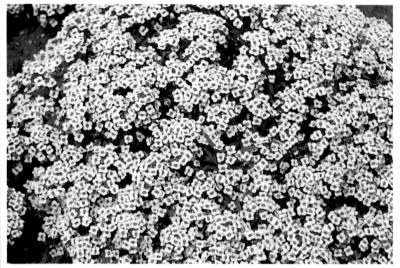

Alyssum maritimum 'Carpet of Snow'

Althaea rosea (single yellow)

a wide range of colors. This cultivar is an annual, so seeds sown in spring produce flowering plants in summer.

Cultivation
Hollyhocks like a heavy, rich soil and, preferably, a sheltered site. For biennial plants, sow seeds outdoors in early summer to midsummer, 9 in (23 cm) apart. Thin the seedlings to 2 ft (60 cm) apart in early fall to midfall.

For annual plants, sow indoors in late winter for planting out in midspring, or sow directly in the final site in midspring and thin to 15 in (38 cm) apart.

Water well during dry weather, and stake tall cultivars in exposed sites. For perennial growth, cut the plants to 6 in (15 cm) above ground in fall.

Pests/diseases Rust, which affects the leaves and stems, is often a problem with older plants, a reason why hollyhocks are best grown as annuals or biennials.

❑ Height 3-6 in (7.5-15 cm)
❑ Planting distance 9 in (23 cm)
❑ Flowers early summer to early fall
❑ Any well-drained soil
❑ Full sun
❑ Perennial grown as hardy annual

Although perennial by its native Mediterranean, sweet alyssum *(Alyssum maritimum,* or correctly *Lobularia maritima)* is grown elsewhere as an annual. It forms low, dense cushions that help edge beds, fill cracks between paving stones, and add color to rock gardens and containers. From early summer to early fall, sprays of tiny flowers appear in great profusion, in white, pink, lilac, purple, and red.

It is an easy annual to grow, tolerating any well-drained garden soil, even poor soil.

Popular species and cultivars
The species itself is rarely grown, but it is represented by readily available cultivars.

'Carpet of Snow' bears clusters of white flowers and reaches 3 in (7.5 cm) high.

'Easter Bonnet' is a mixture of shades of pink, purple, and white on 5 in (12.5 cm) plants.

'Minima' has white flowers, which form a low carpet just 3 in (7.5 cm) high.

'Oriental Night' has deep purple flowers on 4 in (10 cm) high plants.

'Pastel Carpet' reaches up to 5 in (12.5 cm) high and comes in a mixture of shades from white to

cream, pink, as well as pale violet.

'Rosie O'Day' has early-flowering rose-colored blooms and reaches 3-4 in (7.5-10 cm) high.

'Royal Carpet' has scented lilac-purple flowers and reaches 3-4 in (7.5-10 cm) high.

'Snow Crystal' grows to 4 in (10 cm) tall and bears large clusters of pure white flowers on compact plants.

'Trailing Rosy Red' bears pink flowers along its trailing stems. It is good for hanging baskets.

'Wonderland Red' has deep red flowers that last well. It grows 3-4 in (7.5-10 cm) high.

Cultivation
Sweet alyssum needs a sunny spot but grows in any well-drained garden soil, provided it isn't too rich.

Sow the seeds thinly in the flowering site from early spring to midspring and again in late summer. Alyssum is not heat resistant and needs renewal to bloom in fall. Thin the seedlings to 9 in (23 cm) apart when they are large enough to handle.

For early flowering, sow seeds in flats in late winter or early spring, and maintain a temperature of 50-55°F (10-13°C). Prick out into flats of potting soil and then harden off, before planting out in midspring.

Deadhead regularly by trimming lightly with scissors for a longer flowering season.

Pests/diseases Slugs may eat young plants.

Amaranthus
amaranthus

Amaranthus tricolor 'Flaming Fountains'

Amaranthus caudatus

- ❏ Height 2-5 ft (60-150 cm)
- ❏ Planting distance 1-3 ft (30-90 cm)
- ❏ Flowers midsummer to midfall
- ❏ Deep, rich soil
- ❏ Full sun
- ❏ Half-hardy annual

These tall dramatic plants, some with long, drooping crimson flower tassels and others with brilliantly colored foliage, deserve to be grown as focal points in formal beds of annuals. They can also be grown as pot plants in the greenhouse. The flowers are long-lasting when cut and can also be dried.

Popular species and cultivars
Amaranthus caudatus, commonly known as love-lies-bleeding, is the most popular species. Its 1½ ft (45 cm) long plumes of blood-red flowers appear from late summer to midfall on plants 3-4 ft (90-120 cm) high. Space the plants 1½ ft (45 cm) apart. The cultivar 'Pigmy Torch' grows to only 2 ft (60 cm) and has deep maroon upright flower spikes. 'Viridis' has pale green flowers, which are popular for flower arranging.
Amaranthus hypochondriachus,

also known as prince's feather, has erect plumes of bright red flowers 6 in (15 cm) long. These appear from midsummer to midfall. The plants reach 4-5 ft (120-150 cm) high and have bronze-tinted leaves. Space the plants 3 ft (90 cm) apart. One of the cultivars developed from this species is 'Green Thumb,' which has vivid green

Amaranthus caudatus 'Viridis'

spikes on plants 2 ft (60 cm) tall. *Amaranthus tricolor* is chiefly grown for its spectacular foliage: oval-shaped scarlet leaves, overlaid with yellow, bronze, and green. The plants are up to 2-3 ft (60-90 cm) high and should be set 1-1½ ft (30-45 cm) apart. Cultivars include 'Flaming Fountains' (crimson willowlike leaves), 'Illumination' (scarlet, orange, yellow, green, and bronze leaves all on one plant), and 'Joseph's Coat' (a vigorous cultivar with leaves similar to those of the species). All make good pot plants.

Cultivation
Sow seeds indoors in early spring, and keep them at a temperature of 70°F (21°C) — amaranthus seeds require very warm soil for germination. Prick out the seedlings into pots; harden them off before planting outdoors in late spring after all danger of frost is past. In the South (zones 8-10) sow seeds directly in the flowering site in late spring, and then thin to the required planting distance (see individual species entries above).

A. caudatus and its cultivars will tolerate poor soil, but the other species and their cultivars prefer soil enriched with compost. All need a sunny location.
Pests/diseases Aphids sometimes infest the plants.

Anagallis
scarlet pimpernel

Anagallis arvensis caerulea

❏ Height 1-2 in (2.5-5 cm)
❏ Planting distance 6 in (15 cm)
❏ Flowers midsummer to midfall
❏ Ordinary well-drained soil
❏ Full sun
❏ Hardy annual

Scarlet pimpernel *(Anagallis arvensis)* is also called poor-man's-weatherglass because its small scarlet flowers close on cloudy days. A weed in Europe, it makes a fine garden plant here.

The plants reach only 1-2 in (2.5-5 cm) high and form thick, bushy clumps with a spread of 10 in (25 cm), excellent for edging borders or growing in rock gardens. The popular variety *caerulea* produces a mass of rich gentian-blue starlike flowers from midsummer to midfall; mixed seed packs will also include red-flowered plants.

Cultivation
Sow seeds in the flowering site in early spring to midspring. The plants grow in ordinary well-drained garden soil but must have full sun. Thin to 6 in (15 cm) apart when the seedlings are large enough to be handled.
Pests/diseases Trouble free.

Anchusa
anchusa

Anchusa capensis 'Blue Angel'

❏ Height 9-18 in (23-45 cm)
❏ Planting distance 9 in (23 cm)
❏ Flowers mid- to late summer
❏ Ordinary garden soil
❏ Sunny, open site
❏ Tender annual

Anchusa capensis, the only annual in a predominantly perennial genus, bears some of the few truly blue flowers. Like the forget-me-not, which it closely resembles, it flowers over a long season, from mid- to late summer. Only at the season's end do the plants begin to look bedraggled, with many more spent flowers than new ones.

The plants form compact domes of narrow, pointed, midgreen leaves, making them suitable for the front of a border; the dwarf cultivar 'Blue Angel' is also useful for window boxes.

Popular species and cultivars
Striking cultivars have been developed from *Anchusa capensis.*
'Blue Angel' produces ultramarine-blue flowers and forms domes that are 9 in (23 cm) high.
'Blue Bird' has vivid indigo-blue flowers and reaches 1½ ft (45 cm).
'Dawn Hybrids' grow 9 in (23 cm) tall and come as a mixture of white, pink, pale blue, and deep blue starlike flowers.

Cultivation
In the South (zones 8-10), sow in flowering sites in fall and thin to 9 in (23 cm) apart. In the North, start seeds indoors and set seedlings out as soon as the danger of frost is past. Grow in any well-cultivated soil in an open site in full sun. The plants generally do best in groups.

In summer, remove all faded flower stems to encourage more blooms. Water well.
Pests/diseases Cucumber mosaic virus may cause yellow spots on the leaves.

ANGEL'S TRUMPET —
see *Datura*

Antirrhinum
snapdragon

Antirrhinum majus 'Princess'

❏ Height ½-4 ft (15-120 cm)
❏ Planting distance ½-1½ ft (15-45 cm)
❏ Flowers summer to first frost
❏ Well-drained soil enriched with compost
❏ Full sun or light shade
❏ Hardy annual

Antirrhinum majus 'Coronette Hybrids'

Snapdragons are among our most ancient garden plants and, if they were not so susceptible to rust, would still be among the most popular. Coming in an enormous range of colors and a variety of sizes, they make excellent plants for mixed borders and formal beds throughout summer. The taller cultivars can form a spectacular display along the back of a herbaceous border. Medium-size cultivars are useful for formal or informal beds, while dwarf cultivars are ideal as edging and carpeting or for rock gardens.

Popular species and cultivars
Snapdragons grown in gardens have all been developed from *Antirrhinum majus*. They are classified in three groups according to plant size. Some come as single colors, others as mixed colors. Below is a selection of readily available cultivars.
Dwarf cultivars reach only 6 in (15 cm) high and have a compact bushy habit.
'Dwarf Bedding,' a mixed cultivar, comes in numerous colors.

'Floral Carpet' has a profusion of large flowers in mixed colors.
'Floral Showers Hybrids' bear flowers of mixed colors, some bicolored.
'Little Darling' is early flowering and comes in mixed colors. It is rust resistant.
'Magic Carpet' is of trailing habit and available in mixed colors.
'Pixie' has open-petaled butterflylike flowers early in the season. It is free flowering and comes in crimsons, reds, oranges, yellows, and whites.
'Royal Carpet Hybrids' are some of the best carpeting cultivars, being vigorous, long-lasting, and rust resistant. They come in mixed colors, just orange ('Royal Carpet Orange'), or just pink ('Royal Carpet Pink').
'Sweetheart Hybrids' have small, double azalea-type flowers in red, bronze, pink, yellow, or white. They are rust resistant.
'Tahiti' mixtures are compact and closely packed with flowers in pure colors and some bicolors.

'Tom Thumb' is a neat plant bearing flowers in bright mixed colors.
'Trumpet Serenade' has open-petaled freesialike flowers that are long-lasting and come in mixed colors. The plant grows to 1 ft (30 cm).
Intermediate cultivars are the most popular group. They reach 15-18 in (38-45 cm) high.
'Black Prince' is a compact plant that has deep crimson flowers and bronze foliage.
'Bright Eyes' is an F1 hybrid with bright yellow flowers marked with red in the center.
'Cinderella' forms bushy plants with dense flower spikes in a range of colors.
'Coral Monarch' has warm coral-pink flowers and is resistant to rust.
'Coronette Hybrids' are neat plants with flowers in mixed colors. They are both rust and weather resistant.
'Crimson Monarch' has crimson flowers and is rust resistant.

Antirrhinum majus 'Yellow Monarch'

Antirrhinum majus 'Dwarf Bedding'

'Double Supreme Hybrids' bear double flowers in cream, crimson, yellow, rose, and white, and are able to stand the summer heat well.

'Lavender Monarch' has lilac-blue flowers and strong resistance to rust.

'Monarch Mixed' comes in white, yellow, coral, scarlet, and crimson. Like other 'Monarch' strains, it is bred to be resistant to rust.

'Popette' is an F2 hybrid, with uniform early and long-lasting flowers that are bicolored white and purple-rose.

'Princess Hybrids' bear a profusion of long-lasting flowers in a wide range of mixed colors.

'Rembrandt' has orange flowers with yellow tips to the petals.

'Sawyers Mixed' is a rust-resistant mixture in a range of strong colors.

'White Monarch' bears white flowers and is strongly resistant to rust.

'Yellow Monarch' has clear yellow flowers and is strongly resistant to rust.

Tall cultivars will grow 3-4 ft (90-120 cm) high and are good as cut flowers.

'Giant Forerunner Hybrids' have densely clustered flowers in a wide range of mixed colors.

'Liberty Hybrids' are sturdy, thick-stemmed plants with long flower spikes in a range of colors. They are early flowering.

'Madame Butterfly' has double azalealike blooms in mixed colors.

'Ruffled Super Tetra' has large ruffled, veined flowers in mixed colors.

Cultivation
Sow the seeds in flats indoors in late winter to early spring and keep at a temperature of 61-64°F (16-18°C). Water seeds gently with a fine spray. After they germinate, water with diluted liquid fertilizer.

When the seedlings are large enough to handle, prick them out into flats of potting soil. Harden off before planting out in late spring, or grow on as pot plants in the greenhouse.

For early-flowering snapdragons, sow seeds in early summer to midsummer, and pot them in early fall; if you have a warm, sheltered site, they can be planted outdoors in fall.

In the garden, set tall cultivars 18 in (45 cm) apart, intermediate cultivars 10 in (25 cm) apart, and dwarf cultivars 8 in (20 cm) apart.

For the best results plant snapdragons in well-drained light to medium soil enriched with compost, though any well-cultivated garden soil is suitable. The site should be in sun or light shade.

When the plants reach 3-4 in (7.5-10 cm) high, pinch the growing tips to encourage bushy growth. Deadhead to prolong the flowering season, and stake tall cultivars that are in exposed sites.
Pests/diseases Rust is often associated with snapdragons. If your garden is troubled by this disease, grow only rust-resistant cultivars. Damping-off may affect seedlings, and mildew can be a problem with young plants. Look for aphids on young plant growth in summer.

APPLE-OF-PERU —
see *Nicandra*

Arctotis
African daisy

Arctotis hybrids

- ❏ Height ½-2 ft (15-60 cm)
- ❏ Planting distance 1 ft (30 cm)
- ❏ Flowers midsummer to first frost
- ❏ Ordinary garden soil
- ❏ Open, sunny site
- ❏ Half-hardy annual

Bold, brightly colored daisylike flowers and woolly silver-gray leaves make this a striking plant to grow in borders and containers. Though tempting to cut for flower arranging, the blooms last only a short while in water.

In the garden, the flower heads tend to close in the afternoon or during dull, overcast weather, so position them where they will receive plenty of light — and can be appreciated in the morning. This plant is a good choice for southwestern gardeners since it tolerates a considerable degree of both heat and drought.

Popular species and cultivars
Arctotis venusta (sometimes sold as *A. stoechadifolia* or *A. grandis)* has large white to primrose-yellow flowers with blue centers and

pale lavender on the reverse (the petals' backsides). They appear from midsummer until the first frost. The plant grows up to 2 ft (60 cm) high.

Hybrids come in brilliant shades of red, yellow, apricot, orange, carmine, cream, and white. They reach 1-2 ft (30-60 cm) high, making them popular for borders and beds. The long-stemmed flowers tend to last longer than the species in water.

Cultivation
Sow seeds directly in the flowering site in mid- to late spring, and thin to 1 ft (30 cm) apart.

For earlier flowers, sow seeds indoors in flats of seed-starting mix in early spring. Keep at a temperature of 64°F (18°C). Prick out the seedlings into flats of potting soil, and harden off before planting out after all danger of frost is past.

African daisies grow in most soils, but perform best in sandy, well-drained ones, and they need a sunny site. When the plants are

Arctotis venusta

4-5 in (10-12 cm) high, pinch the growing tips to encourage bushy growth. Support the tall cultivars with twiggy sticks, and deadhead to extend the flowering season.

Pests/diseases Aphids may infest young growth, and gray mold can sometimes be a problem in wet weather.

Argemone
prickly poppy

Argemone mexicana

❑ Height 3 ft (90 cm)
❑ Planting distance 1 ft (30 cm)
❑ Flowers early to late summer
❑ Light, well-drained soil
❑ Sunny site
❑ Half-hardy annual

The prickly poppy *(Argemone mexicana)* from Central America has majestic orange and yellow flowers from early to late summer. Their sweet scent attracts bees and other insects. The flowers are carried 3 ft (90 cm) above ground on sprawling prickly stems with gray-blue thistlelike leaves. The flowers can be up to 3 in (7.5 cm) wide.

Grow prickly poppies in informal plantings in borders, preferably where they can be left alone to scatter their seeds.

Cultivation
Prickly poppies grow best in light, well-drained soil in a sunny border. Sow directly in the flowering site in spring as soon as the soil has warmed, and thin to 1 ft (30 cm) apart when seedlings are large enough to handle.

Staking is not a good idea as it may damage the succulent stems. Deadhead to encourage a longer flowering season.

For flowers in early summer, sow seeds indoors in early spring in peat pots to avoid disturbing the roots. Keep them at 64°F (18°C). Harden off and plant out in late spring.
Pests/diseases Trouble free.

Asperula
annual woodruff

Asperula orientalis

❑ Height 1 ft (30 cm)
❑ Planting distance 3-4 in (7.5-10 cm)
❑ Flowers midsummer
❑ Ordinary moist soil
❑ Partial shade
❑ Hardy annual

Annual woodruff *(Asperula orientalis)* is the only hardy annual in this genus of 200 species — all other woodruffs are perennials. Its strongly scented pale blue flowers appear in midsummer on top of 1 ft (30 cm) tall stems clothed with narrow green lance-shaped leaves. The leaves are arranged in attractive whorls up the stems.

This plant is useful for garden decoration as, unlike most annuals, it tolerates partial shade and likes moist soil. With its compact habit, it is also suitable for rock gardens. The flowers are good for cutting.

Cultivation
Scatter seeds over the flowering site in midspring, and rake them gently into the soil. When the seedlings are strong enough to handle, thin them to 3-4 in (7.5-10 cm) apart.
Pests/diseases Trouble free.

Atriplex
orach

Atriplex hortensis

❑ Height 3-4 ft (90-120 cm)
❑ Planting distance 16 in (40 cm)
❑ Foliage plant
❑ Well-drained good garden soil
❑ Open, sunny site
❑ Hardy annual

The cultivars of *Atriplex hortensis* are grown for their deep crimson-purple leaves covered, when young, with fine, glistening white powder. The flowers are insignificant. The cultivar 'Rubra' has bright blood-red foliage.

In rich soil, orach rapidly grows to 3-4 ft (90-120 cm) high, so use it as an instant hedge or simply to fill an awkward gap at the back of an ornamental border.

Cultivation
Sow the seeds indoors in early spring and transplant outdoors in late spring. Alternatively, sow them straight in the ground after the risk of frost is past. Thin the seedlings to 16 in (40 cm) apart.

Any good, well-drained soil in full sun is suitable. The plants prefer warm weather; they are wind resistant and flourish in an open site and in seaside gardens.
Pests/diseases Trouble free.

Begonia
wax begonia

Begonia x semperflorens-cultorum 'Lucia'

- ❏ Height 6-9 in (15-23 cm)
- ❏ Planting distance 8-10 in (20-25 cm)
- ❏ Flowers early summer to early fall or first frost
- ❏ Rich, moist, well-drained soil
- ❏ Sunny or lightly shaded site
- ❏ Half-hardy annual

The wax begonia *(Begonia × semperflorens-cultorum)* and its cultivars are grown as annuals and used as summer bedding and pot plants.

The plants, which generally reach 6-9 in (15-23 cm) high, are smothered with small white, pink, or red flowers from early summer until early fall. The foliage, too, is attractive: succulent and glossy, pale or dark green, purple, or coppery brown. Fill containers with wax begonias to brighten a patio, window box, or hanging basket, or use them in formal beds. In fall you can lift wax begonias and take them indoors as winter pot plants, and flowering will continue if the room is well lit.

Popular species and cultivars
Begonia × semperflorens-cultorum is now represented by an increasing number of cultivars.
'Cocktail Hybrids' have white, pink, rose, salmon, and red flowers with glossy deep bronze foliage. Notable members of this group are 'Gin,' which bears deep pink flowers with reddish leaves, and 'Whiskey,' a white-flowered cultivar that has light, bronze-green foliage.
'Coco Hybrids' come in mixed colors and have bronze foliage.
'Danica Red' has brick-red flowers and glossy bronze leaves.
'Danica Scarlet' has large scarlet flowers and bronze foliage.
'Frilly Dilly Hybrids' have scarlet and pink flowers with frilled petals. The foliage is green.
'Olympia Hybrids' have exceptionally big flowers, which are pink, white, red, or bicolored.
'Options Hybrids' have green or bronze foliage and pink, carmine, or white flowers, often picoteed.

'Organdy Hybrids' come in a wide range of flower colors and have green and bronze foliage. The plants are very compact.
'Pink Avalanche' has delicate pink flowers and green foliage.
'Viva' has pure white blooms and dark green leaves.
'Wings Hybrids' bear white, rose-pink, and bright red flowers that are very large, opening to a width of as much as 3 in (7.5 cm).

Cultivation
Sow seeds indoors in flats of seed-starting mix in late winter to early spring at 61°F (16°C). Prick seedlings out into boxes of potting compost when the first true leaf appears. Harden off and then plant out in beds or containers in late spring, setting them 8-10 in (20-25 cm) apart. The soil should be rich and moist but well drained, and the site should be in sun or light shade.
Pests/diseases Powdery mildew shows as a white coating on leaves and stems.

Bellis
English daisy

Bellis perennis 'Bright Carpet'

❑ Height 4-8 in (10-20 cm)
❑ Planting distance 6-9 in (15-23 cm)
❑ Flowers late spring to midsummer
❑ Ordinary garden soil
❑ Sun or partial shade
❑ Hardy biennial zones 8 and south; tender annual to north

From the wild English daisy come several bigger, brighter cultivars, ideal for edging or mixing with other plants in window boxes. White, pink, and red moplike flowers bloom profusely from late spring to midsummer on 4-8 in (10-20 cm) high stems. Loose rosettes of evergreen leaves form a dense carpet on the ground.

Bellis perennis

Popular species and cultivars
The following cultivars are all developed from *Bellis perennis*.
'Bright Carpet' has small double red, white, and rose blooms.
'Goliath' has large double blooms in shades of red, salmon-pink, pink, and white.
'Kito' bears double flowers with incurved cherry-red petals.
'Pomponette' produces a mass of very small double flowers in reds, pinks, and whites.

Cultivation
Where winters are mild, sow the seeds in late summer directly in the garden to bloom the next spring; in the North, start inside in midwinter and plant out once the soil can be worked in the spring. Thin or transplant seedlings to 6-9 in (15-23 cm) apart. Deadhead to prevent seeding.
Pests/diseases Trouble free.

BELLS OF IRELAND —
see *Moluccella*
BLACK-EYED SUSAN —
see *Rudbeckia*
BLANKET FLOWER —
see *Gaillardia*
BLAZING STAR —
see *Mentzelea*
BLUEBELL — see *Phacelia*
BLUE LACEFLOWER —
see *Trachymene*

Brachycome
Swan River daisy

Brachycome iberidifolia

❑ Height ½-1 ft (15-30 cm)
❑ Planting distance 9 in (23 cm)
❑ Flowers early summer to early fall
❑ Rich, moisture-retentive soil
❑ Sunny, sheltered site
❑ Half-hardy annual

The Swan River daisy (*Brachycome iberidifolia*) is covered with sweetly scented daisy flowers throughout the summer and into early fall. They are set on slender stems carrying pale green filigree leaves on compact plants. These daisies are ideal for low summer bedding and in pots, window boxes, and other containers.

Seeds are available in mixtures, producing white, pink, lavender, and blue flowers, or as single colors, such as 'Purple Splendor' and 'White Splendor.'

Cultivation
From zone 8 southward, sow seed directly in the garden in early spring; to the north, sow indoors 6 weeks before the last frost date, keeping the soil at a temperature of 64°F (18°C). Prick out the seedlings when large enough to handle, and maintain a temperature of 61°F (16°C) until they are growing strongly. Harden off the young plants and transplant to the flowering positions in late spring.

Swan River daisies thrive in rich, moisture-retentive soil and need full sun, preferably with some shelter.
Pests/diseases Trouble free.

Brassica
ornamental cabbage

Brassica oleracea

❏ Height 9-18 in (23-45 cm)
❏ Planting distance 14 in (36 cm)
❏ Foliage plant
❏ Any well-drained soil
❏ Sunny site
❏ Hardy annual

Ornamental cabbages *(Brassica oleracea)* are foliage plants and popular in summer and fall beds for their brightly colored leaves. The foliage opens out from the center and is frilled or deeply wavy, varying from pale to deep green with the midribs often in contrasting colors. The creamy white, pink, or carmine centers look like full-blown flowers. Ornamental cabbages usually grow about 9 in (23 cm) tall, while ornamental kale is twice as high, with colorful feathery centers rising above the foliage. Seeds come in mixed colors.

Fall- and winter-growing ornamental cabbages, suitable for container growing, come in single colors or in mixtures.

Cultivation
For spring planting, sow seeds indoors 8-10 weeks before the expected date of the last frost. Transplant outdoors as soon as the soil can be worked. For a fall display, sow outdoors in late summer in a seedbed or directly in the flowering site. In either case, space plants 14 in (36 cm) apart in any good garden soil and in full sun for the colors to develop properly. Sow container-grown winter plants in late summer.
Pests/diseases Cabbage aphids and caterpillars may attack the leaves.

Briza
quaking grass

Briza maxima

❏ Height 2 ft (60 cm)
❏ Planting distance 6-9 in (15-23 cm)
❏ Flowers late spring to midsummer
❏ Ordinary well-drained garden soil
❏ Sunny site
❏ Hardy annual

Quaking grass *(Briza maxima),* with its silvery green spikelets dancing and rustling on slender 2 ft (60 cm) high stems, is deservedly the most popular ornamental grass. The spikelets appear from late spring to midsummer, forming upright tufts with their bright green narrow, pointed leaves.

Grow quaking grass in large clusters in borders with flowering plants. When the flower heads are well formed, the stems can be cut and dried for indoor flower arrangements.

Cultivation
In the South, sow seeds thinly in the flowering site in early fall; or in North or South, sow in early spring to midspring. Choose a sunny site with well-drained soil. When the seedlings are large enough to handle, thin to 6-9 in (15-23 cm) apart.

Cut the flower stems for drying in sunny weather, when the spikelets are fully developed but before they set seeds. Hang up to dry in a cool place.
Pests/diseases Trouble free.

Browallia
browallia

Browallia speciosa 'Blue Bells'

❏ Height 8-12 in (20-30 cm)
❏ Planting distance 8 in (20 cm)
❏ Flowers early summer to early fall
❏ Any good garden soil
❏ Sunny site
❏ Half-hardy annual

This South American plant *(Browallia speciosa)* is a popular greenhouse and house plant, but it can also be grown outdoors for summer bedding. It is prized for its profusion of violet-shaped white-eyed flowers, up to 2 in (5 cm) wide, handsomely offset by bright green slender and pointed leaves.

Hybrid cultivars are more often seen than the species and include dwarf types for growing in window boxes, pots, and hanging baskets. 'Blue Bells' has violet-blue flowers with prominent white centers; 'Blue Troll' is bright blue; and 'White Bells' is pure white.

Cultivation
Sow seeds indoors at a temperature of 64°F (18°C) in early spring. Prick out the seedlings into pots. For outdoor plants, harden them off before setting them out in their flowering positions when all danger of frost is past. Browallias thrive in loamy soil, but will grow in well-drained soil, even a poor one. They require full sun.
Pests/diseases Trouble free.

BUSY LIZZY — see *Impatiens*
BUTTERFLY FLOWER —
see *Schizanthus*

Calceolaria
slipper flower

Calceolaria integrifolia

❏ Height 8-60 in (20-150 cm)
❏ Planting 12-15 in (30-38 cm)
❏ Flowers early summer to midfall
❏ Well-drained acid soil
❏ Sheltered, sunny or partially shaded site
❏ Half-hardy annual

The kidney-shaped blooms of the slipper flower were favorites in Victorian times for formal beds and greenhouse displays. Two Chilean species, *Calceolaria crenatiflora* and *C. integrifolia,* and their cultivars can be grown outdoors. They do best in sunny spots in temperate summers that are free from both frost and excessive heat. Their bright flowers in various yellows, either plain or blotched, look cheerful among the pale fresh green wrinkled leaves. The flowers are borne in succession from early summer until midfall.

Popular species and cultivars
The cultivars here have been bred for summer bedding.
'Little Sweeties' is a seed mixture producing plants up to 15 in (38 cm) tall with an abundance of small pouch-shaped flowers in pale yellow, orange, pink, and scarlet, often with contrasting speckles. The plants will grow in the shade.
'Midas' bears golden yellow blooms, renowned for their long flowering season. The neat, bushy and branching plants reach 10-15 in (25-38 cm) high.
'Sunshine' is a free-flowering hybrid, bearing bright yellow flowers throughout the summer. It reaches 8-10 in (20-25 cm) high and has a bushy, compact habit.

Cultivation
Sow 10-12 weeks before the projected date of the last frost. Handle tiny seeds carefully. Prick the seedlings out into flats when they are large enough to handle. In late spring harden off and plant outdoors. They will grow in ordinary garden soil, but do best in well-drained, rich acid soil. The site must be sheltered, in sun or partial shade.
Pests/diseases Both aphids and slugs may be troublesome.

Calendula
pot marigold

C. officinalis 'Fiesta Gitana Hybrids'

❏ Height 1-2 ft (30-60 cm)
❏ Planting distance 12-15 in (30-38 cm)
❏ Flowers late spring to first frost
❏ Any well-drained garden soil
❏ Sunny site
❏ Hardy annual

The pot marigold is one of the easiest hardy annuals to grow and, with its glowing orange or yellow daisylike flowers, one of the brightest. The flowers and light green lance-shaped leaves were formerly used in cooking, hence the name "pot marigold."

Most cultivars grow 1½-2 ft (45-60 cm) tall, though several 1 ft (30 cm) high dwarf cultivars are also available. Pot marigolds will grow well in borders even if the soil is poor. The long-stemmed cultivars make good cut flowers and last well in water.

Popular species and cultivars
All garden cultivars are developed from *Calendula officinalis,* which grows 2 ft (60 cm) high and bears a profusion of single daisy flowers, up to 4 in (10 cm) wide, in shades of bright orange or yellow.
Dwarf cultivars
'Apricot Bon Bon,' grows 12-15 in (30-38 cm) high and bears double, warm apricot flowers.
'Double Lemon Coronet' has large grapefruit-yellow flowers on 1 ft (30 cm) high plants.
'Dwarf Gem Hybrids' produce 3 in (7.5 cm) wide double flowers in shades from apricot to lemon-yellow on 1 ft (30 cm) tall plants.
'Fiesta Gitana Hybrids' come

27

Calendula officinalis 'Pacific Beauty'

Calendula officinalis

in mixed colors — oranges, yellows, and creams. They grow 1 ft (30 cm) high and wide and bear masses of double flowers with dark centers.

Tall cultivars

'Art Shades' is a mixture, 2 ft (60 cm) tall, that comes in apricots, oranges, pale yellows, and creams. The flowers are large and graceful.

'Indian Prince' has semidouble, dark orange flowers with mahogany-brown centers. It grows 18-20 in (45-50 cm) tall.

'Kablouna Gold,' 20 in (50 cm) tall, has bright yellow flowers with chocolate-brown centers.

'Kablouna Stormy Sunset' bears 3½ in (9 cm) wide crested double flowers with contrasting brown centers.

'Lemon Queen' has double, clear lemon-yellow flowers on 2 ft (60 cm) high plants.

'Pacific Apricot,' 2 ft (60 cm) high, has large double, soft apricot flowers with dark brown centers and orange tips to the petals.

'Pacific Beauty' is a mixture, 2 ft (60 cm) or more tall, with double orange, apricot, yellow, and primrose flowers on long stems. Some are bicolored.

'Pacific Cream Beauty' has cream-yellow flowers with dark brown centers.

'Pacific Lemon Beauty' has lemon-yellow blooms with dark brown centers.

'Radio Extra Selected,' 1½-2 ft (45-60 cm) tall, has orange blooms similar to cactus dahlias. It is excellent for cutting.

Cultivation

Pot marigolds thrive with little attention and in the poorest soil. For the best results, however, grow them in well-drained, good garden soil.

Sow the seeds in their flowering site in early spring for summer flowering or, in the South, in early fall for late-spring flowering. Cover with ½ in (1 cm) of soil. Thin out to 12-15 in (30-38 cm) apart. Deadhead to prolong the flowering season and prevent self-seeding.

Pests/diseases Powdery mildew may develop on the leaves. Caterpillars, white flies, and red spider mites may also create problems.

CALIFORNIA POPPY — see *Eschscholzia*

Calendula officinalis 'Kablouna Gold'

Callistephus
China aster

Callistephus chinensis 'Powderpuff'

Callistephus chinensis 'Milady'

❑ Height ½-2½ ft (15-75 cm)
❑ Planting distance 1-1½ ft (30-45 cm)
❑ Flowers midsummer to first frost
❑ Well-drained garden soil
❑ Open, sunny site
❑ Half-hardy annual

Just one species, *Callistephus chinensis,* is responsible for the many cultivars of China asters on the market — dwarf and tall, single-flowered and double-flowered, mixed colors or one color. The flowers may look like daisies or, depending on the cultivar, may be pomponlike or mimic chrysanthemums or even peonies. In color China asters range from pink, red, purple, blue, and cream to white. Flowering from midsummer to the first frost, they provide excellent color in borders and containers. As they last well in water, they are also suitable for cutting.

Popular species and cultivars
The dwarf cultivars of Chinese aster reach 6-12 in (15-30 cm) high and the tall cultivars 15-30 in (38-75 cm). Single blooms have clearly visible central disks, while double blooms have more petals, concealing the centers.

Dwarf cultivars
'**Blue Skies**' grows only about 6 in (15 cm) high but is almost smothered with a mass of double, pale lavender-blue flowers.
'**Carpet Ball**' has tightly packed double flowers in a good color range.
'**Comet**' is an early-flowering mixture, with double flowers in white and shades of blue and red.
'**Crimson Sunset**' bears double, deep red flowers.
'**Lilliput Duet**' has small pomponlike flowers in rose, carmine, pink, and blue.
'**Milady**' has large, double incurved chrysanthemumlike flowers in a range of rich colors. It is long-lasting and especially weather resistant.
'**Pinocchio**' is a compact seed mixture, bearing a mass of small, double, ball-shaped blooms.

Tall cultivars
'**All Change**' has double pomponlike flowers bicolored red and white or blue and white.
'**Duchess,**' in shades of rose-pink, yellow, crimson, blue, and pure white, is late flowering. It is good for cutting and with flowers like incurved chrysanthemums.
'**Early Ostrich Plume Finest Mixed**' bears double flowers of feathery, recurving petals in purples, pinks, and white, on 1½ ft (45 cm) tall plants.
'**Florette Champagne**' has quilled flowers of soft creamy pink on sturdy stems.
'**Giant Single Andrella**' has single, many-petaled flowers in white, rose, scarlet, lavender, or blue. Each blossom has a prominent yellow center.
'**Gusford Supreme,**' 15 in (38 cm) tall, is wilt resistant, with scarlet, white-centered flowers.
'**Operetta**' is a color mixture of large, double chrysanthemum-like flowers with incurved petals.
'**Ostrich Plume**' has double flowers with curled and feathery petals in a range of colors.
'**Pastel**' is a wilt-resistant mixture with double flowers in soft pastel shades.
'**Powderpuff Hybrids**' produce upright, compact plants with an abundance of tightly double flowers in shades of pink, blue, and purple as well as white.
'**Prinette Pink**' bears double flowers of pink petals frosted silver at the tips. The 2-ft (60-cm) tall plants are resistant to aster diseases.
'**Super Princess Symphonie**'

Campanula
Canterbury bells

Campanula medium

Callistephus chinensis 'Comet'

is a color mixture with large flowers that have tightly quilled petals.

Cultivation
Sow the seeds indoors in early spring at 61°F (16°C). Harden the seedlings off before planting out in late spring — wait until the nights are growing warmer. Alternatively, sow directly in the flowering site as soon as all danger of frost is past, and thin tall cultivars to 15-18 in (38-45 cm) apart and dwarf cultivars to 12 in (30 cm) apart.

Choose an open, sunny site with shelter from wind for the taller cultivars. A medium loam is best, though ordinary garden soil still gives good results.

Remove the first dead flowers to encourage blooms on the side shoots.

Pests/diseases A fatal fungal disease, callistephus wilt, may attack plants as they are about to flower. To prevent this disease, avoid using the same bed 2 years running and do not plant China asters near calendulas. Leafhoppers and aphids feed on China asters, and eliminating these sucking insects is essential, since they spread aster yellows, an incurable and lethal viral disease.

❑ Height 2-4 ft (60-120 cm)
❑ Planting distance 1 ft (30 cm)
❑ Flowers late spring to midsummer
❑ Ordinary well-drained garden soil
❑ Sunny or lightly shaded site
❑ Hardy biennial, sometimes grown as an annual

Canterbury bells *(Campanula medium)* is an old-fashioned cottage-garden plant that is easily grown and showy when in flower, but it contributes nothing to the garden at other times. It is best planted in small groups where it will not leave large gaps after blooming is finished.

'Cup and Saucer Mixed' is the only cultivar of Canterbury bells

other than the species type that is generally available. The flowers are delicate shades of pink, blue, and white.

Cultivation
Sow the seeds outside in a seedbed in late spring or early summer in the North or in fall in the South. In cold-weather regions, protect seedlings over the winter with a blanket of evergreen boughs. Move to the flowering site the following spring, setting the plants 1 ft (30 cm) apart. By sowing seeds indoors in midwinter, plants may be brought into flower in their first year, but their bloom will be much smaller and less handsome. Any ordinary well-drained soil is suitable, in sun or light shade.

Pests/diseases Slugs and snails may damage the leaves.

CAMPION — see *Silene*
CANDYTUFT — see *Iberis*
CAPE MARIGOLD —
see *Dimorphotheca*
CAPER SPURGE —
see *Euphorbia*
CASTOR-OIL PLANT —
see *Ricinus*
CATCHFLY — see *Silene*
CATHEDRAL BELLS —
see *Cobaea*

Campanula medium 'Cup and Saucer Mixed'

Celosia
cockscomb

Celosia 'Apricot Brandy'

Celosia 'Dwarf Fairy Fountains'

❏ Height 4-24 in (10-60 cm)
❏ Planting distance 9-12 in (23–30 cm)
❏ Flowers midsummer to early fall
❏ Rich, well-drained soil
❏ Sheltered, sunny site
❏ Tender annual

Celosia has large, bright, crested or plumed flowers in reds, oranges, and yellows. The cultivars with crested flowers suggest the common name; the plumed ones look more like feathers. Both types are excellent for beds and containers.

Popular species and cultivars
All garden cultivars have been developed from *Celosia argentea cristata* or *C. a. plumosa*.
'Apricot Brandy' has deep orange plumed flowers on branching plants 20 in (50 cm) high.
'Dwarf Fairy Fountains' has plumed flowers in pastel shades. It grows up to 12-15 in (30-38 cm) high.
'Flamingo Feather' grows to 2 ft (60 cm) tall and bears bicolored rose and deep pink flower spikes. It is ideal for drying.

'Jewel Box Dwarf Hybrids' have crested blooms in red, pink, salmon, gold, and yellow. The plants grow 9 in (23 cm) high.
'Kimono Mixed' grows only 4 in (10 cm) high and is good for containers. The plumes are cream, golden yellow, orange, or scarlet.

Cultivation
Sow seeds in flats of seed-starting mix in spring 6 weeks before the last frost date, and keep at 64°F (18°C). Harden off before planting out in a bed or pots in early summer, after all risk of frost is over and nights and days are dependably warm. Set the plants 9-12 in (23-30 cm) apart in rich, well-drained soil in a warm, sheltered site.
Pests/diseases Root rot, caused by a fungus, can affect the roots, making the plants wilt or collapse. As a rule, celosias are untroubled by pests.

Celosia 'Jewel Box Dwarf Hybrids'

Centaurea
bachelor's button, cornflower

Centaurea cyanus 'Polka Dot'

❏ Height 1-3 ft (30-90 cm)
❏ Planting distance 9-12 in (23-30 cm)
❏ Flowers early summer to early fall
❏ Any well-drained soil
❏ Sunny site
❏ Hardy annual

The cornflower is one of our oldest and best-loved hardy annuals, easy to grow and excellent for cutting. Its wiry stems carry sprays of blue, white, pink, purple, maroon, or deep red flowers and long, narrow silver-gray leaves.

Grow cornflowers on their own in beds and borders or as part of a meadow garden mixture, perhaps grouped with poppies and corn cockles.

Popular species and cultivars
The following cultivars have been developed from *Centaurea cyanus,* which was originally native to Europe but is now a wildflower found in North America.
'Blue Diadem' bears large, double, dark blue flowers on 2½ ft (75 cm) tall plants.
'Dwarf Blue Midget' has large, blue double flowers and reaches 1 ft (30 cm) high.
'Frosty' has pink, blue, red, and maroon flowers, edged white, and white flowers flushed pink. It reaches 2 ft (60 cm) high.
'Jubilee Gem' has large, double, dark blue flowers and reaches 1 ft (30 cm) high.
'Polka Dot' produces a mixture of blue and red colors. It stands 15-18 in (38-45 cm) high.
'Tall Double Mixed' comes in shades of pink, red, maroon, blue, purple, and white and reaches 3 ft (90 cm) high.
Centaurea moschata (sweet sultan) is an Oriental species with large scented flowers and gray-green toothed leaves. It has spawned the following cultivars.
'Dairy Maid' has large golden yellow flowers with fringed petals and prominent centers. It grows to 2 ft (60 cm) high.
'The Bride,' pure white and exceptionally fragrant, reaches a height of 16-24 in (40-60 cm).

Cultivation
Grow in any well-drained garden soil in a sunny site. In the South, sow the seeds in the final site in early fall; elsewhere, in early spring to midspring at 2-week intervals. When they are big enough to handle, thin dwarf cultivars to 9 in (23 cm) apart and tall cultivars to 1 ft (30 cm) apart.

Stake tall cultivars in exposed sites with twiggy sticks. Deadhead all cornflowers.
Pests/diseases Mildew and rust can be problems.

Cheiranthus
wallflower

Cheiranthus × allionii 'Golden Bedder'

❏ Height ½-2 ft (15-60 cm)
❏ Planting distance 10-15 in (25-38 cm)
❏ Flowers midspring to early summer
❏ Well-drained soil, preferably alkaline or neutral
❏ Full sun
❏ Hardy biennial in zone 8 and south; half-hardy annual elsewhere

With its dense spikes of richly colored blooms and its heady fragrance, the wallflower deserves its reputation as the queen of spring and early-summer biennials. *Cheiranthus* is the name used in most nursery catalogs, although botanists have reclassified the plants as *Erysimum*. In any case, many cultivars are now available. These provide the gardener with an enormous range of colors to choose from: shades of yellow, apricot, pink, and purple, or strong, clear reds, oranges, and yellows. All have spikes of freely produced flowers and green lance-shaped leaves.

Most cultivars are anything up to 2 ft (60 cm) high — excellent for growing in borders and formal beds or as cut flowers. But there are dwarf kinds only ½-1 ft (15-30 cm) high, which are useful for rock gardens and small informal patches placed near the house so that their scent can waft through open windows.

Popular species and cultivars
Cheiranthus × allionii (Erysimum allioni), the Siberian wallflower, has had a few cultivars developed

Cheiranthus cheiri — mixture of tall cultivars

Cheiranthus cheiri

from it. They form compact plants with yellow or orange flowers appearing from late spring to early summer.

'Aurora' grows 10-12 in (25-30 cm) tall and bears flowers in shades of orange, brown, apricot, and purple.

'Glasnost Hybrids' are 1 ft (30 cm) high plants, with fragrant flowers in a range of pastel colors, including lilac.

'Spring Jester' is a seed mixture producing plants 1 ft (30 cm) high with flowers in shades of apricot, orange, golden yellow, lemon, lilac, and occasionally white.

Cheiranthus cheiri (now reclassified as *Erysimum cheiri)* has spawned numerous cultivars, dwarf and tall. The following are some of the most readily available cultivars.

Dwarf cultivars
'Dwarf Mixed' includes a good range of colors and reaches 1 ft (30 cm) high.

'Golden Bedder' has large gold-en yellow flowers and reaches 10 in (25 cm) high.

'Orange Bedder' has rich orange flowers, shading to apricot, and reaches 10 in (25 cm) high.

'Primrose Bedder' has primrose-yellow flowers and reaches 10 in (25 cm) high.

'Scarlet Bedder' has rich scarlet flowers and reaches 10 in (25 cm) high.

'Tom Thumb Hybrids' produce late-flowering blooms in mixed colors; the plants grow only 6-9 in (15-23 cm) high.

Tall cultivars
'Blood Red' has early, deep velvety red flowers and reaches 15 in (38 cm) high.

'Cloth of Gold' has large, golden sweet-scented flowers and reaches 15 in (38 cm) high.

'Eastern Queen' has salmon-red flowers and reaches 15 in (38 cm) high.

'Fair Lady Hybrids' come in mixed pastel shades and stand 12-15 in (30-38 cm) high.

'Fire King' offers bright scarlet-orange flowers and reaches 15 in (38 cm) high.

'White Dame' has cream-white flowers and is 15 in (38 cm) high.

Cultivation
In regions with mild winters (zone 8 and south), sow the seeds thinly in a seedbed in early fall. When the first true leaves appear, thin the seedlings to about 6 in (15 cm) apart.

In midfall, plant them out in their flowering site, setting the tall cultivars 12-15 in (30-38 cm) apart and the dwarf cultivars 10-12 in (25-30 cm) apart. Where winters are severe, start wallflowers indoors in January. Prick out the seedlings into peat pots, and in late winter set the seedlings outdoors in a cold frame or a cool but frost-free spot. Transplant into the garden after all danger of frost is past. Most well-drained garden soils are suitable, though acid soils should be dressed with lime. The planting site must be in full sun.

When the plants reach 5-6 in (12-15 cm) high, pinch the tips to encourage bushy growth.

Pests/diseases Cabbage root fly maggots may cause the roots to rot and plants to wilt. Or the plants can become stunted as a result of club root — swellings on the roots.

CHERRY-PIE —
see *Heliotropum*
CHINA ASTER —
see *Callistephus*

Chrysanthemum
chrysanthemum

Chrysanthemum carinatum

Chrysanthemum frutescens

- ❏ Height ½-3 ft (15-90 cm)
- ❏ Planting distance ½-1½ ft (15-45 cm)
- ❏ Flowers late spring to early fall
- ❏ Ordinary garden soil
- ❏ Sunny site
- ❏ Hardy or half-hardy annual

Chrysanthemums are familiar groups of garden plants. Botanists have recently reclassified many, giving them new botanical names, but the traditional names are used here because they are listed in catalogs. Some chrysanthemums are grown as hardy and half-hardy annuals and greenhouse plants; others are true hardy perennials. Most annual species are hardy and free flowering. They form well-branched, bushy plants and produce an abundance of daisylike flowers from early summer to early fall. Grow them in informal beds, as border edgings, in tubs or hanging baskets, or for cutting.

Popular species and cultivars
Chrysanthemum carinatum (now *Ismelia carinatum*) bears single flowers from early summer to early fall. These have purple central disks surrounded by ray petals banded in different colors. The plants reach 2 ft (60 cm) high

and should be spaced 1 ft (30 cm) apart. Popular cultivars include 'Court Jesters' (red, pink, orange, yellow, maroon, and white banded with red or orange). 'Polar Star,' up to 3 ft (90 cm), bears showy flowers of pale yellow banded with golden orange on stiff stems, and is ideal for cutting. 'Rainbow Mixture' has 2½ in (6 cm) wide flowers brightly banded in various combinations of yellow, scarlet, red, rose-lavender, bronze, orange, and white. 'Zebra' is a branching plant with brilliant scarlet flowers.

Chrysanthemum coronarium has double, semidouble, or single flowers ranging from white to golden yellow in mid- and late summer. 'Golden Gem,' the most popular cultivar, reaches 1-1½ ft (30-45 cm) high and has golden yellow flowers. Plant 15 in (38 cm) apart. 'Primrose Gem' is similar, but has pale yellow flowers.

Chrysanthemum frutescens (now *Argyranthemum frutescens*) is really a perennial, but is grown as a half-hardy annual for containers and summer beds. It bears large white or pale yellow flowers from late spring to midfall and reaches 1-1½ ft (30-45 cm) high. Space the plants 1-1½ ft (30-45 cm) apart.

Chrysanthemum multicaule (now *Coleostephus multicaule*) and its cultivar, 'Gold Plate,' have small, single golden yellow flowers. Growing ½-1 ft (15-30 cm) high, they are useful for window boxes, tubs, and rock gardens. Plant these 9 in (23 cm) apart.

Chrysanthemum paludosum (now *Hymenostemma paludosum*) has an abundance of small white flowers with yellow centers, like mini marguerites, throughout the summer. Use the 1 ft (30 cm) high plants in window boxes or tubs, or as edging. Set them 9 in (23 cm) apart.

Chrysanthemum parthenium (feverfew; now *Tanacetum parthenium*) is popular in pots and window boxes and as edging for summer beds. It is a compact

Chrysanthemum coronarium

Cladanthus
Palm Springs daisy

Chrysanthemum parthenium 'Golden Ball'

Cladanthus arabicus

half-hardy plant, up to 1 ft (30 cm) high, studded from midsummer to early fall with masses of small flowers. Its light green leaves have a pungent aroma. A popular cultivar is 'Golden Ball,' with small, rounded gold flowers. *Chrysanthemum segetum* bears single yellow flowers with brown central disks from midsummer to early fall. Plant this 1½ ft (45 cm) high species and its cultivars 1 ft (30 cm) apart in a border. 'Eastern Star' (also known as 'Prado') has primrose-yellow flowers.

Cultivation
Annual chrysanthemums will grow and flower freely in any soil, but they do best in fertile, well-drained soil in a sunny site. Sow the seeds in their flowering site as soon as the ground can be worked in the spring. Cover the seeds with a sprinkling of soil. When large enough to handle, thin the seedlings to the required spacing. In mild districts (zone 8 and south), a fall sowing gives earlier flowers.

   C. frutescens can be increased only from 2-3 in (5-7.5 cm) long cuttings of nonflowering side shoots taken in early fall and rooted indoors.

Pests/diseases Mildew, aphids, and caterpillars can all cause problems.

❑ Height 2½ ft (75 cm)
❑ Planting distance 1 ft (30 cm)
❑ Flowers from early summer to fall
❑ Any well-drained soil
❑ Full sun or partial shade
❑ Hardy annual

The Palm Springs daisy *(Cladanthus arabicus)* deserves to be better known, for it is an easy and accommodating plant, thriving in a wide range of conditions and sites and producing an abundance of flowers from early summer until the first fall frosts. It grows up to 2½ ft (75 cm) tall and forms a steadily increasing mound of pale green feathery leaves. These, like the flowers, are pungently aromatic.

   The dainty foliage is almost completely hidden by a succession of single daisylike flowers, golden yellow and fragrant and about 2 in (5 cm) wide.

   Palm Springs daisies are ideal for growing in groups of five to seven plants in herbaceous and annual borders. They are not suitable for cutting.

Cultivation
Palm Springs daisies will grow in any kind of soil, even poor soils, and in partial shade, but they do best in light, well-drained soil in a sunny spot.

Sow the seeds thinly in the flowering site in early spring to midspring, covering them lightly with soil. When the seedlings are large enough to handle, thin them to stand 1 ft (30 cm) apart. When flowering begins, deadhead the blooms regularly to extend the flowering season.

Pests/diseases Generally trouble free.

Clarkia
clarkia

Clarkia amoena

- ❏ Height 1-3 ft (30-90 cm)
- ❏ Planting distance 1 ft (30 cm)
- ❏ Flowers midsummer to early fall
- ❏ Light, loamy soil
- ❏ Sunny site
- ❏ Hardy annual

The tall spikes of clarkias provide a valuable contrast to the rounded blooms of most other annuals. They come in a range of colors — white, pink, salmon, orange, scarlet, purple, and lavender — available as single colors or in mixtures. Blooming from midsummer to early fall, the slender plants are popular for borders, though they can also be grown as pot plants and for cutting.

Popular species and cultivars
Clarkia amoena (formerly listed as *Godetia*) bears loose spikes of lilac or pink to red funnel-shaped flowers. The plants reach 2 ft (60 cm) high.
Clarkia pulchella bears spikes of semidouble lavender flowers that form dainty sprays from midsummer to early fall. It reaches 12-15 in (30-38 cm) high. Mixed seed selections are available.
Clarkia unguiculata is one of the most popular clarkias, bearing 9-12 in (23-30 cm) long spikes of double flowers on erect and branching plants from midsummer to early fall. The plants reach 2 ft (60 cm) high. Several cultivars have been developed from this species, including 'Apple Blossom' (3 ft/90 cm, double, soft pink touched with white), 'Love Affair' (double, red, pink, purple, and white), 'Orange Queen' (double, orange), and 'Royal Bouquet' (double, carnationlike flowers in mixed colors).

Cultivation
Clarkias like a light, slightly acid loam, slightly moist for *Clarkia amoena*. All need plenty of sun.
Where winters are mild (zone 8 and south), sow seed from late summer to fall directly in the flowering site; elsewhere, sow in early spring. Thin when the seedlings are large enough to handle.
Do not feed the plants, as this encourages leaf growth at the expense of flowering.
Pests/diseases Damping-off fungi may attack seedlings, causing them to collapse. Stem rot and stem canker may infect older plants.

CLARKIA RUBICUNDA — see *Godetia*

Cleome
spider flower

Cleome spinosa

- ❏ Height 2-4 ft (60-120 cm)
- ❏ Planting distance 2 ft (60 cm)
- ❏ Flowers midsummer to fall
- ❏ Well-drained fertile soil
- ❏ Full sun
- ❏ Half-hardy annual

The spider flower *(Cleome spinosa)* is a handsome plant with globe-shaped flower heads and elegant green, divided leaves. The fragrant flowers open from midsummer until fall and come in white, delicate pink, and purple. In a tub the plants rarely exceed 2 ft (60 cm), but in well-prepared ground in a border they can grow up to 4 ft (120 cm) tall.

Popular species and cultivars
'Cherry Queen' has carmine-pink flowers.
'Color Fountain' has pink, rose, purple, lilac, and white flowers.
'Helen Campbell' is white.

Cultivation
Sow the seeds indoors 8-10 weeks before the local frost-free date, and keep at a temperature of 64°F (18°C). When the seedlings are large enough to handle, prick them out into small pots. Harden off for a few weeks before planting out in late spring. Grow in fertile, well-drained soil in full sun.
Pests/diseases Aphids may infest young growth.

CLOUD GRASS — see *Agrostis*

Cobaea
cathedral bells, cup-and-saucer vine

Cobaea scandens and 'Alba'

- ❏ Height 10-20 ft (300-600 cm)
- ❏ Planting distance 2 ft (60 cm)
- ❏ Flowers early summer to midfall
- ❏ Ordinary well-drained soil
- ❏ Sunny, sheltered site
- ❏ Tender annual

Cathedral bells *(Cobaea scandens)* is an annual climber, ideal for providing quick decorative cover for pergolas, trelliswork, and other forms of support. The plants may reach 20 ft (600 cm) high, growing vertically at first and then spreading at the top.

From early summer until midfall an abundance of purple bell-shaped flowers appear. These are seen against a backdrop of mid- to dark green leaves. The cultivar 'Alba' has greenish-white flowers.

Cultivation
Sow the seeds indoors — one seed in each 3-in (7.5-cm) pot of potting soil — 8 weeks before the last frost. Keep at a temperature of 64°F (18°C).

Harden off the plants before planting them outdoors in early summer. Choose a sunny, sheltered site with ordinary well-drained soil. Provide stakes, wire mesh, or a trellis for the plants' tendrils to cling to.
Pests/diseases Watch out for aphids.

COCKSCOMB — see *Celosia*

Coix
Job's tears

Coix lacryma-jobi

- ❏ Height 1½-2 ft (45-60 cm)
- ❏ Planting distance 6-9 in (15-23 cm)
- ❏ Flowers midsummer to early fall
- ❏ Fertile, well-drained garden soil
- ❏ Sunny site
- ❏ Half-hardy annual

Job's tears *(Coix lacryma-jobi),* an ornamental grass, is grown for its attractive pearly gray bead-shaped seeds, which form in midsummer and last until early fall. These seeds are carried in small dangling clusters on graceful arching stems, which reach up to 1½-2 ft (45-60 cm) high and are set with pale green broad leaves. The seeds are not suitable for drying.

Cultivation
Sow the seeds indoors in late winter or early spring in flats of seed-starting mix at a temperature of 55-61°F (13-16°C). Transplant the seedlings to their final site in late spring to early summer, when danger of frost has passed. Alternatively, sow the seeds outdoors in midspring.

Grow all Job's tears in well-drained soil that is enriched with humus. The site should be a sunny one — ideally facing south.
Pests/diseases Mildew may attack the plants.

Coleus
flame nettle

Coleus blumei 'Wizard Mixed'

- ❏ Height ½-1½ ft (15-45 cm)
- ❏ Planting distance 1 ft (30 cm)
- ❏ Foliage plant
- ❏ Moisture-retentive soil
- ❏ Sunny site or dappled shade
- ❏ Tender perennial grown as annual

Coleus blumei (now reclassified as *Solenostemon)* and its cultivars are valued for their colorful foliage — nettlelike leaves in various shades and patterns of green, yellow, red, and maroon. Though most commonly grown as indoor pot plants, they look equally effective in formal beds and containers outdoors, where they provide a splendid setting for summer-flowering plants.

The flowers — tiny blue or white tubular bells — are best removed as soon as buds form, to encourage bushy foliage.

Coleus blumei 'Pineapple Beauty'

Coleus blumei mixed

Popular species and cultivars
The following popular cultivars have been developed from *Coleus (Solenostemon) blumei*. Some are in single colors; others are sold as mixtures.

'Dragon' is a mixture with large serrated leaves in reds and maroons edged with gold. It reaches 1 ft (30 cm) high.

'Fairway' has delicate foliage on 8-10 in (20-25 cm) high, neatly growing plants. Its distinct colors come in various combinations.

'Fashion Parade' has elongated or deeply lobed, fringed or serrated leaves in shades of pink, gold, jade, and scarlet. It grows to 1 ft (30 cm) high.

'Milky Way' is a dwarf cultivar, to 6 in (15 cm) tall, with deeply cut leaves in either vivid or pale colors. It is suitable for window boxes and small pots.

'Mini Coral' is tiny, up to 6 in (15 cm) high and wide, with a well-balanced shape and various leaf color combinations.

'Molten Lava' has black and carmine leaves and reaches 9-12 in (23-30 cm) high.

'Pineapple Beauty' has yellow-green leaves with rich maroon markings. It reaches 1-1½ ft (30-45 cm) high.

'Rainbow' comes in a wide range of bright, rich foliage colors. It is a tall cultivar, reaching 1½ ft (45 cm) high.

'Rose Wizard' grows 10-12 in (25-30 cm) high and has foliage in shades of cream, bright green, and pink. It is good for hanging baskets.

'Scarlet Poncho' has maroon leaves with lemon-yellow edging. Its cascading habit makes it an excellent cultivar for hanging baskets. The plants reach 1 ft (30 cm) high.

'Wizard Hybrids' are a mixture of free-branching cultivars, up to 1 ft (30 cm) high, in a range of bright colors. The shoots do not need to be pinched.

Cultivation
Sow the seeds indoors 10 weeks before the last spring frost. Pot on as required, or plant out in early summer, either singly or in groups, spacing them 1 ft (30 cm) apart. *Coleus* grows in any well-drained but moisture-retentive soil in sun or dappled shade.

Pinch the growing tips and remove flower buds when they appear, to encourage side branching and healthy growth. Good color forms can be propagated from tip cuttings taken in late summer and rooted indoors.

Pests/diseases Trouble free.

Collinsia
Chinese houses, collinsia

Collinsia bicolor

- ❏ Height 2 ft (60 cm)
- ❏ Planting distance 6 in (15 cm)
- ❏ Flowers early summer to early fall
- ❏ Any moist soil
- ❏ Light shade
- ❏ Hardy annual

Easily grown and graceful, *Collinsia bicolor* is popular for its long flowering season. The slender stems, up to 2 ft (60 cm) high, carry opposite pairs of lance-shaped midgreen leaves below loose clusters of showy bicolored flowers with white upper lips and lilac lower ones.

Collinsias are suitable for growing in mixed borders and annual beds. They can also be grown in pots on a windowsill.

Cultivation
Sow seeds from early spring to midspring where the plants are to flower. Successive sowings at 2-week intervals will extend the flowering season. When the seedlings are large enough to handle, thin them to stand 6 in (15 cm) apart. Collinsias will grow in most types of soil, though a well-drained but moisture-retentive soil in partial shade gives the best results. Support the plants with twiggy sticks.
Pests/diseases Trouble free.

CONEFLOWER —
see *Rudbeckia*

Convolvulus
dwarf morning glory

Convolvulus tricolor 'Dwarf Rainbow Flash'

- ❏ Height 6-15 in (15-38 cm)
- ❏ Planting distance 6-9 in (15-23 cm)
- ❏ Flowers midsummer to early fall
- ❏ Any well-drained soil
- ❏ Sunny, sheltered site
- ❏ Hardy annual

Dwarf morning glory *(Convolvulus tricolor)*, the only annual in the genus, has all the beauty of its cousin, the white-flowered perennial bindweed *(C. arvensis)*, without its strangling habit.

Its funnel-shaped flowers, which are on display from midsummer until early fall, are a magnificent deep blue with white or yellow throats. Carried on 6-15 in (15-38 cm) high, bushy and erect plants with oval dark green

Convolvulus tricolor 'Royal Ensign'

leaves, they look most effective in formal beds or mixed borders.

Popular species and cultivars
The following favorite cultivars have been developed from *Convolvulus tricolor.*
'Blue Ensign' has brilliant blue flowers with yellow and white centers. It is a dwarf cultivar, 6 in (15 cm) high.
'Dwarf Rainbow Flash' has large flowers in mixed colors: pink, carmine, rose, deep blue, pale blue, purple, and lilac. It is 6 in (15 cm) high.
'Royal Ensign' has blue flowers with white and yellow centers.

Cultivation
In zone 8 and south, sow seeds outdoors after danger of frost is past; farther north, sow seeds indoors in peat pots 6 weeks before the last frost, and keep at a temperature of 59-64°F (15-18°C). Harden off before planting out in late spring, and set out 6-9 in (15-23 cm) apart.

The plants will grow in any well-drained soil, even a poor, dry one, in a sunny, sheltered site. Deadhead regularly.
Pests/diseases Trouble free.

Coreopsis
tickseed

Coreopsis tinctoria

❑ Height 1-2 ft (30-60 cm)
❑ Planting distance 6-9 in (15-23 cm)
❑ Flowers midsummer to early fall
❑ Fertile, well-drained soil
❑ Open, sunny site
❑ Hardy annual

These bushy plants with deeply cut green leaves and profuse daisylike blooms have two great assets — they thrive in hot weather and tolerate pollution.

Annual tickseeds (perennial tickseeds also exist) have flowers in a range of yellows and chestnuts from midsummer to early fall. They look best in borders and can be used for cutting.

Popular species and cultivars
Coreopsis tinctoria (syn. *C. bicolor)* has profuse bright yellow flowers on stiff stems about 2 ft (60 cm) tall. A dwarf cultivar reaches 1 ft (30 cm) high.

Cultivation
Sow the seeds in their flowering site from early spring to early summer for a succession of flowers. In mild climates (zones 8 and south), sow again from late summer through fall for winter and spring bloom. The best results are achieved in fertile, well-drained soil in an open, sunny site. Stake taller plants. Deadhead regularly.
Pests/diseases Trouble free.

CORN COCKLE —
see *Agrostemma*
CORNFLOWER —
see *Centaurea*

Cosmos
cosmos

Cosmos bipinnatus

❑ Height 2-6 ft (60-180 cm)
❑ Planting distance 1½-2 ft (45-60 cm)
❑ Flowers late summer to early fall
❑ Light soil
❑ Full sun
❑ Half-hardy annual

An abundance of delicate, richly colored dahlialike flowers, borne among pretty, light green leaves, makes these half-hardy annuals excellent for late-summer color in borders and containers.

The flowers come in pinks, reds,

Cosmos bipinnatus 'Sensation'

Crepis
hawksbeard

Crepis rubra 'Alba'

Crepis rubra

Cosmos sulphureus 'Sunny Red'

and white with yellow centers, or shades of orange, vermilion, and yellow. Growing on stems 2-6 ft (60-180 cm) high, they are also ideal for cutting.

Popular species and cultivars
Cosmos bipinnatus reaches 3 ft (90 cm) high. It has white, crimson, rose, or pink flowers with yellow central disks and finely cut midgreen leaves. Popular cultivars are 'Candy Stripe' (white with crimson stripes), 'Gloria' (rose-pink with central dark bands; up to 6 in/15 cm wide), 'Psyche' (semidouble and single pink, red, or white, with frilled petals), 'Purity' (white), and 'Sensation' (white, pink, carmine, and crimson).
Cosmos sulphureus reaches just 2 ft (60 cm) high and has yellow flowers accompanied by coarsely cut dark green leaves. Popular cultivars include 'Bright Lights' (small, double, yellow, orange, or scarlet), 'Diablo' (orange-red), 'Lemon Twist' (acid-yellow), 'Sunny Gold' (semidouble, golden yellow), and 'Sunny Red' (double, vermilion).

Cultivation
Sow the seeds indoors 6 weeks before the last spring frost, and keep at a temperature of 61°F (16°C). Harden off before planting out in late spring.

Cosmos prefer poor, light soil in a hot, dry corner. Stake the plants and deadhead regularly.
Pests/diseases Aphids sometimes infest young plants.

COTTON THISTLE —
see *Onopordum*

❏ Height 1 ft (30 cm)
❏ Planting distance 6 in (15 cm)
❏ Flowers early spring or summer
❏ Any well-drained soil
❏ Full sun
❏ Hardy annual

Most species of the genus *Crepis* are weeds, but a few are suitably handsome for garden decoration, including the annual *Crepis rubra*. This accommodating plant has basal rosettes of pale green toothed and lance-shaped leaves above which rise 1 ft (30 cm) high stems. The stems are topped with a mass of loose clusters of double dandelionlike flowers throughout the summer months. They are rose-pink in the species and white in the cultivar 'Alba.' Another cultivar, 'Snowplume,' has feathery white blossoms with pale apricot centers.

These charming plants are suitable for growing at the front of annual and mixed borders and in rock gardens; they are also long-lasting as cut flowers.

Cultivation
In the South, sow seeds directly in the flowering site in fall for early-spring flowering. Where winters may be harsh, sow in early spring to midspring, covering the seeds lightly with soil. Thin all seedlings to stand 6 in (15 cm) apart when they are large enough to handle.

Crepis will grow well in any dry and well-drained soil, even a poor one, provided it is given full sun. It tolerates exposed sites and thrives in coastal regions. Deadhead regularly to prevent self-seeding; cultivars do not come true to type.
Pests/diseases Generally trouble free.

CUP-AND-SAUCER VINE —
see *Cobaea*
CUPFLOWER —
see *Nierembergia*

Cynoglossum
hound's tongue

Cynoglossum amabile

❏ Height 1½-2 ft (45-60 cm)
❏ Planting distance 1 ft (30 cm)
❏ Flowers spring or mid- to late summer
❏ Well-drained fertile soil
❏ Sunny or partially shaded site
❏ Hardy annual or biennial

Sometimes known as Chinese forget-me-not, *Cynoglossum amabile* produces flowers in greater profusion than the ordinary forget-me-not. The tongue-shaped leaves are gray-green and downy. Although a true biennial, hound's tongue will flower in the same year it was started from seed, raising its sprays of turquoise-blue flowers on slender stems above the bushy foliage. The cultivar 'Blue Showers' has sky-blue flowers.

Hound's tongue is suitable for growing in annual and mixed borders, as edging to semiwild areas, and in containers. The flowers last well in water.

Cultivation
In mild-winter regions, sow the seeds directly into the flowering site in the fall to bloom the next spring. In the North, seed directly in early spring. Seeds should germinate in a couple of weeks and flower 2 months later. For best development of the plant, thin seedlings to a spacing of 1 ft (30 cm) apart. The plants self-seed freely and should be deadheaded regularly.

Hound's tongues grow in any good, well-drained soil; they thrive in full sun or partial shade.
Pests/diseases Tobacco mosaic virus may cause mottling of leaves and stunting of plants.

Dahlia
bedding dahlia

Bedding dahlias

❏ Height 1-4 ft (30-120 cm)
❏ Planting distance 1-2 ft (30-60 cm)
❏ Flowers midsummer to first hard frost
❏ Medium to heavy soil
❏ Open, sunny site
❏ Half-hardy annual

A number of dahlia cultivars can be grown from seed for flowering the same year. Known as bedding dahlias, they are more modest cousins of the large perennial border dahlias growing from tubers. They have similar, though smaller, flowers and vary in height from 1 ft (30 cm) to 4 ft (120 cm). The flowers, in white, yellow, orange, scarlet, crimson, and pink, appear in midsummer and continue until the first hard frost.

Use these half-hardy annuals in containers and window boxes, beds, and the foreground of a mixed border.

Popular species and cultivars
The range of cultivars available increases and changes every year. The following are some of the most popular. The majority come in mixed colors.
'Bambino Hybrids' are miniature cultivars, growing 1-1½ ft (30-45 cm) high and carrying a profusion of double flowers. They are good for pots and containers.
'Cactus-Flowered Hybrids' have semidouble and double flowers with quilled petals. They reach 3-4 ft (90-120 cm) high.
'Collarette Dandy' has single flowers, each with a white or yellow collar of inner petals around the central disk. The plants reach 1½-2 ft (45-60 cm) high.
'Coltness Hybrids,' some of the most popular, are dwarf cultivars reaching just 20 in (50 cm) high. The large single flowers are freely produced.
'Diablo' is similar to 'Redskin,' but the semidouble flowers and bronze-green foliage are borne on more compact plants, 15-18 in (38-45 cm) tall.
'Mignon Silver' has pure white flowers shading to pale yellow-green near the center. The plants grow 15-20 in (38-50 cm) high.
'Pompon Mixed' has small ball flowers and reaches 3 ft (90 cm).
'Redskin' has large semidouble flowers and rich bronze foliage. It reaches up to 20 in (50 cm) high. A dwarf mixture produces similar plants, 15 in (38 cm) tall.
'Rigoletto' is an early-flowering dwarf cultivar, 12-20 in (30-50 cm) high, with both double and semidouble blooms.

Datura
angel's trumpet

Dahlia 'Coltness Hybrids'

'**Sunburst**' bears single flowers, up to 5 in (12.5 cm) wide, with broad overlapping petals that form circular blooms. The plant is about 2 ft (60 cm) high.

'**Unwin Hybrids**' produce an abundance of double flowers in a particularly wide range of colors. These blooms are long-lasting and are carried on plants 1½-2 ft (45-60 cm) high.

Cultivation

Sow the seeds indoors 6-8 weeks before the last frost in flats of seed-starting mix. Keep them at a temperature of 61°F (16°C). When large enough to handle, prick out the seedlings into flats and later into 3 in (7.5 cm) pots. Harden off from midspring on, and plant out in late spring to early summer, when danger of frost is past.

Bedding dahlias grow best in a medium to heavy soil in an open, sunny spot. Enrich poor soils with well-decayed compost several weeks before planting out. Water regularly in hot weather, and deadhead for continuous flowering. Staking is unnecessary.

Pests/diseases Aphids and caterpillars may attack, and European corn borers may feed on buds and tunnel down through stems, causing them to wilt. Botrytis can be troublesome on flower stalks, buds, and older flowers in wet summers.

Datura metel 'Aurea'

❏ Height 2-3 ft (60-90 cm)
❏ Planting distance 2-2½ ft (60-75 cm)
❏ Flowers midsummer to early fall
❏ Ordinary soil
❏ Sunny, sheltered site
❏ Perennial grown as a tender annual

Angel's trumpet could be a misnomer, for these exotic plants are poisonous in all their parts and are best kept out of gardens where there are children. But in spite of this and their frost tenderness, they produce an impressive show of trumpet-shaped flowers with a strong fragrance, which is headiest in the evening.

Daturas are technically shrubby perennials but are usually grown as tender annuals in mixed borders and beds. They are ideal as pot and container plants.

Popular species and cultivars
Datura metel grows 2 ft (60 cm) or more high. It forms a shrubby plant with red stems set with ovate dark green leaves. The flowers, 8 in (20 cm) long, are creamy white and held erect. 'Aurea' bears yellow flowers. Pink and purple cultivars also exist.

Datura meteloides, a bushy plant, reaches a height of 3 ft (90 cm) and bears hairy gray leaves with a pungent aroma. The upright, white or pink-flushed flowers, 6 in (15 cm) long, are sweetly scented. The cultivar 'Evening Fragrance' has larger, more strongly scented flowers of pure white,

Datura meteloides

with picotee edges picked out in lavender.

Cultivation

Sow seeds indoors 2-3 months before the last frost, and keep them at 61°F (16°C). When the seedlings are large enough to handle, prick them out into small pots of potting compost and grow on. Harden off the young plants before setting them out when all danger of frost has passed.

In the open garden, daturas grow in any garden soil, in a sunny and sheltered spot. For pot plants, choose an ordinary well-drained potting soil.

Pests/diseases Trouble free.

Delphinium
larkspur

Delphinium consolida

- ❏ Height 1-4 ft (30-120 cm)
- ❏ Planting distance 9-12 in (23-30 cm)
- ❏ Flowers early to late summer
- ❏ Fertile, well-drained soil
- ❏ Sunny or lightly shaded site
- ❏ Hardy annual

One of the most enchanting sights in a summer herbaceous border is a mass of blue, white, and pink delphinium spires soaring into the sky above attractive fernlike foliage. Two species — *Delphinium ajacis* and *D. consolida* (which botanists now call *Consolida ambigua* and *C. orientalis)* and their cultivars — are hardy annuals.

Commonly known as larkspurs, they reach 1-4 ft (30-120 cm), so they should be grown in herbaceous borders where there is plenty of space. Though blue and white are the most common flower colors, shades of pink, lavender, and purple are also available.

Popular species and cultivars
Delphinium ajacis (Consolida ambigua), or rocket larkspur, reaches 1-3 ft (30-90 cm) high and has sparsely branching stems bearing spires of loosely arranged flowers. The hyacinth-flowered hybrids are the most commonly grown — they make excellent cut flowers as well as decoration for borders. They come in blues, purples, pinks, and whites. The cultivar 'Imperial Blue Bell' reaches a height of 3-4 ft (90-120 cm) and bears extra-long spikes of double sky-blue flowers. 'Imperial White King' is similar except that its flowers are white.

Delphinium consolida (Consolida orientalis), or larkspur, is a taller species, reaching 4 ft (120 cm) high, with a more branching habit. The flowers are arranged in densely packed spikes and come in shades of blue, red, purple, pink, and white.

Cultivation
Sow seeds in the flowering site in early spring to midspring. When the seedlings are large enough to handle, thin to 9-12 in (23-30 cm) apart for rocket larkspur and its cultivars, and 12 in (30 cm) for larkspur and its cultivars. In mild areas, sow seeds in early fall for larger, early-flowering plants.

These annuals like fertile, well-drained soil in full sun or partial shade. Support tall cultivars with twiggy sticks, and cut out faded stems after flowering.

Pests/diseases Slugs, snails, and powdery mildew may affect the leaves, stems, and flowers.

Delphinium ajacis

Dianthus
pink, sweet William

Dianthus chinensis

Dianthus barbatus

- ❏ Height 8-24 in (20-60 cm)
- ❏ Planting distance 6-10 in (15-25 cm)
- ❏ Flowers early summer until first frost
- ❏ Well-drained garden soil
- ❏ Full sun
- ❏ Hardy annual or biennial

Dianthus is a large genus of mainly perennials, but it also includes two species that are usually grown as biennials and annuals: *Dianthus barbatus* (sweet William) and *D. chinensis* (Indian pink). Both have fragrant flowers in shades of pink, red, cream, and white. They appear in summer against a foil of narrow green leaves and are excellent as cut flowers.

The annual and biennial dianthuses are particularly useful for urban and seaside gardens, as they tolerate air pollution and salt spray.

Popular species and cultivars
Dianthus barbatus (sweet William) is often grown as a biennial. During early summer and midsummer it bears dense heads of sweetly scented single or double flowers in combinations of white, pink, and red.

An enormous range of sweet William cultivars are available. Most are the standard 1-2 ft (30-60 cm) high, but a few dwarf cultivars, reaching just 8-10 in (20-25 cm) high, can also be found. Popular cultivars include 'Auricula-Eyed' (a mixture of pink, red, and crimson flowers with conspicuous white eyes), 'Dunnet's Dark Crimson' (dark crimson), 'Dwarf Double Pinocchio Hybrids' (dwarf mixture, ideal for containers), 'Excelsior Mixed' (to 1½ ft/45 cm; pinks and reds; fragrant), 'Harlequin' (pink and white ball-shaped flower heads), and 'Indian Carpet' (dwarf bedding mixture with long-lasting flowers).

Dianthus chinensis (Indian pink) has a range of cultivars, which are grown as hardy annuals. The plants are small and compact with pale to midgreen grasslike foliage and attractive flowers with notched petals in shades of red, pink, and white. Often the blooms have patterns or darker central zones. They are borne from midsummer until the first frost.

Indian pinks reach 1 ft (30 cm) high, making excellent edging for borders. They can also be used in formal beds.

Popular cultivars are 'Baby Doll' (mixture of large single flowers in shades of crimson, rose-pink, and white), 'Color Magician' (an F1 hybrid with colors ranging from white through pink to deep rose on the same plant), 'Fire Carpet' (single, bright scarlet), 'Magic Charm' (fringed; pinks, reds, white, or bicolored), 'Snowfire' (white with scarlet center), and 'Telstar' (early flowering; bright crimson, pink, white, and bicolored).

Cultivation
In the North, sow the seeds of sweet William indoors 8 weeks before the local frost-free date; in the South, sow outdoors in fall. Dianthuses flourish in full sun and any well-drained soil. Treat acid soil with lime. Stake only if the site is exposed and the soil is rich.

Indian pinks are grown as hardy annuals. Sow the seeds thinly in the flowering site in midspring. When the seedlings are large enough to handle, thin to 6-10 in (15-25 cm) apart. Grow in well-drained alkaline or neutral soil in full sun.

Pests/diseases Sweet Williams are susceptible to rust.

Dianthus chinensis 'Baby Doll'

Diascia
twinspur

Diascia baberae

❑ Height 15 in (38 cm)
❑ Planting distance 6 in (15 cm)
❑ Flowers late spring to early fall
❑ Any light, well-drained soil
❑ Full sun
❑ Half-hardy annual

The little twinspur *(Diascia barberae)* gets its name from the shape of its shell-like two-spurred flowers. They are rosy pink and borne in loose clusters on top of slender stems from late spring or early summer straight through to fall. Twinspur is a slender plant, clothed with ovate, glossy dark green leaves, and ideal for growing in groups at the front of borders, in beds, and in containers. The cultivar 'Rose Queen' has exquisite blooms in great profusion.

Cultivation
Sow the seeds indoors 6-8 weeks before the last frost at a temperature of 61°F (16°C), covering them lightly. When the seedlings are large enough to handle, prick them out into flats of potting soil. Harden them off in late spring, and transplant the young plants to their flowering sites when all danger of frost is past.

Any light and well-drained soil in full sun is suitable. Pinch the growing point to encourage side branching, and deadhead regularly to maintain continuous flowering.
Pests/diseases Generally trouble free.

Digitalis
foxglove

Digitalis purpurea

❑ Height 3-5 ft (90-150 cm)
❑ Planting distance 1½ ft (45 cm)
❑ Flowers early summer to midsummer
❑ Any moisture-retentive soil
❑ Sun or partial shade
❑ Hardy biennial; may be grown as an annual

Foxglove *(Digitalis purpurea)* combines strength and delicacy, growing 5 ft (150 cm) high in good conditions, yet needing no support for its gracefully arching stems. In early summer and midsummer these stems, rising from rosettes of green leaves, turn into one-sided spires of spotted red-purple or white bell-shaped flowers.

Foxgloves make excellent border plants, even in winter, when their rosettes of foliage form good ground cover. They also look very effective in a semiwild corner of the garden.

Popular species and cultivars
Several cultivars of common foxglove are readily available.

'**Alba**' has pure white flowers, suitable for cutting.
'**Apricot**' has apricot flowers.
'**Excelsior Hybrids**' have tall spikes of maroon-spotted white, cream, pink, and carmine flowers.
'**Foxy**' is a dwarf hybrid strain, about 3 ft (90 cm) tall, with flower spikes in white, cream, pink, and carmine, all spotted with maroon. It blooms during its first year of growth.

Cultivation
In milder climates (zone 7 and south), sow the seeds outdoors from late summer through fall. Scatter them on the soil's surface and then gently rake in. In cold-winter regions, start the seeds indoors 8-10 weeks before the last frost. Thin or transplant seedlings to 1½ ft (45 cm) apart in a sunny or lightly shaded spot. Do not let the soil dry out in summer.

When the central spikes have finished flowering, remove them to encourage side shoots.
Pests/diseases Trouble free.

Dimorphotheca
Cape marigold, star of the veldt

Dimorphotheca sinuata

Dimorphotheca 'Glistening White'

❑ Height ½-1½ ft (15-45 cm)
❑ Planting distance 1-1½ ft (30-45 cm)
❑ Flowers early summer to early fall
❑ Light, well-drained soil
❑ Sunny site
❑ Perennial grown as tender annual

In its native South Africa, star of the veldt grows rapidly and flowers quickly so it can produce its seeds before the dry season sets in. Fortunately, in cooler climates, it lasts longer, producing hundreds of elegant daisylike flowers from early summer until early fall. These are brilliant orange, with dark brown eyes, and are carried on 1-1½ ft (30-45 cm) high stems with narrowly oblong midgreen leaves.

The genus has been reclassified as *Osteospermum*, and seed catalogs may list stars of the veldt under either name. Their popularity has risen steadily due to their long flowering season and the brightness of their daisy flowers, sometimes with yellow, sometimes with purple centers. They look magnificent grown in groups in borders and beds, and the dwarf cultivars are suitable for sunny rock gardens and for patio containers.

The most popular species, *Dimorphotheca (Osteospermum) sinuata*, is a perennial, but it is invariably grown as a tender annual. It will, however, often survive winters outdoors in mild districts if set in a protected spot.

Popular species and cultivars
Several cultivars have been developed from *Dimorphotheca sinuata*, offering a range of colors and sizes. The following are readily available.
'Giant Mixed' grows 1 ft (30 cm) high and produces plants with a profusion of flowers in pastel shades — creamy white, orange, and salmon.
'Glistening White' bears silvery and pure white flowers. It grows 6-9 in (15-23 cm) high.
'Salmon Queen' grows up to 1 ft (30 cm) tall, with large, 2½-in (6-cm) wide blossoms in pastel shades of salmon and apricot. Set these branching plants 1½ ft (45 cm) apart.

'Starshine' bears 2-3 in (5-7.5 cm) wide, glistening flowers in pink, rose, carmine, or white, all with yellow centers. The plants grow to 1½ ft (45 cm) high and almost as much across.
'Tetra Pole Star,' up to 15-18 in (38-45 cm) high, has shiny, 3-in (7.5-cm) wide silvery flowers with bright violet veins.

Cultivation
Sow the seeds indoors 4-6 weeks before the last frost at a temperature of 64°F (18°C). Harden off, and plant out when danger of frost has passed. Space them 1 ft (30 cm) or more apart.

In mild areas seeds can be sown in the flowering site in late summer for fall to winter bloom and a repeat flowering in the spring. All dimorphothecas need a sunny spot with cool temperatures and light, well-drained soil. Thin to 1 ft (30 cm) apart when the seedlings are large enough to handle.

These plants produce the best bloom when the weather is dry and night temperatures hover around 50°F (10°C). Deadhead to encourage repeat flowering.

Cultivars can be increased by 3-in (7.5-cm) tip cuttings taken in late summer and rooted in compost in a cold frame. Overwinter the cuttings in a warm greenhouse.
Pests/diseases Gray mold can affect plants in wet weather.

DUSTY MILLER —
see *Senecio*

Echium
viper's bugloss

Echium 'Dwarf Hybrids'

- ❏ Height 1-2 ft (30-60 cm)
- ❏ Planting distance 9-18 in (23-45 cm)
- ❏ Flowers early to late summer
- ❏ Any well-drained garden soil
- ❏ Sunny site
- ❏ Hardy annual or biennial

Echiums are valuable in summer beds and borders, where their bright, upturned bell-shaped flowers add color throughout the summer and are very attractive to bees. Although of biennial habit, they will flower in their first year from seed and frequently seed themselves.

Popular species and cultivars
Echium lycopsis (syn. *E. plantagineum*) is a bushy, erect annual growing to a height of 2 ft (60 cm), its stems set with midgreen oblong leaves. From early summer on, 10 in (25 cm) long flower spikes are closely packed with purple or blue tubular blooms. Several seed selections, ideal for containers, are available, including 'Blue Bedder' (1 ft/30 cm high, bearing deep blue flowers), and 'Dwarf Hybrids' (1 ft/30 cm tall, in a mixture of white, pink, rose, and various shades of blue and purple).

Echium vulgare is a biennial usually grown as an annual. It is about 2 ft (60 cm) high, of bushy but compact habit, with leaves that are lance-shaped and dark green. The tubular flowers are borne in shorter but dense and profuse spikes; they are purple in bud and open violet-blue.

Cultivation
Sow seeds in the flowering site in fall in zone 8 and south, in early spring elsewhere. Thin the seedlings when large enough to handle, to stand 1½ ft (45 cm) apart for *Echium lycopsis* and 9 in (23 cm) for dwarf cultivars and *E. vulgare*. In areas with long, cold winters, start seeds indoors 6-8 weeks before the last frost.

Echiums will grow in any kind of soil and site, but flower most profusely in light, well-drained soil in full sun.

Pests/diseases Trouble free.

Emilia
tassel flower

Emilia javanica

- ❏ Height 1½-2 ft (45-60 cm)
- ❏ Planting distance 10 in (25 cm)
- ❏ Flowers early to late summer
- ❏ Well-drained garden soil
- ❏ Sunny site
- ❏ Half-hardy annual

Tassel flowers are excellent half-hardy annuals for providing a splash of orange, scarlet, and gold in sunny, dry borders in seaside gardens. Their tassellike flowers, carried on wiry stems throughout the summer, look most effective planted in mixed bedding displays, though they also make excellent subjects for containers, and as cut flowers they are long-lasting in water. Only one species, *Emilia javanica*, is grown in the United States. It reaches up to 1½-2 ft (45-60 cm) high. Mixed seed selections with orange and gold flowers are available.

Cultivation
Sow the seeds in their flowering site — a hot, dry sunny spot with well-drained soil — in late spring. Thin to 10 in (25 cm) apart when the seedlings are large enough to handle. Deadhead to encourage flowering all summer long.

Pests/diseases Trouble free.

ENGLISH DAISY — see *Bellis*

Eschscholzia
California poppy

Eschscholzia californica 'Monarch Hybrids'

Eschscholzia californica

- ❏ Height 5-15 in (13-38 cm)
- ❏ Planting distance 6 in (15 cm)
- ❏ Flowers early summer to midfall
- ❏ Any garden soil
- ❏ Sunny site
- ❏ Hardy annual

The fragile delicate charm of this group of poppies is apparent from the moment the conical green hats split open around their buds of crumpled silk until the petals fall to reveal long, cylindrical seed heads. Produced from early summer to midfall, the bright flowers are complemented by exquisitely cut blue-green foliage.

Two species and their cultivars are popular in gardens, where they can be grown in borders with poor sandy soil or on sunny banks. They produce self-sown seedlings, so you can rely upon them to appear year after year.

Popular species and cultivars
Eschscholzia caespitosa (syn. *E. tenuifolia)* has small yellow flowers, which appear freely between early summer and early fall. It is a dwarf species, reaching just 5 in (13 cm) high, so it looks best as edging at the front of a border or in a rock garden. Space the plants 6 in (15 cm) apart. The popular cultivar 'Sundew' bears scented lemon-yellow blooms.

Eschscholzia californica bears masses of bright orange-yellow flowers from early summer until midfall, followed by long cylindrical blue-green seedpods. The plants reach 12-15 in (30-38 cm) high. Popular cultivars include 'Ballerina' (double red, orange, pink, and yellow flowers, sometimes striped white), 'Dalli' (bicolored scarlet and yellow flowers on compact plants), 'Monarch Hybrids' (single and semidouble blooms in yellow, orange, red, and carmine-pink), 'Orange King' (translucent orange flowers), and 'Purple-Violet' (unusual purple flowers with a hint of red in them).

Cultivation
Where winters are mild, sow the seeds in the flowering site in fall, covering them with just a sprinkling of soil; in the North, sow as soon as the soil can be worked in spring. Thin seedlings to 6 in (15 cm) apart, when they are large enough to handle.

These poppies will grow in any soil, but thrive in poor, sandy soil and in full sun, which encourages an abundance of flowers with strong colors.

For plants the following year, delay clearing the site until the seeds have scattered.

Pests/diseases Trouble free.

Eschscholzia caespitosa

49

Euphorbia
euphorbia

Euphorbia marginata

Euphorbia lathyris

- ❏ Height 1½-3 ft (45-90 cm)
- ❏ Planting distance 1-1½ ft (30-45 cm)
- ❏ Foliage plant
- ❏ Ordinary garden soil
- ❏ Sun or partial shade
- ❏ Hardy or half-hardy annual

Annual euphorbias are usually grown in borders for their elegant foliage. They do have flowers in summer, but these seem insignificant beside the scarlet or cream petallike bracts, which are modified leaves.

The plants form neat bushes 2-3 ft (60-90 cm) high. They tolerate partial shade as well as sun, and grow in any ordinary garden soil. Indeed, the foliage colors become more intense when the plants are grown in poor soil.

Popular species and cultivars
Euphorbia heterophylla, commonly known as fire-on-the-mountain or annual poinsettia, is a neat, bushy half-hardy annual, with dark green oval or lance-shaped leaves. At the end of each shoot a 4 in (10 cm) wide whorl of red bracts appears from midsummer to early fall with small crimson-orange flowers.

Euphorbia lathyris, or caper spurge, is attractive with long, thin green leaves arranged symmetrically on upright stems. In early summer to midsummer small yellow flowers appear in leafy heads. The plants reach 3 ft (90 cm) high.

Euphorbia marginata (snow-on-the-mountain) has bright green oval leaves, which become edged and veined with white as the plant matures. Insignificant white flowers appear in early fall. 'Summer Icicle,' heavily variegated, is 1½ ft (45 cm) tall.

Cultivation
Sow in a sunny site when spring has warmed the soil; the seeds need temperatures of 70-75°F (21-24°C) to germinate. When seedlings are large enough to handle, thin to 1 ft (30 cm) apart.

Where the growing season is short, sow seeds indoors 6 weeks before the last frost. Harden off and plant out in late spring.
Pests/diseases Trouble free.

Felicia
felicia

Felicia bergerana

❏ Height ½-1½ ft (15-45 cm)
❏ Planting distance 6-9 in (15-23 cm)
❏ Flowers early summer to early fall
❏ Ordinary well-drained garden soil
❏ Sunny, sheltered site
❏ Half-hardy annual

This little-known South African plant is rather special as it is one of the few daisy look-alikes with blue flowers. These appear in great profusion throughout the summer, with slender blue petals arranged around a yellow central disk. The plants form attractive domes of gray-green foliage and make excellent window-box fillers or edging for borders.

Popular species and cultivars
Felicia amelloides (blue marguerite) has sky-blue flowers, standing 1½ ft (45 cm) above domes of midgreen foliage from early until late summer.
Felicia bergerana (kingfisher daisy) is a dwarf species (6 in/15 cm high) with gray-green foliage and steel-blue flowers from early summer to early fall.

Cultivation
Sow the seeds indoors in flats of seed-starting mix in late winter to early spring, and keep at a temperature of 61°F (16°C). When the seedlings are large enough to handle, prick out into flats or pots of potting soil and grow on at 50°F (10°C). Harden off and plant out once all danger of frost is past. They will grow in any ordinary well-drained garden soil in a sunny, sheltered spot.

Deadhead by lightly shearing after the first flush to ensure a second display of flowers.
Pests/diseases Trouble free.

FEVERFEW —
see *Chrysanthemum*
FIELD POPPY — see *Papaver*
FIRE-ON-THE-MOUNTAIN —
see *Euphorbia*
FLAME NETTLE — see *Coleus*
FLAX — see *Linum*
FLOSSFLOWER — see *Ageratum*
FORGET-ME-NOT —
see *Myosotis*
FOUR O'CLOCK —
see *Mirabilis*
FOXGLOVE — see *Digitalis*
FRENCH MARIGOLD —
see *Tagetes*

Gaillardia
blanket flower

Gaillardia pulchella

❏ Height 1-2 ft (30-60 cm)
❏ Planting distance 1 ft (30 cm)
❏ Flowers midsummer to midfall
❏ Any well-drained soil
❏ Sunny site
❏ Hardy annual

This genus of bright daisylike flowers has one annual species, *Gaillardia pulchella,* or blanket flower. Its single red flowers are edged in yellow from midsummer to midfall. They are suitable for herbaceous borders and also make good cut flowers.

Popular species and cultivars
These popular cultivars come from *Gaillardia pulchella.*
'**Double Mixed,**' 2 ft (60 cm) high, has 3 in (7.5 cm) wide, double flowers in cream-white, gold, crimson, and bicolors.
'**Red Plume**' has double, round-headed red, gold, or yellow flowers. It grows 1 ft (30 cm) high.
The variety *G.p. lorenziana* has double, round-headed red, gold, or yellow flowers. It grows 1 ft (30 cm) tall.

Cultivation
Blanket flowers grow reasonably well in a variety of sites, but a light, well-drained soil in a sunny exposure gives the best results. In mild-winter regions, sow the seeds in the flowering site and thin to 1 ft (30 cm) apart; where winters are severe, start seed indoors 6 weeks before the last frost. Support with twiggy sticks may be necessary; deadhead to prolong the flowering period.
Pests/diseases Downy mildew may affect the leaves.

Gazania
gazania

Gazania species

❏ Height 8-15 in (20-38 cm)
❏ Planting distance 1 ft (30 cm)
❏ Flowers midsummer to first frost
❏ Well-drained soil
❏ Sunny site
❏ Half-hardy annual

Large daisylike flowers in bright yellows are the main feature of this mat-forming 9 in (23 cm) high South African plant. The flowers appear from midsummer to the first frost, but open only in bright sunshine — even then they close in midafternoon. The leaves are deep green, with white-felted undersides.

Gazanias are excellent for beds and make good cut flowers. They are wind resistant and thrive in seaside gardens and in the Southwest; a combination of heat and humidity is fatal to gazanias.

Popular species and cultivars
Most garden cultivars are developed from *Gazania × hybrida*.
'Carnival Hybrids,' an F1 mixture, grow to 14 in (35 cm) tall, with silver-green foliage and flowers in pink, rose, bronze, and red shades, sometimes striped or bicolored.
'Chansonette,' up to 1 ft (30 cm) tall, bears 3-in (7.5-cm) wide flowers in lemon, orange, gold, apricot, and pink-red shades.
'Harlequin Hybrids,' 15 in (38 cm) tall, have brightly colored flowers in shades of yellow, orange, brown, pink, and red, each with a brown zone around the central disk.
'Mini Star Hybrids' have bright yellow, red, pink, and orange flowers on neat, compact plants, 8 in (20 cm) tall.
'Talent Mixed' has short stems, to 8 in (20 cm) high, set with finely cut silvery leaves and flowers in pastel and strong colors.

Cultivation
Sow the seeds indoors 6-8 weeks before the last frost, and keep at a temperature of 61°F (16°C). Prick out into 3-in (7.5-cm) pots, and harden off before planting out after the risk of frost is past.

Set gazanias 1 ft (30 cm) apart in well-drained to dry soil in a sunny spot.
Pests/diseases Botrytis can damage or kill the plants in wet weather.

GERANIUM — see *Pelargonium*

Gilia
gilia

Gilia capitata and *Gilia tricolor*

❏ Height 2-3 ft (60-90 cm)
❏ Planting distance 9 in (23 cm)
❏ Flowers early summer to early fall
❏ Light, well-drained soil
❏ Sunny site
❏ Hardy annual

Gilias are grown for their attractive feathery midgreen foliage and showy flowers, which appear from early summer on. They are good for massing in beds and borders and as cut flowers.

Popular species and cultivars
Gilia capitata has pincushionlike heads of lavender-blue flowers from early summer to early fall on 3-ft (90-cm) high stems.
Gilia tricolor, 2 ft (60 cm) tall, has clusters of pale violet bell-shaped flowers, ringed maroon at the base, in early summer.

Cultivation
In mild-winter regions sow in the flowering site in fall for flowering in early summer of the next year; in the North sow in early spring for flowering later in summer. Ordinary garden soil suffices, but a light, well-drained soil is best. The site should be in full sun. Thin seedlings to 9 in (23 cm) apart when they are large enough to handle — leave fall-sown ones until spring.
Pests/diseases Trouble free.

GLOBE AMARANTH —
see *Gomphrena*

Godetia
godetia

Godetia

Godetia 'Dwarf Show Mixed'

- ❏ Height 9-36 in (23-90 cm)
- ❏ Planting distance 6 in (15 cm)
- ❏ Flowers early to late summer
- ❏ Ordinary well-drained soil
- ❏ Sunny site
- ❏ Hardy annual

Godetia, an old favorite among border plants, is listed here under its traditional name, although botanists have recently reclassified it as *Clarkia.* Godetias owe their popularity to their bushy habit, abundance of brightly colored flowers, and the ease with which they can be grown. The funnel-shaped blooms — single, double, semidouble, and frilled — are carried at the top of upright leafy spikes from early to late summer.

They are suitable for beds, borders, pots, or containers, and as cut flowers.

Popular species and cultivars
Only *Godetia grandiflora* (now *Clarkia rubicunda)* is commonly grown, but many cultivars have been developed from it.

'Azalea-Flowered' has semi-double flowers with wavy-edged petals in shades of pale pink, carmine-pink, salmon-pink, and white. The plants stand 15-18 in (38-45 cm) high.

'Crimson Glow,' a dwarf plant reaching 9 in (23 cm) high, has single red flowers.

'Double White,' growing 15-20 in (38-50 cm) high, has double white flowers.

'Duchess of Albany,' 12-15 in (30-38 cm) high, has satin-white frilled flowers.

'Dwarf Show Mixed,' 9-12 in (23-30 cm) high, bears single flowers in mixed colors on compact plants.

'Firelight' is bright crimson on 12-15 in (30-38 cm) high plants.

'Grace Hybrids,' a tall F1 hybrid mixture up to 2½ ft (75 cm) high, bear flowers marbled in lavender, salmon, pinks, and reds.

'Salmon Princess' is a compact plant, 10-12 in (25-30 cm) high, with salmon-pink flowers.

'Sybil Sherwood' has lilac-pink flowers edged with white. The plants are 15 in (38 cm) high.

'Tall Double Mixed' has pink, red, rose, and purple double flowers on 2½-3 ft (75-90 cm) high stems.

Cultivation
Godetias like a well-drained but moisture-retentive soil in a sunny site. If the soil is too rich, excessive foliage will grow at the expense of the flowers.

Where winters are mild, sow seeds in their flowering site from late summer through fall; in cold-weather regions sow as soon as the soil can be worked in spring. Thin the seedlings to 6 in (15 cm) apart. Stake the taller cultivars in exposed sites, and water during dry weather.

Pests/diseases Overwatering can cause yellow, brown, or khaki patches on the leaves, which then fall off prematurely.

Godetia 'Azalea-Flowered'

Gomphrena
globe amaranth

Gomphrena globosa 'Full Mix'

❏ Height ½-2 ft (15-60 cm)
❏ Planting distance 6-9 in (15-23 cm)
❏ Flowers midsummer to early fall
❏ Ordinary well-drained soil
❏ Sunny site
❏ Half-hardy annual

Globe amaranths grow wild in India; in North America they thrive in areas with hot, humid summers, making them one of the best annuals for the Deep South.

One species and its cultivars are generally grown. Botanically known as *Gomphrena globosa,* it bears cloverlike flowers in bright orange, yellow, purple, pink, and white, with hairy, light green leaves. The 1 ft (30 cm) high stems are upright. The flowers last well and are excellent as dried flowers. In the garden use them in beds.

Popular species and cultivars
Single and mixed color strains are available.
'Buddy Hybrids' are compact, dwarf forms that reach a height of 6 in (15 cm). Their flowers are a vivid deep purple.
'Full Mix' is a mixture with orange, purple, pink, red, lavender, or white flowers, also available as single colors. The plants grow up to 1½-2 ft (45-60 cm) high.

Cultivation
Sow the seeds indoors in flats of seed-starting mix 6-8 weeks before the last frost, and keep them at a temperature of 59-64°F (15-18°C). When the seedlings are large enough to handle, prick them out into flats. Harden off before planting out in late spring when danger of frost has passed. Plant in ordinary well-drained garden soil in a sunny site.

For dried flowers, cut the blooms just before they are fully open and hang upside down in bunches in a cool, airy place to dry. Gather the blooms in dry weather.
Pests/diseases Trouble free.

Gypsophila
baby's breath

Gypsophila elegans 'Covent Garden'

❏ Height 2 ft (60 cm)
❏ Planting distance 1 ft (30 cm)
❏ Flowers late spring to early fall
❏ Any well-drained garden soil
❏ Sunny site
❏ Hardy annual

The soft gray-green foliage and clouds of tiny white or pink flowers that this annual produces from late spring to early fall serve as a good foil for other border plants and are also good for cutting. Several garden cultivars have been developed from *Gypsophila elegans.*

Popular species and cultivars
The following seed strains are readily available.
'Covent Garden' has large white flowers, excellent for cutting.
'Giant White' has exceptionally large white flowers.
'Improved Hybrids' come in shades of shell-pink, carmine-rose, and pure white.
'Red Cloud' bears a mass of carmine-pink blooms.

Cultivation
In mild-winter regions, sow the seeds in their flowering site in fall; elsewhere, start in spring, sowing at 2-week intervals to ensure a succession of flowers. Thin to 1 ft (30 cm) apart. Baby's breath will thrive in any well-drained soil in a sunny spot; treat acid soils with lime. Support with twiggy sticks.
Pests/diseases Trouble free.

HARE'S TAIL GRASS —
see *Lagurus*
HAWKSBEARD — see *Crepis*

Helianthus
sunflower

Helianthus annuus

Helianthus annuus 'Teddy Bear'

❏ Height 2-10 ft (60-300 cm)
❏ Planting distance 1-1½ ft (30-45 cm)
❏ Flowers late summer to early fall
❏ Well-drained garden soil
❏ Sunny site
❏ Hardy annual

Sunflowers usually conjure up the image of a solitary yellow flower gazing down to earth from the top of a stem 10 ft (300 cm) high, sparsely clad with huge bristly leaves. Fortunately for owners of small gardens, not all sunflowers are this tall. A number of lower-growing cultivars of *Helianthus annuus*, with more foliage but equally spectacular blooms, are now available. They offer a large variety of flower forms — double as well as single — and come in varying shades of yellow, orange, red, and cream.

Sunflowers look best grown at the back of a border. They also make extremely attractive temporary screens.

Popular species and cultivars
The following is a selection of the most popular annual sunflower cultivars.

'Italian White' has cream flowers with black central disks and gold zones. The plants reach 4 ft (120 cm) high.
'Lemon Queen' has classic lemon-yellow, brown-centered flowers suitable for cutting. It grows 5 ft (150 cm) tall.
'Music Box Mixed' is low growing, to 28 in (70 cm) high, with medium-size flowers that range from yellow and cream to mahogany-red, with black centers.
'Orange Sun Double,' about 3½ ft (105 cm) high, bears fully double apricot-orange flowers.
'Queen Series' sunflowers bear deep velvety red or lemon-yellow, 4-5 in (10-12.5 cm) wide blossoms on 5 ft (150 cm) high stems.
'Russian Mammoth' has large single yellow flowers (reaching 1 ft/30 cm wide) and grows 10 ft (300 cm) high.
'Sunburst Hybrids' have crimson, gold, bronze, and lemon flowers. These branching cultivars reach 4 ft (120 cm) high.
'Sunspot,' only 2 ft (60 cm) high, has 10 in (25 cm) wide golden yellow flowers with huge yellow-green centers.

'Teddy Bear' is a dwarf cultivar 2 ft (60 cm) high, with double golden blooms.

Cultivation
Sow the seeds in well-drained garden soil in a sunny site during the early spring, as soon as the soil can be worked. Sunflowers are one of the few annuals that look effective grown as solitary plants. Sow two or three seeds in each flowering site and remove the weakest, leaving just the strongest to grow on. Sunflowers growing in a row or group should be thinned to 1-1½ ft (30-45 cm) apart.

Support tall sunflowers with strong stakes. Remove dead flowers to prevent self-seeding.
Pests/diseases Botrytis can cause flowers to rot in wet weather late in the season.

Helianthus annuus 'Sunburst Hybrids'

55

Helichrysum
everlasting, strawflower

Helichrysum 'Bright Bikini'

❏ Height 1-4 ft (30-120 cm)
❏ Planting distance 1 ft (30 cm)
❏ Flowers midsummer to early fall
❏ Light, well-drained soil
❏ Open, sunny site
❏ Half-hardy annual

Helichrysum is a large genus including annuals, perennials, and shrubs. The most common annual species is *Helichrysum bracteatum,* and a number of cultivars have been developed from it, offering the gardener a wide choice of flower colors.

The showy daisylike flowers of the annual species are familiar to flower arrangers, who often dry them for winter decoration. In the garden they are used to provide color from midsummer to early fall in borders and bedding displays — the dwarf species are also suitable for containers. The plants have midgreen lance-shaped leaves.

Popular species and cultivars
The following cultivars are readily available.

'Bright Bikini' is a mixture of dwarf plants, 12-15 in (30-38 cm) high, bearing a profusion of flowers in bright colors.
'Candy Pink' has particularly large, double candy-pink colored blooms, 3 in (7.5 cm) wide and grows 3-4 ft (90-120 cm) tall.
'Golden' has golden flowers and reaches 3-4 ft (90-120 cm) high.
'Hot Bikini' is a dwarf cultivar reaching 12-15 in (30-38 cm) high with rich scarlet flowers.
'Monstrosum' has double flowers in white and shades of rose, crimson, yellow, and orange. The plants grow 1 ft (30 cm) high.
'Rose' has rose-pink flowers and reaches 3-4 ft (90-120 cm) high.
'Salmon Rose' has salmon-pink blooms and reaches 3-4 ft (90-120 cm) high.
'Silvery Rose' is a mixture of 2½-3 ft (75-90 cm) tall plants with large double flowers of sulfur-yellow and clear rose-pink overlaid with silvery white.
'Snowhite' has double pure white flowers and reaches 3-4 ft (90-120 cm) high.

Cultivation
Sow the seeds indoors in flats of seed-starting mix 6-8 weeks before the last frost, and keep at a temperature of 64°F (18°C). Prick out into flats and harden off before setting out in the flowering site in mid- to late spring. An open, sunny site with light, well-drained soil is ideal. Rich soil encourages more blooms but reduces the strength of their colors.

Deadhead to encourage flowering on the side shoots.

Cut flowers for drying before they open fully and show the central disks. Tie them in bunches and hang them upside down in a cool room or shed until they are dry. Avoid hanging them in sunlight — the colors fade and the stems become brittle.

Pests/diseases Downy mildew, a white fungal growth, can affect the leaves, eventually causing them to drop off.

Heliotropium
cherry-pie, heliotrope

Heliotropium arborescens 'Marine'

❑ Height 14-24 in (35-60 cm)
❑ Planting distance 1 ft (30 cm)
❑ Flowers late spring to midfall
❑ Fertile, well-drained garden soil
❑ Sunny, sheltered site
❑ Evergreen shrub treated as
  tender annual

The hybrid heliotropes *(Heliotropium arborescens)* received their common name "cherry-pie" because the heavy fragrance of their small forget-me-not-like flowers is similar to that of cherry-pie filling. Great favorites in the formal gardens of Victorian times, they are still much used as accent plants in formal bedding displays in warm, sheltered gardens — heliotropes will not tolerate cold, exposed sites.

Dwarf types are suitable for pots and containers and for sunny window boxes.

The flowers range in color from dark purple through lilac to white. They appear from late spring until midfall and are carried above attractive dark green, finely wrinkled leaves.

Popular species and cultivars
The following are the most readily available heliotrope cultivars.
'Marine' bears large clusters of deep purple flowers, accompanied by dark foliage. It reaches 1½ ft (45 cm) high.
'Marine Dwarf' is a dwarf mixture growing 14-16 in (35-40 cm) tall. The plants are compact but bushy, branching from the base, and have large violet-purple flower clusters and dark green, near-bronze foliage.

Cultivation
Sow the seeds indoors 10-12 weeks before the last frost in pots or flats of seed-starting mix. Germinate them at a temperature of 61-64°F (16-18° C). Prick out the seedlings when they are large enough to handle into flats of potting soil. When 3 in (7.5 cm) high, pinch the growing tips to encourage bushy growth. Harden off before planting out 1 ft (30 cm) apart in late spring, when all danger of frost is past.

Outdoors use heliotrope in bedding displays and for filling containers. They thrive in fertile, well-drained soil and need full sun and shelter from winds.
Pests/diseases Trouble free.

Helipterum
Swan River everlasting

Helipterum manglesii

❑ Height 1-2 ft (30-60 cm)
❑ Planting distance 6 in (15 cm)
❑ Flowers midsummer to early fall
❑ Any well-drained soil
❑ Sunny site
❑ Hardy annual

These hardy everlastings are now classified as members of the genera *Acroclinium, Pteropogon,* and *Rhodanthe* but are still commonly listed in catalogs under their traditional name. They make enchanting contributions to herbaceous borders, rock gardens, and bedding displays. The daisylike flowers have a strawlike texture, which makes them ideal for drying. They are easily grown plants, reveling in poor soil and full sun and tolerating exposure to winds and sea spray.

Popular species and cultivars
Helipterum humboldtianum (now *Pteropogon humboldtianum*) grows 1½ ft (45 cm) tall and has erect flower stems with narrow, pointed leaves that are silvery green and woolly. From midsummer to early fall the stems are crowned with fragrant clusters of golden yellow flowers, which turn green after drying.
Helipterum manglesii (now *Rhodanthe manglesii),* up to 15 in (38 cm) tall, has erect and wiry stems sparsely set with oblong gray-green leaves and topped with a single red or white, yellow-eyed daisy flower. The flowering season extends from midsummer to early fall. Cultivars include

Hibiscus
hibiscus

Helipterum roseum

Hibiscus 'Southern Belle'

Hibiscus moscheutos 'Disco Belle'

'Mixed,' to 1 ft (30 cm) tall, of compact growth and with a mass of carmine, pink, rose, or white flowers. There is also a separate 'Rose' color.

Helipterum roseum (now *Acroclinium roseum*) grows 15 in (38 cm) tall; it resembles *H. manglesii* but bears semidouble rose-colored flowers in mid- and late summer. The grandiflorum varieties are 1-1½ ft (30-45 cm) high and have double flowers in pink, red, or white, with yellow or black centers. The seed strain is available as a mixture or as single colors of red, rose, and white. 'Sensation Giants' bear large pink to deep rose flowers with bright yellow centers on long, sturdy stems and are exceptionally floriferous.

Cultivation
Sow the seeds in the flowering site in late spring. The plants grow best in poor but well-drained soil in a sunny site. Thin the seedlings to stand 6 in (15 cm) apart. Avoid transplanting.

Cut the flowers for drying before they are fully open; tie them in bunches and hang them upside down to dry in a cool, airy place.
Pests/diseases Aphids may attack young plants.

❑ Height 15-96 in (45-240 cm)
❑ Planting distance 9-24 in (23-60 cm)
❑ Flowers late summer to early fall
❑ Rich, moist, well-drained soil
❑ Sunny, sheltered site
❑ Hardy or half-hardy annual

There are few more exotic-looking plants than the hibiscus hybrids with their wide, funnel-shaped richly colored flowers. They are showy but rather short-lived, though more blooms follow in quick succession. The plants are suitable as accent plants in mixed borders, for bedding displays, and for growing in tubs on the patio.

Popular species and cultivars
Hibiscus moscheutos is a moderately hardy perennial usually treated as a half-hardy annual. The species is rarely grown, having been superseded by F1 hybrids such as 'Disco Belle' (syn. 'Les Belles'). Some of these hybrids grow up to 8 ft (240 cm) tall and bear huge near-circular flowers, 8 in (20 cm) or more wide; they are pure white, sometimes with rosy centers, or pink or deep cerise-red. A pure white form, 'Disco Belle White,' is also available.

Hibiscus trionum (flower-of-an-hour) is a hardy bushy annual, up to 4 ft (120 cm) tall, with dark green coarsely toothed leaves. The five-petaled creamy white flowers with chocolate-maroon centers are much smaller, about 2 in (5 cm) wide, and very short-lived, but they are produced continuously during late summer and early fall. The cultivar 'Sunnyday' (15 in/38 cm high) has cool lemon-yellow blooms with purple-black centers.

Cultivation
Sow seeds of *Hibiscus trionum* in the flowering site in midspring, and thin the seedlings to 9 in (23 cm) apart. The species will frequently self-seed if the soil is left undisturbed.

Sow seeds of the half-hardy hybrids indoors 8-10 weeks before the last spring frost at a temperature of 61-64°F (16-18°C). When the seedlings are large enough to handle, prick them out singly into 3 in (7.5 cm) pots of compost and grow on at the same temperature. Harden off before planting out in a sheltered site when all danger of frost has passed.

All annual hibiscuses perform best in rich, moist but well-drained soil in a sunny site.
Pests/diseases Trouble free.

HOLLYHOCK — see *Althaea*
HONESTY — see *Lunaria*

Hordeum
squirreltail grass

Hordeum jubatum

- ❏ Height 1-2 ft (30-60 cm)
- ❏ Planting distance 4 in (10 cm)
- ❏ Flowers early to late summer
- ❏ Well-drained fertile soil
- ❏ Sunny site
- ❏ Hardy annual

Hordeum jubatum — commonly referred to as squirreltail grass — bears 1 ft (30 cm) high, slender feathery flower heads, similar to ripe barley but without the grain. These appear from early to late summer.

It looks best planted in large clusters, perhaps in a bed of annuals to provide welcome relief from bright flower colors. But it is also a popular ornamental grass for flower arrangers.

To dry squirreltail grass for winter decoration, cut it in warm, dry weather in late summer and hang the grasses upside down to dry in a cool place.

Cultivation
Squirreltail grass should be grown in well-drained fertile soil in a sunny site.

Sow the seeds outdoors in mid-spring, sprinkling them thinly across the ground and covering them with only a little soil. When the seedlings are large enough to handle, thin them to 4 in (10 cm) apart.
Pests/diseases Trouble free.

HOUND'S TONGUE —
see *Cynoglossum*

Iberis
candytuft

Iberis umbellata

- ❏ Height ½-1½ ft (15-45 cm) high
- ❏ Planting distance 6-9 in (15-23 cm)
- ❏ Flowers early summer to early fall
- ❏ Ordinary well-drained soil
- ❏ Sunny site
- ❏ Hardy annual

Easy to grow and generous with their white and pink flowers, candytufts are popular annuals. As they tolerate smoke and dirt, they are a good choice for urban gardens, where they can be grown in borders and rock gardens, for decoration, or for cutting.

Two species and their cultivars are found in gardens.

Popular species and cultivars
Iberis amara (syn. *I. coronaria*), commonly known as rocket candytuft, is an upright plant that reaches 15 in (38 cm) high. Its fragrant flowers are excellent for cutting and border decoration.
Iberis umbellata is a spreading plant (6-15 in/15-38 cm high) with compact clusters of white, pink, and lavender flowers. Popular cultivars include 'Cream Flash' (9-12 in/23-30 cm high; creamy white flowers), 'Dwarf Fairy' (10 in/25 cm high; pink, red, maroon, white, and lavender flowers), 'Pinnacle' (15-18 in/38-45 cm high; pure white, dense and fragrant flowers), and 'Red Flash' (15 in/38 cm high; carmine flowers).

Cultivation
In mild-winter regions sow the seeds in their flowering site in fall; where winters are severe, sow in very early spring. Sowing at 2-week intervals from spring through early summer ensures continuous summer-long blooms. Thin the seedlings to 9 in (23 cm) apart. Candytuft does well in full sun in any well-drained garden soil, including poor soil. Deadhead regularly.
Pests/diseases Trouble free.

ICE PLANT —
see *Mesembryanthemum*
IMMORTELLE —
see *Xeranthemum*

Impatiens

busy Lizzy, patience plant

Impatiens 'Super Elfin Hybrids'

Impatiens 'Firelake Hybrids'

❏ Height ½-2½ ft (15-75 cm)
❏ Planting distance 1 ft (30 cm)
❏ Flowers midspring to midfall
❏ Fertile, well-drained but moisture-retentive soil
❏ Sunny or partially shaded site
❏ Tender annual

Impatiens are very popular house plants, but introductions of robust F1 hybrids have encouraged gardeners to use them for summer beds, window boxes, tubs, and hanging baskets as well.

The hybrids can be relied upon to produce a mass of flowers in shades of red, pink, and white throughout the summer. Combined with the small leaves, they form an attractive ground carpet.

Popular species and cultivars
Impatiens balsamina (rose balsam) has pale green lance-shaped leaves and pink flowers from early summer until early fall. Up to 2½ ft (75 cm) high, it looks effective in beds. Two popular cultivars come from it.
'Camellia-Flowered Hybrids' have white, pink, rose, and scarlet blossoms resembling those of a camellia. These plants have a spreading habit and reach up to 16-28 in (40-70 cm) high.

'Extra Dwarf Tom Thumb Hybrids' have double blooms in shades of red, carmine-pink, salmon-pink, coral, and white. The dwarf plants reach just 8-12 in (20-30 cm) high and are drought resistant.
Impatiens wallerana hybrids include the following.
'Accent Hybrids' grow up to 6 in (15 cm) high, spreading and bearing large flowers. Seeds are available in single or mixed colors of white, pink, salmon, crimson, and violet.
'Blitz Orange' bears many large flowers in warm orange; it grows 9-12 in (23-30 cm) high.
'Double Confection Hybrids' grow 9-12 in (23-30 cm) high, with semi- or fully double flowers in a range of colors.
'Firelake Hybrids,' 1-1½ ft (30-45 cm) tall, have 2 in (5 cm) wide flowers in a mixture of colors set among foliage variegated dark red, green, white, or cream.
'Futura Hybrids' have brightly colored flowers and a pendulous habit, making them excellent for hanging baskets. The plants reach 8-12 in (20-30 cm) high. The flowers come in reds, oranges, pinks, and white, either plain or striped.

'King Kong Hybrids' have large flowers in a mixture of reds, pinks, oranges, and whites. The very bushy plants reach 9-12 in (23-30 cm) high.
'Mega Orange Star' is 8-10 in (20-25 cm) high and weather resistant. The orange-red flowers have white star markings.
'Novette Hybrids,' just 6-8 in (15-20 cm) high, carry big bright red, pink, and orange flowers early in the summer.
'Novette Star Hybrids' are a bicolored mixture of bright red, orange, rose-pink, and violet.
'Pastel Hybrids' are a mixture of dwarf plants (9-12 in/23-30 cm high), bearing flowers in coral, pink, salmon, and white.
'Picotee Swirl' grows to 10 in (25 cm) tall and is early flowering; the white to soft-rose flowers have fuchsia edges to the petals.
'Starbright Hybrids' have spectacularly large bicolored flowers in shades of orange, pink, rose, and violet. The plants grow 6-8 in (15-20 cm) high.
'Super Elfin Hybrids,' 8-10 in (20-25 cm) high, are available as mixtures or single colors.
'Tempo Hybrids,' up to 10 in (25 cm) tall, are of branching and pendulous habit. They are available in seed mixtures and single colors of white, blush-pink, apricot, red, and lavender.
New Guinea impatiens, hybrids bred from plants collected in that Southeast Asian island, are remarkable more for their colorful red- and cream-striped leaves, which may measure 8 in

Ipomoea
morning glory

Impatiens 'Novette Star Hybrids'

(20 cm) long, than for their flowers. Most must be propagated by cuttings, but two superior cultivars may be started from seed and bear attractive flowers.
'Spectra Hybrids,' about 1 ft (30 cm) high, have white, pink, lilac, and carmine flowers and variegated cream or bronze foliage.
'Tango' bears large deep orange flowers amid bronze-green foliage. The plants are up to 15 in (38 cm) high.

Cultivation
Sow seeds in pots or flats of seed-starting mix indoors 6-8 weeks before the last frost at a temperature of 61-64°F (16-18°C). When the seedlings are large enough to handle, prick out into flats and then into 3-in (7.5-cm) containers of potting soil. Harden off and plant out a couple of weeks after the last frost, setting the seedlings 1 ft (30 cm) apart.

Give patience plants a site in sun or light shade with fertile, well-drained but moist soil. Pinch the growing tips to encourage bushy growth.

They can also be grown from 3-4 in (7.5-10 cm) long cuttings of tips on vigorous shoots between summer and early fall. Root at a temperature of 61°F (16°C). When they have rooted, prick out individually into 3-in (7.5-cm) pots. Harden off before planting out.
Pests/diseases Aphids may infest leaves and stems, weakening the plants.

Ipomoea tricolor

❏ Height 8-10 ft (240-300 cm)
❏ Planting distance 8-12 in (20-30 cm)
❏ Flowers midsummer to early fall
❏ Rich, well-drained soil
❏ Sunny, sheltered site
❏ Half-hardy annual

Morning glory is widely regarded as one of the most beautiful climbers. Grown as an annual, its wiry stems twist their way up walls, trellises, pergolas, or simple pea-stick supports, decorating them with heart-shaped light green leaves and magnificent trumpet-shaped flowers in either a heavenly blue color fading to

Ipomoea purpurea

white in the center or red-purple.

Popular species and cultivars
Ipomoea purpurea (syn. *Convolvulus purpureus)* bears purple flowers singly or in small clusters. It is a vigorous climber, to 10 ft (300 cm) high. 'Scarlet Star' is cerise with a white star.
Ipomoea tricolor is a half-hardy perennial usually grown as an annual. A free-flowering species, it carries large red-purple to blue flowers. The plant reaches 8 ft (240 cm) high. 'Heavenly Blue' is sky-blue and white-throated.

Cultivation
To speed germination, nick the seed's hard coat with a razor blade and soak in water 24 hours before planting. Sow after danger of frost has passed, setting seeds ½ in (1.25 cm) deep and 8-12 in (20-30 cm) apart.

Grow morning glory in rich and well-drained soil in a sheltered, sunny site — against a wall or fence or up poles or pea-sticks. Deadhead to prolong the flowering period.
Pests/diseases Aphids may infest young plants.

JOB'S TEARS — see *Coix*
KINGFISHER DAISY —
see *Felicia*

Kochia
burning bush, summer cypress

Kochia scoparia trichophylla — summer

❑ Height 2-5 ft (60-150 cm)
❑ Planting distance 2-3 ft (60-90 cm)
❑ Foliage plant
❑ Ordinary well-drained soil
❑ Open, sunny site
❑ Half-hardy annual

Untidy forms of this intriguing foliage plant grow in the wild from southern Europe to Japan — and many Europeans regard it as a weed. But in gardens in North America summer cypress is grown as a half-hardy annual, its mass of pale green foliage providing relief in beds of brightly colored flowering annuals.

The most commonly grown variety is *Kochia scoparia trichophylla* (now reclassified as *Bassia scoparia tricophylla*). This forms a neat, symmetrical dome and gradually turns a rich crimson-purple in fall, giving it the name "burning bush."

Cultivation
In warmer regions (lower zone 7 and south) sow seeds in the final site in midspring, in well-drained

Kochia scoparia trichophylla — fall

soil in an open, sunny spot. Thin seedlings to 2-3 ft (60-90 cm) apart.

In regions with short growing seasons, give plants a head start by sowing seeds into peat pots indoors 8 weeks before the last frost. Keep at 61° F (16° C). Harden off seedlings gradually before planting out in late spring after the danger of frost has passed.

Stake plants in exposed sites.
Pests/diseases Trouble free.

Lagurus
hare's tail grass

Lagurus ovatus

❑ Height 1 ft (30 cm)
❑ Planting distance 6 in (15 cm)
❑ Flowers early summer to early fall
❑ Well-drained soil
❑ Sunny site
❑ Hardy annual

Hare's tail grass *(Lagurus ovatus)* is a hardy annual often grown in mixed borders for its decorative flowers — delightful 1½ in (3 cm) long, fluffy white heads resembling the tail of a hare or rabbit. These appear from early summer to early fall carried on slender stems that are 1 ft (30 cm) high.

The long, narrow, hairy gray-green leaves present a pleasant contrast to the soft, furry flower heads.

To dry the grass for winter decoration, gather in dry weather in late summer.

Cultivation
Sow the seeds indoors in flats of seed-starting mix 8 weeks before the last frost. Harden off the seedlings and set them out in midspring, spacing them 6 in (15 cm) apart. A well-drained fertile soil in a sunny spot is suitable.
Pests/diseases Trouble free.

LARKSPUR — see *Delphinium*

Lathyrus
sweet pea

Lathyrus odoratus 'Old-Fashioned Mixed'

- ❏ Height 4-120 in (10-300 cm)
- ❏ Planting distance 6-10 in (15-25 cm)
- ❏ Flowers late spring to early fall, or winter in South
- ❏ Well-drained medium loam, ideally slightly alkaline
- ❏ Sunny site
- ❏ Hardy annual

A favorite of our grandparents' day, the sweet pea deserves a revival since it is not only a beautiful flower but also a versatile one. Planted against a wall, fence, or another plant, it may climb to a height of 10 ft (300 cm). It can be grown up through a circle of interlaced twigs in a vegetable patch to provide cut flowers. Or it can be grown without support in a mixed annual border — dwarf cultivars look most effective beside such cottage-garden plants as clarkias, candytufts, and cornflowers.

This plant prefers cool weather; in temperate areas such as the Pacific Northwest, it blooms in early summer and, if deadheaded, may continue flowering until early fall. Elsewhere, the plant fades in hot weather; in the South it is best cultivated as a winter flower.

Sweet peas come in a range of colors — reds, pinks, salmons,

Lathyrus odoratus 'Multiflora'

purples, and white, either one color or bicolored. Most are scented, some more than others.

Popular species and cultivars
All sweet pea cultivars grown in the garden are developed from *Lathyrus odoratus*. While many different ones have been introduced over the years, the distinctions between them are slight. For convenience, sweet peas may be divided into a few groups.
Dwarf cultivars, reaching 4-42 in (10-105 cm) high, can be grown

Lathyrus odoratus 'Maggie May'

without supports. Use them at the front of borders or to fill window boxes and containers. The following are dwarf cultivars.
'Bijou Mixed' produces bushy plants 15 in (38 cm) tall with flowers that range in color from scarlet to blue, white, pink, and salmon.
'Continental Mixed,' up to 3-3½ ft (90-105 cm) high, bears fragrant flowers of mixed colors. Because it requires no staking to stand upright, it is ideal as a fast-growing and colorful small hedge.
'Jet Set Hybrids' have sweetly scented frilled flowers in a wide range of colors. They reach 3 ft (90 cm) high.
'Pink Cupid' has large (up to 1½ in/3 cm wide) bicolored flowers in shades from bright carmine to white. It grows to a height of 4-6 in (10-15 cm) and has a spread of 1½ ft (45 cm).
'Super Snoop' has waved flowers in a range of colors, carried on long stems, making them suitable for cutting. The plants are without tendrils and grow with a neat habit up to 2½-3 ft (75-90 cm) high.
Galaxy cultivars are tall, vigorous cultivars, reaching 6-10 ft (180-300 cm) high. Grown for their early, long-lasting display, they produce numerous large flowers in a wide range of colors and are offered as 'Galaxy Hybrids.' These plants need to be trained on tall supports.
Old cultivars have largely been replaced by the more robust, bigger-flowered Spencer cultivars.

Lathyrus odoratus

Lathyrus odoratus 'Butterfly Hybrids'

Available now mainly in seed mixtures ('Old-Fashioned Mixed'), they have small, dainty flowers with a strong, sweet fragrance. Train up a wall, fence, pergola, or pea sticks – they grow 6-10 ft (180-300 cm) high.

Another group of old cultivars is the 'Multiflora Hybrids.' Multifloras, up to 6 ft (180 cm) high, carry five or six ruffled flowers on each stem.

Spencer cultivars, the most commonly grown climbing sweet peas, carry four or five particularly large blooms on each stem. Reaching up to 10 ft (300 cm) high, they are effective as climbers and suitable for garden decoration, cutting, and exhibition. A few have a strong scent.

'Anniversary' has soft white flowers edged with rose-pink and is delicately scented.

'Blue Danube' is a blue-flowered cultivar with frilled petals.

'Butterfly Hybrids' have cream or white flowers marked, streaked, and edged with red, pink, orange, blue, or purple.

'Elizabeth Taylor' has clear, rich purple flowers.

'Hunter's Moon' bears sweetly scented lemon-cream flowers.

'Leamington' has deep lavender-blue flowers with a sweet scent.

'Maggie May' bears wavy-edged, strongly fragrant blooms of sky-blue flushed with white.

'Mrs. R. Bolton' has blossoms of a delicate pale pink that shades almost to white.

'Noel Sutton' is rich blue-purple and has a very strong fragrance.

'Pageantry' bears large flowers of dark (almost black) red-purple.

'Pennine Floss' is strongly scented and has red-purple wavy flowers.

'Princess Elizabeth' has cream to salmon-pink flowers.

'Red Ensign,' a strong grower, has scented deep scarlet flowers.

'Rosy Frills' has white flowers with frilled petals edged deep rose-pink.

'Superstar' bears lightly fragrant, wavy-petaled blossoms of deep rose-pink veined with white.

'White Supreme' has strongly scented pure white flowers.

'World's Children' is free flowering, with long-stemmed flowers bicolored in fiery red and orange.

Cultivation

Many sweet pea cultivars have seeds with thick coats, so it pays to nick them with a sharp knife or soak them in water for 12 hours to speed up germination.

Sow the seeds in flats or shallow pots of seed-starting mix in early spring in the North or early fall in the South. Keep the seeds at a temperature of 61°F (16°C). Put the seedlings into 3 in (7.5 cm) pots of potting soil. When they reach 4 in (10 cm) high, pinch the growing tips to encourage strong side shoots. Harden off before planting out in spring (North) or late fall (South).

Alternatively, sow the seeds directly into the garden in early spring (as soon as the soil can be worked) in the North or in late fall in the South. Thin seedlings to 6 in (15 cm). Covering the soil with a clear-plastic mulch and then planting seeds through slits cut with a knife will improve germination in cold-weather regions.

Sweet peas will grow in any ordinary garden soil in a sunny site. But for the best results plant them in deeply dug, well-fertilized and well-drained, slightly alkaline loam.

Deadhead and remove any seedpods to prolong the plants' blooming season.

Pests/diseases The anthracnose fungus may attack sweet pea stems, leaves, and flowers, whitening the foliage and then spreading downward toward the roots as a general wilt. Aphids may attack the roots as well as the leaves and stems. Viral diseases can also be a problem.

Lathyrus odaratus 'Madrid Jet Set Scarlet'

Lavatera
tree mallow

Lavatera trimestris 'Silver Cup'

Layia
tidytips

Layia platyglossa

❏ Height 1½ ft (45 cm)
❏ Planting distance 10 in (25 cm)
❏ Flowers early summer to midfall, or spring and fall
❏ Any well-drained soil
❏ Sunny site
❏ Hardy annual

❏ Height 20-36 in (50-90 cm)
❏ Planting distance 1½ ft (45 cm)
❏ Flowers midsummer to early fall
❏ Ordinary well-drained soil
❏ Sunny site
❏ Hardy annual

One species of mallow *(Lavatera trimestris)* and its cultivars are commonly grown as annuals. This bushy plant, some 2-3 ft (60-90 cm) high, has attractive trumpet-shaped hibiscuslike flowers in shades of pink and white. These appear in the summer and are shown off most effectively in herbaceous borders.

Popular species and cultivars
Several cultivars have been developed from *Lavatera trimestris,* including the following.
'Loveliness' is an old cultivar producing rose-pink flowers in late summer and early fall. The plants are 3 ft (90 cm) high.
'Mont Blanc' has glistening large white flowers in midsummer on dwarf compact plants, 20-24 in (50-60 cm) high.

'Ruby Regis' grows 2 ft (60 cm) high and bears a profusion of large, deep cerise-red flowers.
'Silver Cup' has bright pink flowers shaded silvery pink. It stands 2 ft (60 cm) high.
'Tanagra' has large, glistening cerise-pink blooms. It is a tall cultivar, reaching 3 ft (90 cm).

Cultivation
Mallows prefer cool weather; sow seed outdoors in early fall in the South and in midspring (after the last frost) in the North, just covering the seeds with soil. Mallows flourish in most well-drained garden soils, though very rich soils should be avoided, since they encourage leafy growth instead of flowers. Thin the seedlings to stand 1½ ft (45 cm) apart.

Mallow seeds itself freely and produces plants the following season if the soil around is left undisturbed.
Pests/diseases Generally trouble free.

The charm of tidytips *(Layia platyglossa)* lies in the neat white tips of the pale yellow petals. The petals themselves surround a bright yellow central disk.

Tidytips is a bushy, well-branched plant, some 1½ ft (45 cm) high, with pleasantly scented gray-green leaves. Suitable for herbaceous borders and summer annual beds, it provides a succession of daisylike flowers from early summer until midfall where summers are cool; where summers are hot, it blooms in spring or fall. Tidytips are useful for cutting as well as garden decoration.

Cultivation
In cold-winter regions, sow the seeds outdoors in early spring, just covering them with soil. In California, sow seed at the end of the summer dry season. Tidytips prefer cool weather and will tolerate a light frost. Well-drained sandy soil gives the best results, though the plants will grow in any soil provided they receive plenty of sunlight.

Thin the seedlings, when large enough to handle, to stand 10 in (25 cm) apart.
Pests/diseases Trouble free.

Leptosiphon
leptosiphon

Limnanthes
marsh flower, meadow foam

Leptosiphon

❑ Height 4-6 in (10-15 cm)
❑ Planting distance 3-4 in (7.5-10 cm)
❑ Flowers early summer to early fall
❑ Ordinary well-drained soil
❑ Sunny, open site
❑ Hardy annual

Often classified as *Linanthus grandiflorus* or *Gilia grandiflora*, this plant is a gem by any name. Those who encounter the hybrids of this unjustly neglected annual are enchanted by them. The tiny flowers are scattered in profusion over the plant and come in a random collection of pink, red, orange, yellow, cream, and white. They appear from early summer to early fall on straight slender stems above finely divided deep green foliage, which forms mounds 4-6 in (10-15 cm) high.

Use leptosiphon hybrids to edge borders or to cheer up earth-filled cracks in paving or small pockets of soil between rocks or stones. They are also suitable for growing in window boxes and other shallow containers.

'Stardust Hybrids Mixed' is the mixture most commonly sold in garden centers or found in mail-order catalogs.

Cultivation
Sow the seeds, barely covering them, in ordinary well-drained soil in an open, sunny site in early spring, as soon as the soil can be worked. Thin the seedlings to 3-4 in (7.5-10 cm) apart.
Pests/diseases Trouble free.

Limnanthes douglasii

❑ Height 4-12 in (10-30 cm)
❑ Planting distance 6 in (15 cm)
❑ Flowers late spring to late summer
❑ Ordinary garden soil
❑ Open, sunny site
❑ Hardy annual

The color scheme of this flower recalls a breakfast table setting: the disk of petals is colored white around the edges with a center of yolk-yellow, giving it the appearance of a poached egg. Bowl-shaped, softly waved, and with a delicate fragrance, these blooms are set off to perfection by glossy, pale yellow-green, deeply cut foliage. Bees and other nectar-loving insects find them irresistible.

Limnanthes reaches 4-12 in (10-30 cm) high and spreads quickly. It looks best grown in clumps in rock gardens, at the front of borders, or along the edges of paths — where the seedlings will swiftly fill the cracks between paving stones.

Cultivation
Limnanthes thrives in ordinary garden soil in an open, sunny site, though it needs a cool root run. Such conditions are usually found along paths or between rocks and paving.

This species prefers cool weather. In California and the Deep South, sow the seeds directly into the garden at the beginning of the fall rains; where winters are cold, sow in early spring. In either case, cover seeds with just a little soil. Thin to 6 in (15 cm) apart. If sown in the fall in the mid-South, protect the seedlings through the coldest winter months by covering them with a blanket of evergreen boughs.

The plants usually seed themselves prolifically, so be ready for more flowers in successive years. These plants are unlikely to be as strong and robust as those grown from fresh packets of seeds.
Pests/diseases Trouble free.

Limonium
sea lavender, statice

Limonium suworowii

❏ Height 1-2½ ft (30-75 cm)
❏ Planting distance 1 ft (30 cm)
❏ Flowers midsummer to early fall
❏ Ordinary well-drained soil
❏ Open, sunny site
❏ Half-hardy annual

Statice, or sea lavender, is perhaps more often seen in dried flower arrangements than in gardens. Its tiny bright yellow, purple, pink, blue, and white blooms provide an invaluable splash of color indoors in winter. The individual funnel-shaped flowers are tiny, but they are clustered together in spikes at the top of tall, stout stems. Flower spikes are accompanied by small midgreen lance-shaped and stem-clasping leaves. If you wish to dry statice, cut the stems before the flowers have opened fully, tie them in bundles, and hang them upside down to dry in a cool, airy, and shady place.

Statice is best suited for growing in large clumps in herbaceous borders. Two species and their various cultivars are generally available.

Popular species and cultivars

Limonium sinuatum is a tender perennial species usually grown as a half-hardy annual. The 2½ ft (75 cm) long stems carry 3-4 in (7.5-10 cm) long clusters of white or blue flowers surrounded by green bracts from midsummer to early fall. This is the most commonly grown statice, and the one used for drying. Popular cultivars developed from it include 'Beidermeier Hybrids' (12-15 in/30-38 cm high; white, rose, blue, apricot, yellow, and purple) and 'Formula Mixture' (rose, cream-yellow, light blue, and white).

Limonium suworowii (now reclassified as *Psylliostachys suworowii* but still listed in catalogs as a statice) is a half-hardy annual grown for its cut flowers — it is unsuitable for drying. The 1½ ft (45 cm) high plants have tall, thin spikes of tiny rose-pink flowers.

Cultivation

Sow the seeds thinly in peat pots of seed-starting mix indoors 8 weeks before the last frost, and keep at a temperature of 55-61°F

(13-16°C). Since seedlings resent transplanting, do not prick out or move to large pots. Harden off before planting out in late spring.

Plant statice in ordinary well-drained soil in a sunny site.

In regions with a long frost-free growing season, you can sow seeds directly into the garden in midspring and thin to the appropriate spacings. The blooms will appear later and may be damaged by fall frosts in cooler regions.

Pests/diseases Aster yellows and fungal leaf spots may afflict statices. Root-knot nematodes are common animal parasites.

Limonium sinuatum 'Beidermeier Hybrids'

Linaria
toadflax

Linaria maroccana 'Fairy Bouquet'

- ❏ Height 9-24 in (23-60 cm)
- ❏ Planting distance 6 in (15 cm)
- ❏ Flowers late spring, summer, or winter
- ❏ Ordinary well-drained soil
- ❏ Sunny site
- ❏ Hardy annual

Moroccan toadflax *(Linaria maroccana)* is a narrow upright plant some 9-24 in (23-60 cm) high, with slender light green leaves. It bears spikes of narrow tubular flowers, resembling miniature snapdragons, which can be bright yellow, red, pink, or mauve, often blotched with white.

Flowering throughout the summer in regions such as the Pacific Northwest, where summers are cool, toadflax blooms in late spring to early summer or winter where summers are hot. It is suitable for annual and mixed borders, rock gardens, and edging a path. For best effect, grow in groups of five or seven plants.

Popular species and cultivars
The following cultivars have been developed from the species *Linaria maroccana*.
'Fairy Bouquet' is a seed mixture producing compact plants reaching just 9 in (23 cm) high. The flowers come in shades of red, pink, purple, yellow, and cream, all with white throats. This is a particularly easy toadflax to grow.
'Northern Lights' reaches 2 ft (60 cm) high and has flowers in shades of bronze, red, purple, pink, yellow, and cream. Some of the flowers are bicolored.

Cultivation
In the South and along the Pacific Coast, sow the seeds directly into the garden in early fall for large early flowers. In cold-winter regions, sow in early spring, as soon as the soil can be worked. Make successive sowings to extend the flowering season. Thin the seedlings to 6 in (15 cm) apart.

Toadflax seeds itself freely, so plants will appear the following year if the surrounding soil is left undisturbed.

Moroccan toadflax grows in any ordinary well-drained garden soil. If soil is of particularly heavy clay, it's advisable to add some grit to aid drainage. A sunny site is essential.
Pests/diseases Trouble free.

Linum
flax

Linum grandiflorum 'Rubrum'

- ❏ Height 1-2 ft (30-60 cm)
- ❏ Planting distance 6 in (15 cm)
- ❏ Flowers early to late summer
- ❏ Well-drained garden soil
- ❏ Open, sunny site
- ❏ Hardy annual

Flaxes have elegant brightly colored flowers and slender fresh green leaves. *Linum grandiflorum,* the most widely grown of the annual species, displays rose-red cup-shaped flowers from early to late summer in moderate climates. Elsewhere, this is an early-summer flower.

Popular species and cultivars
Cultivars are more popular than the species.
'Bright Eyes' has ivory-white flowers with crimson centers. It is up to 1½ ft (45 cm) high.
'Rubrum' (scarlet flax) grows about 1 ft (30 cm) high, with brilliant crimson satiny flowers.

Cultivation
Sow the seeds in the flowering site in early fall in the South and on the Pacific Coast, or early spring to midspring in cold-winter regions. For a prolonged floral display, resow monthly in the spring. Thin to 6 in (15 cm) apart.

To achieve their full brilliance, flax flowers need full sun. Flax grows in any well-drained ordinary soil, flourishing in limy soil but also tolerating an acid one.
Pests/diseases Trouble free.

LIVINGSTONE DAISY —
see *Mesembryanthemum*

Lobelia
lobelia

Lobelia erinus 'Mrs. Clibran'

Lobelia erinus 'Color Cascade Hybrids'

- ❏ Height 4-9 in (10-23 cm)
- ❏ Planting distance 4 in (10 cm)
- ❏ Flowers late spring to fall
- ❏ Fertile, moisture-retentive soil
- ❏ Sunny or partially shaded site
- ❏ Half-hardy perennial grown as hardy annual

Though grown as an annual, *Lobelia erinus* is correctly a half-hardy perennial. It is a small plant, only 4-9 in (10-23 cm) high, with light green leaves, and it produces a mass of small blue flowers from late spring until the fall frosts.

More popular than the species are the many cultivars, which may be either compact, making neat domes 4-6 in (10-15 cm) high, or trailing in a spread 1 ft (30 cm) wide. These cultivars may be white, pale blue, deep purplish-blue, or wine-red.

Compact cultivars are good for edging, while those with a trailing habit make an attractive display in hanging baskets, window boxes, and other containers.

Popular species and cultivars
The following cultivars are readily available.

Lobelia erinus 'Rosamund'

'Blue Moon' is a compact, early-flowering cultivar. The large flowers are clear blue.
'Cambridge Blue' is neat and compact with light blue flowers.
'Color Cascade Hybrids' are a mixture of cascading cultivars coming in blue, purple, red, and white, usually with white eyes.
'Crystal Palace' is a compact cultivar bearing rich deep blue flowers. The foliage is bronze-colored.

'Lilac Fountain' is a trailing cultivar, with pale lilac-pink flowers. Other strains in this series include white and blue cultivars.
'Mrs. Clibran' is a compact plant bearing rich violet-blue flowers with white eyes.
'Red Cascade' is a trailing cultivar with wine-red, white-eyed flowers.
'Rosamund' is a compact cultivar bearing crimson flowers with white eyes.
'Sapphire' is a trailing cultivar with white-eyed, glossy deep blue flowers.
'Snowball' is a compact cultivar with white flowers, though some are slightly tinged with blue.

Cultivation
Sow seeds in late winter in flats of seed-starting mix, and keep at a temperature of 61-64°F (16-18°C). Prick out the seedlings in groups of three or four — they're too small to prick out individually — and grow on at a temperature of 55-61°F (13-16°C). Harden off and plant out in late spring.

Plant lobelias in rich, well-drained soil in a sunny or partially shady spot — afternoon shade is essential in the South.
Pests/diseases Damping-off and root rot can cause the plants to wilt. In some areas, wireworms may damage lobelias.

LOVE-IN-A-MIST — see *Nigella*
LOVE-LIES-BLEEDING — see *Amaranthus*

Lunaria
honesty, money plant, moonwort

Lunaria annua

❑ Height 2½ ft (75 cm)
❑ Planting distance 1 ft (30 cm)
❑ Flowers midspring to early summer
❑ Any well-drained soil
❑ Partially shaded site
❑ Hardy biennial

Although *Lunaria annua* (syn. *L. biennis)* can be grown as an annual, it is naturally a biennial and, treated as such, produces finer flowers. These are borne in loose, fragrant clusters from midspring to early summer. The true species has pale lavender flowers; the cultivars range from white to rich purple and red.

In summer silvery white seedpods follow the flowers and can be used for indoor display.

Popular species and cultivars
'Mixed' has rich purple or purple-red flowers that are sometimes marked with white, as well as pure white ones.
'Stella' bears pure white flowers and foliage strongly variegated with creamy white.

Cultivation
Sow the seeds outdoors directly into the garden in early spring in northern cold-winter regions and in fall where winters are mild. Thin seedlings to a spacing of 1 ft (30 cm) apart. Honesty prefers cool weather and grows best in well-drained soil in partial shade.
Pests/diseases Trouble free.

Lupinus
lupine

Lupinus nanus 'Pixie Delight'

❑ Height 1½ ft (45 cm)
❑ Planting distance 8-10 in (20-25 cm)
❑ Flowers midsummer to midfall
❑ Acid to neutral, well-drained soil
❑ Sun or partial shade
❑ Hardy annual

To most people, lupines are the perennial Russell lupines, but a few annual types are also grown. *Lupinus nanus,* the best known of these, is generally available only in its 1½ ft (45 cm) high dwarf form 'Pixie Delight.' This is a mixed strain, whose flowers may be white, pink, red, lavender, purple, blue, or bicolored.

'Pixie Delight' has colorful spikes, which appear from midsummer to midfall, persisting long after perennial lupines have faded. Carried on bushy plants with leaves divided into soft, hairy green leaflets, they are excellent for producing a band of color at medium height in a mixed border. But they also look effective when grown on their own in a mass or in containers on the patio.

Cultivation
Soak the hard seeds in water for 12 hours before sowing them outdoors in their flowering site in early fall in mild parts of the country or in early spring where winters are severe. Thin the seedlings to stand 8-10 in (20-25 cm) apart.

Lupines grow in sun or partial shade. They do best in light, neutral to acid soils and thrive in poor soil.

'Pixie Delight' should not require any support. Deadhead regularly — the poisonous seedpods appeal to children and, if eaten, cause upset stomachs.
Pests/diseases Trouble free.

Malcolmia
Virginia stock

Malcolmia maritima

- ❑ Height 1 ft (30 cm)
- ❑ Planting distance 3 in
- ❑ Flowers midspring to fall
- ❑ Ordinary well-drained soil
- ❑ Sunny site
- ❑ Hardy annual

The flowers of *Malcolmia maritima,* an easily grown 1 ft (30 cm) high hardy annual, have a delightfully old-fashioned look. The little cross-shaped blooms come in white, pink, red, lavender, and purple (usually sold as a mixture) and have a sweet scent. If sown in succession from early spring to midsummer, where summers are mild, they will produce flowers from midspring to fall. Expect flowering to begin 4 weeks after sowing and to continue for 6-8 weeks. Where summers are hot, treat Virginia stock as a midspring to early-summer flower.

Cultivation
Sow the seeds thinly, beginning as soon as the soil can be worked in the North, and in fall in the Deep South and southern California. Virginia stocks flourish in ordinary well-drained soil, preferably in a sunny site. Rake the seed into the soil, so that it is only just covered; thin seedlings to 3 in apart. Or leave seedlings to grow into one another to form a cluster. Virginia stock self-seeds freely.
Pests/diseases Trouble free.

MALLOW — see *Lavatera*

Malope
malope

Malope trifida

- ❑ Height 3 ft (90 cm)
- ❑ Planting distance 9 in (23 cm)
- ❑ Flowers early summer to early fall
- ❑ Ordinary garden soil
- ❑ Sunny site
- ❑ Hardy annual

Malope is one of the easiest — and showiest — hardy annuals. Its trumpet-shaped flowers add bright colors to annual and mixed borders all summer, and they are also good for cutting. The species, *Malope trifida,* grows up to 3 ft (90 cm) high, bearing its blooms in large clusters. The most widely available form is 'Grandiflora,' whose large flowers are borne in great profusion.

Seed mixtures producing white, rose-pink, crimson, or rich purple blooms are available, as are single-colored strains, such as 'Pink Queen' and 'White Queen.'

Cultivation
Sow seeds outdoors as soon as the soil can be worked, just covering them with soil. When the seedlings are large enough to handle, thin them to 9 in (23 cm) apart.

Malopes will grow in any kind of soil, preferably light and well drained; they do best in a sunny spot. Self-sown seedlings will grow if the surrounding soil is left undisturbed.
Pests/diseases Trouble free.

MARGUERITE, BLUE — see *Felicia*
MARIGOLD — see *Calendula* and *Tagetes*
MARVEL OF PERU — see *Mirabilis*
MASK FLOWER — see *Alonsoa*

Matthiola
stock

Matthiola incana 'Ten Week Stock'

- ❑ Height 8-30 in (20-75 cm)
- ❑ Planting distance 1 ft (30 cm)
- ❑ Flowers early to late summer; winter and spring in South
- ❑ Fertile garden soil
- ❑ Sunny or lightly shaded site
- ❑ Hardy annual or biennial

Their heavenly scent and dense spikes of pastel and rich-colored flowers have made stocks favorites for cottage gardens, formal beds, mixed borders, and cut flowers. The spikes are borne on erect stems clothed with narrow, gray-green downy leaves.

Popular species and cultivars
Most garden cultivars have been developed from *Matthiola incana,* commonly known as stock.
'Brompton Stocks' are upright bushy plants reaching up to 1½ ft (45 cm) high. These late-spring-flowering stocks have single or double blooms of red, pink, purple, yellow, and white. Usually sold as a mixture, they should be treated as biennials.
'Cinderella Hybrids' produce dwarf plants 8-10 in (20-25 cm) tall. Double blossoms of carmine-red, rose, purple, and white open 7 weeks after sowing, making these one of the earliest-flowering stocks. Treat these plants as annuals.
"Night-Scented Stock," the common name for *Matthiola longipetala bicornis,* is a 15 in (38 cm) high, bushy annual. The lilac-gray or purple flowers, borne

Mentzelia
blazing star

Mentzelia lindleyi

❏ Height 2 ft (60 cm)
❏ Planting distance 9 in (23 cm)
❏ Flowers mid- to late summer in North; winter in Southwest
❏ Well-drained garden soil
❏ Sunny site
❏ Hardy annual

Matthiola incana 'Brompton Stocks'

from mid- to late summer, remain closed during the day, but open at night to release the sweet fragrance for which they are known. **'Ten Week Stocks'** are exceptionally fragrant early-flowering cultivars in mixed colors. As the name implies, they will flower 10-12 weeks after being sown. They make ideal bedding plants. Cultivars include 'Dwarf,' a compact plant 1 ft (30 cm) high, carrying large flowers in mixed pastel and rich colors.

Cultivation
Stocks are easily grown but will not tolerate hot weather. In the North, sow the annual stocks — 'Cinderella,' "Night Scented," and 'Ten Week' — directly in the flowering site in very early spring for an early-summer display. In the South, sow in late summer for winter and spring bloom. Sow shallowly, just covering the seeds with soil. Stocks grow in any fertile garden soil in either sun or partial shade. Thin the seedlings to stand 1 ft (30 cm) apart.

For early flowering in the North, sow indoors in late winter to early spring and keep at a temperature of 55-59°F (13-15°C). Prick out into flats and harden off in a cold frame before planting them out in mid- to late spring.

Strains with double flowers, such as the Cinderella Hybrids, should be sown indoors as already described, with the temperature lowered to 50°F (10°C) for a couple of days before pricking out. This drop in temperature will exaggerate the difference in seedling leaf color between the pale yellow-green double plants and green singles. Discard the singles only if double-flowered plants are wanted.

'Brompton Stocks' are treated as biennials. Sow the seeds in a nursery bed in late summer. Thin when the seedlings are large enough to handle and then transfer to the flowering site in fall, setting the plants 1 ft (30 cm) apart.

All stock cultivars thrive in fertile soil in sun or light shade.
Pests/diseases Flea beetles may attack seedlings, eating small holes in the leaves. Caterpillars feed on the leaves of older plants, and aphids can be a problem. Troublesome diseases include club root and mildew.

MEADOW FOAM —
see *Limnanthes*

Mentzelia lindleyi, sometimes called *Bartonia aurea*, is a robust, freely branching, slightly sprawling annual some 2 ft (60 cm) high. Best adapted to mild, dry climates, it will bloom from mid-to late summer in cooler regions and in the winter in the Southwest. It produces a long succession of fragrant brilliant yellow flowers that open from gracefully pointed buds into flowers, each composed of five broad petals arranged around a mass of slender golden stamens. The small, narrow leaves are rich green and set on succulent stems.

A California native, this annual should be grown in full sun. If the weather becomes cloudy and cool, the flowers may fail to open properly. However, the plant stands up well to wind.

Cultivation
In the North, sow the seeds outdoors in very early spring in a sunny site; on the Pacific Coast, time the sowing to coincide with the arrival of the fall rains. Blazing stars grow best in light, fertile soil, though any well-drained soil gives good results. Barely cover the seeds with soil. Thin to 9 in (23 cm) apart.
Pests/diseases Trouble free.

Mesembryanthemum
ice plant, Livingstone daisy

Mesembryanthemum 'Magic Carpet Hybrids'

- ❏ Height 4-6 in (10-15 cm)
- ❏ Planting distance 6 in (15 cm)
- ❏ Flowers early to late summer
- ❏ Any well-drained soil
- ❏ Sunny site
- ❏ Tender annual

The Livingstone daisy, originally from South Africa, has astonishingly brilliant pink, lavender, red, orange, and yellow daisylike flowers with slender petals. The dazzling display will last from early to late summer, if they are grown in a dry, sunny spot. The thick pale green leaves have a glistening, frosty appearance — hence the name "ice plant."

Since the plants are less than 6 in (15 cm) high and have a trailing habit, they are most attractive on banks, in rock gardens, and along the edges of borders. Grow them in large clusters.

Popular species and cultivars
Garden cultivars, developed from *Mesembryanthemum criniflorum*

(syn. *Dorotheanthus bellidiformis),* are more available than the true species.

'Lunette' has flowers with clear yellow petals arranged around deep rust-red central disks.

'Magic Carpet Hybrids' are a mixture of red, orange, pink, lavender, and yellow flowers; some have a white band around the dark central disks.

Cultivation
Sow the seeds indoors in early spring, and keep at a temperature of 59°F (15°C). Prick out the seedlings into flats when they are large enough to handle, and harden off before planting out in late spring. Set the plants 6 in (15 cm) apart. Choose a site in full sun and with well-drained soil. The plants thrive in sandy soil.

Seeds can be sown directly in the flowering site, after all danger of frost is past, but they won't flower as early as plants started indoors. Thin to 6 in (15 cm) apart.

Mesembryanthemum 'Magic Carpet Hybrids'

Pests/diseases Plants are susceptible to the southern root-knot nematodes.

MIGNONETTE — see *Reseda*

Mimulus
monkey flower

Mirabilis
four o'clock, marvel of Peru

Mirabilis jalapa

❑ Height 2-3 ft (60-90 cm)
❑ Planting distance 1 ft (30 cm)
❑ Flowers midsummer to early fall
❑ Light, moderately rich soil
❑ Sheltered, sunny site
❑ Tender perennial grown as tender annual

Marvel of Peru, or four o'clock *(Mirabilis jalapa),* has fragrant trumpet-shaped flowers in yellow, red, crimson, rose-pink, or white, often striped, veined, or mottled with contrasting colors. These usually open from mid- to late afternoon and fade the following morning, though in cool, cloudy weather they open earlier and stay fresh longer the following day. Appearing from midsummer to early fall, the blooms are carried on erect 2-3 ft (60-90 cm) high plants and are set against a foil of heart-shaped midgreen leaves.

The plants look best growing in clumps in sunny borders.

Cultivation
In mild-climate regions of the Pacific Coast and South, sow seed outdoors in spring or fall. In cold-winter regions, sow indoors in late winter to early spring and germinate at a temperature of 64°F (18°C). Prick out the seedlings into flats when large enough to handle, and harden off before planting them out in late spring to early summer. Set the plants 1 ft (30 cm) apart in groups of five or seven.
Pests/diseases Aphids may infest young growth.

Mimulus x hybridus 'Queen's Prize'

❑ Height ½-1 ft (15-30 cm)
❑ Planting distance 9 in (23 cm)
❑ Flowers early summer to midfall
❑ Moisture-retentive soil
❑ Sunny or lightly shaded site
❑ Half-hardy annual

Mimulus is a large genus of mainly perennial garden plants, but some hybrids from Chile — a race of mixed parentage known as *Mimulus × hybridus* — are grown as half-hardy annuals. These produce flowers (said to resemble the face of a grinning monkey) in profusion from early summer until midfall where summers are not too hot. The blooms may be bright red, orange, or yellow.

The annual monkey flower is one of the few bedding plants to tolerate light shade and flourish in damp soil. It is useful for filling window boxes and hanging baskets out of direct sun or for edging lightly shaded borders.

Popular species and cultivars
Several cultivars are available.
'Calypso Hybrids' produce robust plants, to 1 ft (30 cm) high, bearing a mass of orange, yellow, burgundy, and pink flowers, singly or in bicolors.
'Magic' is an early-flowering mixture in bright red, orange, yellow, and crimson, as well as pink,

Mimulus x hybridus 'Red Emperor'

pale yellow, and several bicolors. It grows 6 in (15 cm) high.
'Queen's Prize' has mixed-color flowers (some are mottled or spotted). It grows 1 ft (30 cm) high.
'Red Emperor' has dazzling scarlet flowers and reaches 6 in (15 cm) high.

Cultivation
Sow the seeds indoors 10 weeks before the last frost, and keep at a temperature of 55-61°F (13-16°C). When the seedlings are large enough to handle, prick them out into flats. Harden off before planting out after all danger of frost is past.

Monkey flowers grow in any moisture-retentive soil in sun or light shade.
Pests/diseases Trouble free.

75

Moluccella
bells of Ireland, shellflower

Myosotis
forget-me-not

Myosotis alpestris

❏ Height ½-1½ ft (15-45 cm)
❏ Planting distance 6 in (15 cm)
❏ Flowers midspring to early summer
❏ Fertile, well-drained but moisture-retentive soil
❏ Partial shade
❏ Biennial often grown as hardy annual

Forget-me-nots offer a delightful succession of tiny pure blue or pink flowers, each with a white or yellow eye, from midspring to early summer. They are planted mainly in beds with spring-flowering bulbs, though they also make attractive long-lasting cut flowers — only when the sprigs are taken indoors are the neatness and delicate coloring of the tiny flowers fully appreciated. They are also useful at the front of mixed borders, in woodland gardens, and at the edges of garden shrubbery.

Popular species and cultivars
The plant's cultivars all stem from *Myosotis alpestris* and *M. sylvatica*.
'Blue Ball' forms compact ball-shaped plants that are just 6-8 in (15-20 cm) high and bear indigo-blue blossoms. It is excellent for edging.
'Blue Bird' is 1 ft (30 cm) tall, bearing bright blue flowers. Because of its height, this cultivar is better adapted to planting within a border or to naturalization in a woodland setting.
'Carmine King' carries rich pink flowers on compact plants

Moluccella laevis

❏ Height 2-3 ft (60-90 cm)
❏ Planting distance 9 in (23 cm)
❏ Flowers late summer to early fall
❏ Well-drained rich soil
❏ Open, sunny site
❏ Half-hardy annual

Bells of Ireland — a misnomer, as the species *Moluccella laevis* comes from Syria — is a favorite among flower arrangers, not because of its flowers, which are small and insignificant, but because of the large pale green bell-like calyxes that surround them. These are arranged in tall, graceful spikes 9 in (23 cm) long and borne on erect stems clothed with rounded light green leaves.

These plants make unusual border plants and last for months in water as cut flowers. In addition, they can be dried for display. To do so, pick them in dry, warm weather near summer's end.

Cultivation
Sow the seeds indoors in early spring at a temperature of 59°F (15°C), just covering them with soil. Prick out the seedlings into flats, and harden off in a cold frame before planting out in late spring, 9 in (23 cm) apart. Bells of Ireland will grow in any ordinary garden soil, though well-drained rich soil in an open, sunny site provides the perfect conditions.

As the plants are moderately hardy, seeds can also be sown in the flowering site in early spring. In mild regions, sow into deep, well-moistened furrows in late summer.
Pests/diseases Trouble free.

MONEY PLANT — see *Lunaria*
MONKEY FLOWER —
see *Mimulus*
MOONWORT — see *Lunaria*
MORNING GLORY —
see *Convolvulus* and *Ipomoea*
MOROCCAN TOADFLAX —
see *Linaria*
MULLEIN — see *Verbascum*

and grows up to 8 in (20 cm) high. **'Royal Blue'** will grow up to 1 ft (30 cm) high, producing loose sprays of indigo-blue flowers. It is one of the earliest cultivars to bloom.

'Victoria Hybrids' form mounds 6-8 in (15-20 cm) tall with flowers that may be gentian-blue, all-white, rose, or pink.

Cultivation

These annuals will perform better in cool weather. In the South, sow seeds in fall for a spring bloom; in the North, sow them in early spring, as soon as the soil can be worked. Except in the most temperate regions, forget-me-nots will typically die with the onset of summer heat, but may self-sow first to appear anew in the fall. This sort of spontaneous reseeding is particularly common among plants naturalized along stream banks or woodland edges — the situations to which this flower is best adapted. Because forget-me-nots hybridize easily, self-sown plants are not likely to perpetuate the superior colors of their cultivated parents.

For the best results, grow forget-me-nots in fertile, well-drained but moisture-retentive soil in partial shade, though ordinary garden soil in sun or shade is usually quite adequate.

Pests/diseases Downy mildew, blight, and aster yellows can cause problems.

Nemesia
nemesia

Nemesia strumosa 'Carnival Hybrids'

❑ Height 7-24 in (18-60 cm)
❑ Planting distance 4-6 in (10-15 cm)
❑ Flowers early to late summer
❑ Moist, rich soil
❑ Sunny site
❑ Half-hardy annual

This bushy annual, with its mass of funnel-shaped blooms in many vivid colors, grows well on the Pacific Coast but is hard to grow in other climates. It offers a splendid summer-long show of bright flowers. Plant nemesias in beds and containers. They are long-lasting as cut flowers.

Popular species and cultivars

Several cultivars are derived from *Nemesia strumosa*.

'Carnival Hybrids' produce compact plants 9 in (23 cm) high, which become smothered with a mixture of brightly colored blooms.

'Funfair,' also compact (up to 9 in/23 cm high), blooms in bright shades of red, orange, and gold.

'Mello Red and White' bears bicolored flowers on 7-9 in (18-23 cm) plants.

'Triumph Red,' up to 10 in (25 cm) tall, is compact and early flowering, with bright red blossoms.

Cultivation

On the West Coast, sow seeds directly into the garden in fall, barely covering them with soil. Elsewhere, start seeds indoors in late winter or very early spring, sowing them into flats of seed-starting mix kept at a temperature of 59°F (15°C). Prick out the seedlings into flats, and harden off before planting out in late spring, after all danger of frost is past. Ideally, grow nemesias in fertile, moist soil in full sun.

Pests/diseases Root rot may cause the plants to collapse.

Nemesia strumosa

NASTURTIUM —
see *Tropaeolum*
NATAL GRASS —
see *Tricholaena*

Nemophila
baby blue eyes, nemophila

Nicandra
apple-of-Peru, shoo-fly plant

Nicandra physalodes

❏ Height 4-8 ft (120-240 cm)
❏ Planting distance 3-4 ft (90-120 cm)
❏ Flowers early to late summer
❏ Deep, moist, rich soil
❏ Sunny site
❏ Half-hardy annual

If you're looking for an unusual plant to fill a gap in a border, *Nicandra physalodes* is worth considering. It is a vigorous plant, easily grown and robust, with branching growth reaching 4-8 ft (120-240 cm). It has lush mid-green toothed leaves, small but pretty lilac-blue bell-shaped flowers, and fruits enclosed in attractive green lanternlike calyxes. Another benefit is its supposed ability to repel flies, giving it the common name "shoo-fly plant."

The flowers appear from early to late summer, though they open only for a few hours at midday. Expect the fruits to form between late summer and midfall; when dried, they are suitable for winter decoration.

Nemophila menziesii

❏ Height 6-9 in (15-23 cm)
❏ Planting distance 6 in (15 cm)
❏ Flowers early to late summer
❏ Moist good garden soil
❏ Sun or partial shade
❏ Hardy annual

The two garden species, *Nemophila maculata* and *N. menziesii,* are compact bushy plants used in the front of beds and edging. They do best in climates with cool summers or in the sunny, high mountain regions of the West.

Popular species and cultivars
Nemophila maculata has white flowers with purple veins and purple blotches on the petal tips. The spreading stems carry lobed leaves and reach 6 in (15 cm) high and 1 ft (30 cm) long.
Nemophila menziesii (baby blue eyes) has sky-blue white-centered flowers. Reaching 9 in (23 cm) high with stems 1 ft (30 cm) long, the plants bear feathery leaves. 'Pennie Black' has deep purple, near-black flowers edged with silvery white.

Cultivation
In mild-winter regions, sow seeds shallowly in their flowering site in fall; if winters are severe, sow seeds in early spring. In mid-spring thin to 6 in (15 cm) apart. Nemophilas like some afternoon shade. While they adapt to ordinary soil, a moist, rich soil is best.
Pests/diseases Aphids may infest young shoots.

Nemophila maculata

Cultivation
Sow the seeds indoors in early spring at a temperature of 59°F (15°C). Prick out the seedlings into 3 in (7.5 cm) pots. Harden off before planting out in late spring, 2-3 weeks before the last frost. Set the plants 3-4 ft (90-120 cm) apart. Or sow the seeds directly into the garden in midspring.

Shoo-fly plant thrives in deep moist and rich soil in a sunny location.
Pests/diseases Trouble free.

Nicotiana
tobacco

Nicotiana 'Nicki Hybrids'

❏ Height 10-60 in (25-150 cm)
❏ Planting distance 9-12 in (23-30 cm)
❏ Flowers early summer to early fall
❏ Rich, well-drained soil
❏ Sunny site
❏ Half-hardy annual

Flowering tobacco plants have long been valued for the heady evening scent of their blooms. Species and cultivars grown in the past mainly flowered in the evening, but modern breeding programs have resulted in hybrids and cultivars with flowers that open during daylight hours.

The plants have rosettes of pale green leaves at the base, from which rise elegant branching stems. The star-shaped blooms are borne in clusters throughout the summer and come in a mixture of white, soft pink, lavender-pink, deep red, and lime-green.

With their long season of bloom, flowering tobacco plants are ideal for group planting in borders and summer beds; the dwarf types will do well in pots and containers.

Popular species and cultivars
Most hybrids and cultivars are developed from *Nicotiana alata*.
'**Domino Hybrids**' are compact plants just 1 ft (30 cm) high, carrying flowers in red, pink, mauve, lilac, lime, and white.
'**Dwarf White Bedder**' bears large white blossoms that remain open throughout the day on 16 in (40 cm) tall plants.
'**Lime Green**' has greenish-yellow flowers and reaches 2½ ft (75 cm) high.
'**Merlin Hybrids**' are a dwarf mixture, up to 9 in (23 cm) high, with blooms in crimson, white, lime-green, and bicolored purple.
'**Nicki Hybrids**' have strongly fragrant flowers in a mixture of colors — pink, white, red, mauve, maroon, and lime-green. They reach 1 ft (30 cm).
'**Sensation Hybrids**' bear flowers in a wide range of colors — white, pink, red, and mauve. They reach 2½ ft (75) cm high.

Cultivation
Sow the seeds indoors in late winter to early spring at a temperature of 64°F (18°C). Prick out the seedlings into flats. Harden off before planting out in late spring, after all danger of frost is past. Set the plants 9-12 in (23-30 cm) apart in rich, well-drained soil in a sunny site. Deadhead the flowers regularly.
Pests/diseases Aphids can attack young plants. Nicotianas are also vulnerable to tobacco mosaic virus.

Nicotiana 'Lime Green'

Nierembergia
cupflower

Nierembergia 'Purple Robe'

- ❏ Height 6-15 in (15-38 cm)
- ❏ Planting distance 8 in (20 cm)
- ❏ Flowers early summer to early fall
- ❏ Moist but well-drained soil
- ❏ Sunny, sheltered site
- ❏ Tender perennial grown as half-hardy annual

Although a perennial, *Nierembergia hippomanica violacea* is tender and usually treated as an annual. Its fine green foliage forms neat mounds, which become covered with small pale lavender flowers with yellow throats from early summer to early fall. 'Mont Blanc' is smothered with glistening white flowers; 'Purple Robe' has deep violet flowers. Cupflower looks most effective as edging to beds and borders, and it may be used in containers and hanging baskets.

Cultivation
Sow the seeds in pots or flats indoors in late winter or early spring at a temperature of 59°F (15°C). Prick out the seedlings into flats, and harden off before planting out in late spring, 2-3 weeks before the expected date of the last frost.

The plants will grow in ordinary soil, although a moist but well-drained soil gives the best results. Choose a sunny, sheltered location.
Pests/diseases Trouble free.

Nigella
nigella

Nigella hispanica

- ❏ Height 2 ft (60 cm)
- ❏ Planting distance 9 in (23 cm)
- ❏ Flowers early summer to early fall
- ❏ Any good soil
- ❏ Sunny site
- ❏ Hardy annual

The blue, white, and pink flowers of this enchanting annual bloom all summer long in a haze of feathery soft green foliage. As the flowers fade, each seedpod swells and ripens into a pale brown, red-banded spiky globe, suitable for drying for winter decoration.

Invaluable for a border, nigella also provides superb cut flowers. Two species and their cultivars are widely grown in gardens.

Popular species and cultivars
Nigella damascena (love-in-a-mist) has showy blue or white flowers surrounded by a leafy green crown of threadlike bracts from early to late summer. Popular cultivars include 'Miss Jekyll,' with large bright blue flowers, and 'Persian Jewels,' with light and dark blue, rose-pink, and white flowers.
Nigella hispanica has larger blue flowers than the more commonly grown love-in-a-mist. Appearing from midsummer to early fall, these have a slight scent and a cluster of red stamens. The seedpods are less inflated than those of love-in-a-mist.

Cultivation
In early spring sow seeds in any well-cultivated soil in a sunny spot, just covering them with soil. Thin to 9 in (23 cm) apart. Deadhead for larger, later flowers, unless you want the seedpods.
Pests/diseases Trouble free.

Nigella damascena 'Persian Jewels'

Ocimum
basil

Ocimum basilicum 'Purpureum'

- ❏ Height 1-2 ft (30-60 cm)
- ❏ Planting distance 1 ft (30 cm)
- ❏ Flowers late summer
- ❏ Any well-drained soil
- ❏ Sunny, sheltered site
- ❏ Half-hardy annual

Better known for its culinary uses, sweet basil *(Ocimum basilicum)* has given rise to several ornamental cultivars, which are popular in summer bedding displays and as container plants. The purple foliage provides strong color contrasts and can also be used in cooking like its green-leaved relation.

The small pinkish-white or purple flower spikes borne on bushy plants are of little significance compared with the shiny purple leaves, wavy-edged in the cultivar 'Purple Ruffles' and almost black in 'Purpureum.'

Cultivation
Sow seeds in pots or flats indoors about 8 weeks before the last frost, at a temperature of 55°F (13°C). Prick the seedlings out into flats or peat pots when large enough to handle, and grow on at the same temperature. Harden young plants off before planting them out in late spring when all danger of frost is past.

Basil thrives in light and well-drained garden soil and needs a sheltered site in full sun. Pinch the flowers to encourage more leaf growth.

Pests/diseases Trouble free.

Oenothera
evening primrose

Oenothera biennis

- ❏ Height 3-6 ft (90-180 cm)
- ❏ Planting distance 1 ft (30 cm)
- ❏ Flowers early summer to midfall
- ❏ Ordinary well-drained soil
- ❏ Sunny site
- ❏ Hardy biennial

Most evening primroses are perennials, but the species *Oenothera biennis* is a hardy biennial. Ideal for the back of a border or a wild garden, its pale yellow funnel-shaped flowers open in the evening from early summer to midfall. The lance-shaped mid-green leaves, arranged in a large rosette on 3 ft (90 cm) high erect stems, make a perfect foil for the slightly fragrant and short-lived flowers.

If allowed to self-seed, evening primrose spreads like a weed.

Cultivation
Sow the seeds in pots or flats of seed-starting mix in a cool but frost-free location in midspring. Prick out the seedlings and grow them on in a nursery bed until midfall, when they can be planted out in the flowering site — preferably in ordinary well-drained soil in an open, sunny spot. Water the plants well in dry weather.

Pests/diseases Mildew can cause a white powdery coating on the leaves.

Onopordum
cotton thistle, Scotch thistle

Onopordum acanthium

- ❏ Height 8 ft (240 cm)
- ❏ Planting distance 2½ ft (75 cm)
- ❏ Flowers mid- to late summer
- ❏ Rich or ordinary garden soil
- ❏ Sunny or partially shaded site
- ❏ Hardy biennial

Scotch, or cotton, thistle *(Onopordum acanthium)* is an excellent specimen plant in a border, large shrubbery, or wild garden. Its dramatic foliage — broad silver-gray spiny leaves — is covered with white cobweblike hairs. Purple thistlelike flowers appear from mid- to late summer.

Cultivation
Sow the seeds directly in the flowering site, and thin to 2½ ft (75 cm) apart. If the plants are to reach their maximum height (8 ft/240 cm), they should be grown in rich soil. However, an ordinary garden soil in full sun or partial shade still gives good results. Remove dead flowers to prevent self-seeding.

Pests/diseases Trouble free.

Papaver
poppy

Papaver somniferum 'Danebrog'

Papaver nudicaule

- ❏ Height 9-48 in (23-120 cm)
- ❏ Planting distance 1-1½ ft (30-45 cm)
- ❏ Flowers early to late summer
- ❏ Ordinary well-drained soil
- ❏ Sunny site
- ❏ Hardy annual or biennial

Poppies' delicate, brightly colored petals are irresistible. Some poppies have single flowers with four broad overlapping petals arranged in a bowl shape, while others have double flowers — ball-like blooms with many petals.

Poppies are suited to a variety of exposures and situations in the garden — though sun is essential.

Popular species and cultivars

Papaver commutatum (formerly a subspecies of *P. rhoeas)* bears single flowers of crimson with large black blotches.

Papaver nudicaule (Iceland poppy) is an elegant poppy that comes from the sub-Arctic. The slender leafless stems carry white or yellow fragrant flowers in early summer. Only at the base of the 1½-2½ ft (45-75 cm) high stems is there a rosette of smooth, soft green leaves. This is one of the few poppies suitable for cutting for bouquets. When you cut it, se-

lect buds just starting to show color. Scald the stems in hot water after cutting to seal the ends.

Many garden cultivars have been developed from the species, offering a wide range of flower colors. 'Champagne Bubbles' has large pink, salmon, apricot, orange, golden yellow, or scarlet flowers, single or bicolored, and reaches 2 ft (60 cm) high. 'Garden Gnome Hybrids' are a compact strain, growing only 1 ft (30 cm) high, with flowers in scarlet, salmon, orange, yellow, or white. *Papaver rhoeas* (field poppy) has scarlet flowers with black centers from early to late summer on erect 2 ft (60 cm) high stems. The blooms are accompanied by pale green deeply lobed leaves. Field poppies look best grown in large clusters on grassy banks or in a semiwild meadow area.

Several garden cultivars have been developed. The most popular are the 'Shirley' strains: 'Shirley Single Hybrids' have single flowers in white, rose, pink, salmon, orange, and red; 'Shirley Reselected Double Hybrids' have similar but double flowers. Both types will grow to 2 ft (60 cm) tall. *Papaver somniferum* (opium pop-

py) has large white, red, pink, or purple flowers from early to late summer, followed by bulbous, flat-capped poisonous seedpods in fall. The plants reach up to 4 ft (120 cm) high and carry smooth, pale green deeply lobed leaves.

Cultivars include: 'Danebrog,' with single blood-red flowers, fringed petals, and a prominent white center; 'Paeonia Flowered Hybrids,' with a mixture of white, pink, or purple flowers resembling peonies; and 'White Cloud,' with extra-large white flowers on 3 ft (90 cm) tall stems.

Cultivation

Poppies grow in ordinary well-drained soil in a sunny site. Sow biennials *(Papaver nudicaule)* in the flowering site in early summer where the weather does not get too hot, or in the fall in the South and Southwest. Thin seedlings to 1-1½ ft (30-45 cm) apart the following spring.

Sow annuals in the flowering site in early spring in the South, just covering them with soil. In the North, start indoors in peat pots. Thin or transplant seedlings to a spacing of 1 ft (30 cm) apart. Deadhead regularly to prevent self-seeding. Avoid transplanting. **Pests/diseases** Downy mildew can cause pale blotches on the leaves, and a bacterial blight may cause browning and defoliation.

PATIENCE PLANT —
see *Impatiens*
PEARL GRASS — see *Briza*

Papaver somniferum

Papaver somniferum 'Paeonia Flowered Hybrids'

Papaver commutatum

Pelargonium
geranium, pelargonium

Zonal pelargonium 'Ringo Scarlet'

Zonal pelargonium 'Apple Blossom'

❏ Height ½-3 ft (15-90 cm)
❏ Planting distance 8-18 in (20-45 cm)
❏ Flowers late spring to midfall
❏ Ordinary well-drained garden soil
❏ Full sun
❏ Tender perennial grown as a half-hardy annual

Pelargoniums, grown outdoors as half-hardy bedding plants, come in a wide range of forms. The flowers, in white, red, pink, rose-pink, salmon, and purple, are borne on either upright or pendulous plants, with variously shaped and colored leaves.

Popular species and cultivars
Pelargoniums are grouped according to hybrid provenance, flower type, or growth habit.
Ivy-leaved pelargoniums are trailing plants with stems up to 3 ft (90 cm) long and midgreen fleshy ivylike leaves. They are ideal for hanging baskets and deep window boxes. These hybrids and cultivars are bred from *Pelargonium peltatum.*
'Butterfly' is compact, with double lilac flowers.
'Cornell' has pink flowers with a hint of lavender in them.

'Lulu' trails to 1½ ft (45 cm) and has deep violet flowers.
'Salmon Queen' has deep pink semi- or fully double flowers.
'Snow Queen' has double white flowers tinged with lilac.
'Summer Showers Hybrids' offer a mixture of pink, red, purple, and white flowers.
Martha Washington Pelargoniums, known as *Pelargonium × domesticum,* are erect shrubby hybrid plants up to 2 ft (60 cm) tall, with light green lobed leaves that are lightly toothed. Clusters of exotic blooms may be veined or marked with contrasting colors; petals may be frilled. Plant in containers, outdoors and indoors.
'Applause' has pink flowers with frilled petals.
'Aztec' has pink blooms, veined in maroon, with a white base.
'Grand Slam' is crimson-red.
Scented pelargoniums, grown for the strong scent of their leaves, bear typical five-petaled flowers, but these are small and insignificant. They are suitable for pot and tub cultivation.
'Chocolate Mint' has peppermint-scented leaves and blush-pink flowers.

'Citronella' has white blooms; its leaves have a lemon scent.
'Gray Lady Plymouth' has foliage smelling of eucalyptus and blush-pink flowers.
Zonal Pelargoniums, sometimes listed as *Pelargonium × hortorum,* are the most commonly grown cultivars. The rounded pale to midgreen leaves usually have an obvious brown or maroon zone. From 1-3 ft (30-90 cm) high, these upright plants are suitable for beds and containers. Many seed selections, mainly F1 hybrids, are available, such as:
'Borders Series Hybrids' produce medium-size plants 14-16 in (35-40 cm) tall with 5 in (13 cm) wide blooms of scarlet and cherry-red. Excellent for beds, they may be started from seeds.
'Classic Scarlet' produces huge heads of crimson flowers on 12-15 in (30-38 cm) tall plants. Bred to be grown in containers, it may be started from seeds.
'Eyes Right' has huge flower clusters in shades of pink and rose-red with scarlet eyes. It may be started from seeds.
'Hollywood Hybrids' bear tightly packed rosy pink, white-centered flower heads. These plants may be started from seeds.
'L'Amour Hybrids' are compact plants that branch from the base with semi- or fully double blooms in pink, red, and white.
'Lucky Break Hybrids' grow only 10-12 in (25-30 cm) high, yet they bear blooms in every shade from red through pink to pure white. Excellent bedding plants, they may be started from seeds.

Ivy-leaved pelargonium 'Cornell'

Ivy-leaved pelargonium 'Snow Queen'   Martha Washington pelargonium

Zonal pelargonium 'Mrs. Cox'

Zonal pelargonium 'Hollywood Hybrids'

'Masquerade Hybrids,' a bicolored mixture, has scarlet, pink, cerise, or salmon flowers, all with white eyes. They may be started from seeds.

'Multibloom Hybrids' are compact plants 10-12 in (25-30 cm) high. They flower 2 weeks earlier than most other zonal types and have many more flowering stems per plant. Available in shades of white through pink to scarlet, they may be started from seeds.

'Orange Appeal,' with large, pure orange flower heads, may be started from seeds.

'Orbit Hybrids' are available as a mixture or in pink, deep pink, scarlet, violet, or white. They may be started from seeds. 'Apple Blossom' is a cultivar.

'Ringo Scarlet' has glossy, rich scarlet flowers above dark green zoned foliage.

'Ringo White' has pure white flowers and light green leaves.

'Sensation Mixed,' called floribunda geraniums, come as mixed seeds or in colors of rose, scarlet, cherry, blush-pink, and coral.

'Startel' has dense flower heads in white, pink, and red, and heavily zoned leaves.

Cascading zonal types branch from the base and cascade over their containers. Cultivars are:

'Breakaway Red' and **'Breakaway Salmon,'** both 10 in (25 cm) tall, have deep red or salmon flowers and lightly zoned leaves. They may be started from seeds.

'Red Fountain' has single vermilion flowers above strongly zoned leaves.

Fancy-leaved zonal pelargoniums have heavily marked leaves that outshine the flowers. The following are cultivars.

'Happy Thoughts' has green leaves with yellow markings and red flowers.

'Mrs. Cox' has yellow, green, red, and copper leaves, with salmon-pink flowers.

Miniature zonal pelargoniums, suitable for window boxes and edging, include the following.

'Playboy Speckles,' 9 in (23 cm) high, is compact and bushy, with pink-and-white blooms. It may be started from seeds.

'Video Hybrids,' to 10 in (25 cm) high, come in many clear colors with deep green zoned leaves. They may be started from seeds.

Cultivation

Traditionally pelargoniums have been grown from cuttings. Recent breakthroughs in the breeding process have made it possible to start many zonal and ivy-leaved cultivars from seeds. Starting plants from seeds is both easier and less expensive.

Nevertheless, gardeners will find many fine older cultivars that bear outstanding flowers and are worth propagating by cutting. To propagate older cultivars, buy

Zonal pelargonium

Portulaca
sun plant

Portulaca grandiflora

- ❏ Height 6-9 in (15-23 cm)
- ❏ Planting distance 6 in (15 cm)
- ❏ Flowers early summer to fall
- ❏ Well-drained garden soil
- ❏ Sunny site
- ❏ Tender annual

A swath of sun plants (*Portulaca grandiflora*) make a gloriously bright display. The dense elegant cylindrical succulent leaves, 6-9 in (15-23 cm) high, are smothered in summer by single or double flowers in a range of colors.

Popular species and cultivars
'Extra Double Hybrids' have double flowers in rich shades.
'Sundance Hybrids' are semi-trailing, with double flowers.

Cultivation
Sow the seeds indoors 6-8 weeks before the last frost, keeping pots at a temperature of 64°F (18°C). Prick out the seedlings into flats of potting soil, and harden off before planting out in late spring, when the soil has warmed and the danger of frost is past. Set in a sunny site and well-drained soil.
Pests/diseases Aphids may make the plants sticky.

POT MARIGOLD —
see *Calendula*
PRICKLY POPPY —
see *Argemone*

Primula
polyanthus

Primula x polyantha hybrids

- ❏ Height 4-18 in (10-45 cm)
- ❏ Planting distance 1 ft (30 cm)
- ❏ Flowers early to late spring
- ❏ Moist, fertile soil
- ❏ Partially shaded site
- ❏ Short-lived perennial treated as biennial or hardy annual

Primula is an enormous genus of hardy and half-hardy perennials, but a few are grown as annuals or biennials. One type, the polyanthuses (cultivars of *Primula × polyantha*), are usually grown as biennials or annuals for bedding displays.

The polyanthus has been popular since its introduction in the 19th century. It is developed in part from the common primrose (*Primula vulgaris*) and has retained the characteristic bright green corrugated leaves of that species. But only with the development of the large-flowered hybrids has the polyanthus become widely used in bedding. These large-flowered hybrids produce blooms in compact long-lasting clusters on tall, sturdy stems 9-12 in (23-30 cm) high. The flowers appear from early to late spring in a wide spectrum of colors.

Popular species and cultivars
Primula malacoides (fairy primrose) is grown as an annual. It is 4-18 in (10-45 cm) tall and bears red, pink, or white blossoms in

P. x polyantha 'Elite Pacific Giant Blue'

tiers along its slender upright stems. The dwarf 'First Love' offers fragrant flowers on sturdy 6-8 in (15-20 cm) stems and is an outstanding choice for container plantings.
Primula × polyantha hybrids are available in several seed selections, usually mixed strains.
'Crescendo Hybrids' have giant blooms in primrose-yellow, red, pink, blue, and white, and reach 1 ft (30 cm) high.
'Pacific Giant Hybrids' have enormous blooms coming in a wide range of colors. The plants reach 1 ft (30 cm) high.
Primula vulgaris hybrids are smaller than polyanthus primroses, up to 6 in (15 cm) tall, with clusters of often stemless flowers. They include the following.
'Gold Laced Hybrids' are early

Primula vulgaris

flowering and long blooming, bearing flowers in various shades of red, purple, and violet, each with a golden eye at the center and white picotee edging.
'Rosebud Hybrids' bear clusters of rose-shaped frilled flowers in pink, red, apricot, and orange edged with gold or silver.
'Wanda Hybrids' bloom prolifically and are exceptionally cold resistant. Available as mixtures or in single colors, they have strong, bright colors and often display bronze foliage.

Cultivation
Primulas are commonly purchased as nursery-grown transplants, because propagation from seed is tricky. Do-it-yourselfers should chill seeds in the refrigerator for 3 weeks before sowing them indoors in fall. Germination is often erratic and slow. Prick out in pots or flats of ordinary potting soil, and grow on in a cold frame or other cool but frost-free and well-lit location. Pot on as necessary, harden off, and plant out after the last spring frost, setting the plants 1 ft (30 cm) apart.

Polyanthuses grow best in a partially shaded site in moist, fertile soil. They are not a flower for hot-summer regions, though *Primula malacoides* may be grown as a winter flower in coastal California.
Pests/diseases Slugs and snails sometimes eat the flowers.

PRINCE'S FEATHER —
see *Amaranthus*

Reseda
mignonette

Reseda odorata

❑ Height 1 ft (30 cm)
❑ Planting distance 10 in (25 cm)
❑ Flowers early summer to midfall
❑ Fertile, well-drained soil
❑ Sun or dappled shade
❑ Hardy annual

The unforgettable fragrance of mignonette flowers fills the air between early summer and midfall. This is the plant's great charm; visually it is unimpressive, with leaves that resemble those of spinach and flower spikes that consist of minute yellow-green blooms with tufted brown stamens.

Popular species and cultivars
Several cultivars have been developed from *Reseda odorata*.
'Fragrant Beauty' has strongly scented lime-green and red-tinged flowers on plants 1 ft (30 cm) high.
'Machet Giant,' to 1 ft (30 cm) high, has red-tinged flowers.

Cultivation
Except in very temperate areas, sow seeds in spring and again in fall. A hot summer stifles these cool-weather blooms. Plant in fertile, well-drained soil (ideally alkaline) in full sun or dappled shade. Cover them with just a little soil and press in well. Thin to 10 in (25 cm) apart.

For early-flowering plants, sow the seeds indoors in peat pots in late winter to early spring at a temperature of 55°F (13°C). Harden off before planting out in late spring in the flowering site.
Pests/diseases Trouble free.

Ricinus
castor-oil plant

Ricinus communis

❑ Height 5 ft (150 cm)
❑ Planting distance 3 ft (90 cm)
❑ Foliage plant
❑ Rich soil
❑ Sunny site
❑ Tender shrub grown as tender annual

This tropical plant, whose seeds are used to make castor oil, is a very striking tender annual. Robust and shrubby, it will grow 5 ft (150 cm) high and nearly as wide in the course of a year, making it useful as an eye-catching specimen plant. The leaves, up to 1 ft (30 cm) wide, are hand-shaped. In the species *Ricinus communis* these are green, but cultivars exist with brown, maroon, or bronze-green foliage.

Cultivation
Soak the seeds in water for 24 hours to speed germination, then sow singly in pots indoors 6-8 weeks before the last spring frost. Keep at a temperature of 70°F (21°C). Harden off before planting out after the danger of frost is past. Space the plants 3 ft (90 cm) apart in rich soil in a sunny site. Stake in exposed sites.
Pests/diseases Trouble free.

ROCKET LARKSPUR —
see *Delphinium*
RUBY GRASS —
see *Tricholaena*

Rudbeckia
black-eyed Susan, coneflower

Rudbeckia hirta

- ❏ Height 1½-3 ft (45-90 cm)
- ❏ Planting distance 1½ ft (45 cm)
- ❏ Flowers midsummer to late fall
- ❏ Any well-drained soil
- ❏ Open, sunny site
- ❏ Short-lived perennial grown as half-hardy annual

Rudbeckia hirta 'Rustic Dwarf Hybrids'

Rudbeckia hirta and its cultivars are excellent annuals for producing color in flower borders toward the end of summer. Displaying a mass of large yellow or orange daisylike flowers with conspicuous conelike central disks, the plants stand 1½-3 ft (45-90 cm) high with oblong midgreen leaves and bristly branching stems. Some cultivars may overwinter to flower again for a few years. The blooms are excellent for cutting.

Popular species and cultivars
'Double Gold' bears bright golden yellow double or semidouble flowers that measure up to 4½ in (11 cm) wide. The plants grow to a height of 3 ft (90 cm).
'Gloriosa Daisy' has huge single flowers in shades of yellow, orange, bronze, and mahogany. The plants reach 3 ft (90 cm) high.
'Goldilocks' bears large golden yellow double and semidouble blooms. The plants reach 1½-2 ft (45-60 cm) high and have a particularly long flowering season.
'Green Eyes,' up to 2½ ft (75 cm), is a well-branched cultivar bearing golden yellow, pointed flowers with olive-green centers.
'Marmalade' has golden orange single flowers with black centers and reaches 2 ft (60 cm) high.
'Nutmeg,' 2-2½ ft (60-75 cm) tall,

has double flowers ranging from clear and golden yellow to orange-brown, often with contrasting zones of red.
'Rustic Dwarf Hybrids' bear a mixture of large single flowers in shades of golden yellow, mahogany-red, and bronze.
'Sputnik' ('Kelvedon Star') has large 4-in (10-cm) wide flowers with bright yellow petals around prominent dark brown centers. The plants grow up to 3 ft (90 cm) tall, and the flowers are especially long-lasting when cut.

Cultivation
In regions with mild winters and long growing seasons, sow seeds directly into the garden as soon as the soil has warmed in the spring. Farther north, sow seeds indoors in pots of seed-starting mix 8-10 weeks before the last spring frost. Prick the seedlings out into flats, harden off, and plant out when all danger of frost is past. Set out at 1½ ft (45 cm) intervals in an open, sunny site with well-cultivated and well-drained soil. Tall cultivars need staking in windy sites.

After the first main flowering, give the plants a liquid foliar fertilizer to encourage more blooms.

The 'Gloriosa Daisy' cultivars are often perennial in habit and will flower for a couple of years if the crowns are protected with a deep winter mulch.
Pests/diseases Slugs and snails may eat the leaves and stems.

Rudbeckia hirta 'Goldilocks'

Salpiglossis
painted tongue, velvet flower

Salvia
salvia

Salvia splendens 'Blaze of Fire'

❑ Height 10-48 in (25-120 cm)
❑ Planting distance 1-1½ ft (30-45 cm)
❑ Flowers midsummer to fall
❑ Ordinary well-drained soil
❑ Sunny site
❑ Half-hardy annual or perennial
  grown as annual or biennial

Salpiglossis sinuata 'Splash Hybrids'

❑ Height 1-3 ft (30-90 cm)
❑ Planting distance 1 ft (30 cm)
❑ Flowers early summer to midsummer,
  or into early fall in cooler regions
❑ Rich soil
❑ Open, sunny site
❑ Half-hardy annual

The velvety funnel-shaped blooms of this Chilean half-hardy annual create a dramatic effect in a mixed border with their kaleidoscope of purples, reds, pinks, oranges, and yellows. The flowers, many of which are veined in deeper or contrasting colors, are produced from early summer to midsummer and into fall where summers are cool.

Salpiglossis sinuata is the species usually grown, and its hybrid cultivars make good pot plants in the greenhouse and on the patio; they add a wealth of color to summer borders and last well in water.

Popular species and cultivars
Several seed types are available. **'Bolero Hybrids'** are vigorous cultivars that bear a mixture of richly colored flowers.

'Casino Hybrids' have strongly veined flowers in shades of red, rose, yellow, orange, and purple; they are good for bedding.
'Kew Blue,' a dwarf cultivar that grows only 1 ft (30 cm) high, bears gold-veined blue flowers.
'Splash Hybrids' are a bushy strain with a profusion of brightly colored flowers. They will grow in poor soil.

Cultivation
Sow the seeds indoors 8 weeks before the last spring frost at a temperature of 64°F (18°C). When the seedlings are large enough to handle, prick out into flats. Harden off before planting out in late spring 1 ft (30 cm) apart in rich soil and a sunny site.

The seeds can be sown directly into the flowering site in mid- to late spring in mild-winter areas.

Support the plants with a circle of interlaced twigs, and remove dead flower spikes to increase the size of blooms on the side shoots.
Pests/diseases Aphids may infest the stems, and southern root-knot nematodes may attack roots.

When considering salvia, many gardeners never look beyond *Salvia splendens*, the bedding plant with spikes of aggressively red flowers seen in almost every public garden. But salvias form a large genus incorporating shrubs and perennials as well as annuals. Both annual and tender perennial species used in bedding displays and borders are described here. All have spikes of tubular flowers, but they come in a range of colors.

Popular species and cultivars
Salvia argentea is a short-lived perennial grown as a biennial foliage plant. Reaching 4 ft (120 cm) high, the plant forms attractive rosettes of oval leaves covered with silky, silvery white hairs. If the white flowers flushed with purple do appear, remove them to encourage healthy foliage. Plant 15-18 in (38-45 cm) apart in the rock garden, on a wall, or in a summer border, where its silver leaves will temper the bolder flowers around it.
Salvia farinacea (mealycup sage) is a 2½-3 ft (75-90 cm) tall tender perennial, usually grown as a half-hardy annual. It bears spikes of blue flowers flushed with purple from midsummer to fall.

Salvia argentea

A waxy dusting, which gives it a gray-green "mealy" appearance, covers the stems and foliage. The cultivar 'Victoria,' 1½ ft (45 cm) high, carries dense spikes of violet-blue flowers appropriate in formal bedding displays and mixed borders. The flowers are excellent for cutting.

Salvia patens, a perennial species grown as an annual, is distinguished by its striking clear gentian-blue flowers, which appear from late summer to early fall. These are widely spaced on 3-ft (90-cm) high slender stems. The upright, well-branched plants bear midgreen oval leaves.

Salvia splendens (scarlet sage) has spikes of brilliant red flowers between midsummer and fall, accompanied by rich green foliage. Ranging from 15-36 in (38-90 cm) high, this species and its cultivars are some of the most popular annuals for formal beds. While the red-flowered cultivars are most commonly seen, cultivars with pink and purple blooms are also available. 'Blaze of Fire' is an early-flowering cultivar with vivid scarlet flowers. 'Laser Purple' has rich deep purple flowers. 'Phoenix Hybrids,' up to 10 in (25 cm) tall, have scarlet, purple, white, deep or pale pink, and lilac flowers. 'Rambo' is especially vigorous, growing to 2 ft (60 cm) high, with vivid scarlet flower spikes and deep green foliage. 'Splendisima' is a dwarf (to 1 ft/30 cm) that performs unusually well in cool and wet or hot and humid conditions.

Salvia viridis

Salvia viridis 'Claryssa Pink'

Scabiosa
sweet scabious

Salvia patens

Salvia viridis, an annual, has an upright branching habit and reaches 1½ ft (45 cm) high. The pale pink or purple flowers appear from midsummer to early fall, but it is the deep purple bracts around the flowers that give this species its decorative appeal. 'Claryssa Pink' is a pink-flowered cultivar. The flower spikes can be dried for use in flower arrangements.

Cultivation
Where summers are hot and the growing season long, sow seeds directly into the garden as soon as spring has warmed the soil. Elsewhere, sow seeds in pots of seed-starting mix 10 weeks before the last spring frost, and keep at a temperature of 64°F (18°C). Prick out the seedlings into flats when they are large enough to handle, and harden off before planting out in late spring, when all danger of frost is past. Set the plants about 1 ft (30 cm) apart.

Salvia argentea may be difficult to grow from seeds and is better purchased as plants from a garden center.

Grow all salvias in ordinary well-drained garden soil in a sunny spot. When the plants are 2-3 in (5-7.5 cm) high, pinch the growing tips to encourage branching and bushy growth.

Pests/diseases Trouble free.

Scabiosa atropurpurea

- ❏ Height 1½-3 ft (45-90 cm)
- ❏ Planting distance 9 in (23 cm)
- ❏ Flowers midsummer to early fall
- ❏ Fertile, well-drained soil
- ❏ Open, sunny site
- ❏ Hardy annual

Sweet scabious *(Scabiosa atropurpurea),* a graceful plant with elegantly divided foliage, carries closely packed fragrant flowers in blue, mauve, purple, red, pink, and white on slender stems 3 ft (90 cm) tall. The plant is ideal both for cutting and for beds.

Popular species and cultivars
'Blue Moon' has lavender-blue flowers, ideal for cutting. Left on the plant, the flowers fade to lovely papery blue-eyed seed heads.
'Dwarf Double Mixed' is a short cultivar reaching just 1½ ft (45 cm) high, but it carries large fragrant flowers in mixed colors.
'Stellata' grows to 2½ ft (75 cm) high. Its silvery blue flowers develop into attractive large round seed heads with a greenish, spiny starlike center. They are excellent for dried flower arrangements.

Cultivation
In the South, sow seeds directly into the garden in early spring and again in late summer. Elsewhere, sow seeds indoors 6 weeks before the last spring frost, prick out into flats, then harden off and plant out in late spring when still cool. Scabiosas grow in fertile, well-drained soil in an open, sunny site. Thin seedlings or transplant to 9 in (23 cm) apart. Stake tall cultivars in windy situations. To encourage further flowering, cut the stems at the first joint as blooms fade.

Pests/diseases Slugs and snails often damage young plants. Root rot may cause the plants to collapse, and powdery mildew may appear on the leaves.

SCARLET PIMPERNEL — see *Anagallis*
SCARLET SAGE — see *Salvia*

Schizanthus
butterfly flower, poor man's orchid

Schizanthus pinnatus 'Dwarf Bouquet Hybrids'

- ❏ Height 1-4 ft (30-120 cm)
- ❏ Planting distance 1 ft (30 cm)
- ❏ Flowers late winter to early spring in California; elsewhere, early summer to midsummer
- ❏ Fertile, moisture-retentive soil
- ❏ Sheltered, sunny site
- ❏ Half-hardy annual

This Chilean plant flourishes only in cool weather and grows best in coastal or cooler regions with temperate summers. The orchidlike blooms in pink, red, and purple blotched with yellow make good cut flowers. Each has a pale throat veined with a darker color, set off by pale green, almost fernlike foliage. They bloom in late winter to early spring in California and in early summer to midsummer elsewhere.

Schizanthus pinnatus and its cultivars are often grown as indoor pot plants, but several dwarf cultivars may be grown outdoors.

Popular species and cultivars
'**Butterfly Mixture**,' to 1½ ft (45 cm), has dainty pink, carmine, purple, crimson, or white blooms. '**Disco**' has neat, compact plants 1 ft (30 cm) high covered profusely with flowers in mixed colors. '**Dwarf Bouquet Hybrids**' are 12-15 in (30-38 cm), with red, pink, amber, or salmon blooms.

Cultivation
Sow the seeds directly into the garden in California in fall or early spring, barely covering them with soil. Elsewhere, sow indoors in early spring and keep at a temperature of 61°F (16°C) till they germinate. Prick out into flats, and harden off before planting out in late spring 1 ft (30 cm) apart in fertile, moisture-retentive soil in a sunny, sheltered site.
Pests/diseases Aphids may infest young plants.

SCOTCH THISTLE —
see *Onopordum*
SEA LAVENDER —
see *Limonium*

Senecio
dusty miller, silver-leaved cineraria

Senecio cineraria 'Silverdust'

- ❏ Height 9-30 in (23-75 cm)
- ❏ Planting distance 1 ft (30 cm)
- ❏ Foliage plant
- ❏ Dry to well-drained soil
- ❏ Sunny site
- ❏ Half-hardy perennial grown as annual

Arching sprays of intricately dissected white-felted leaves make *Senecio cineraria* an excellent foliage plant for summer beds.

Silver-leaved cineraria, a half-hardy evergreen, will survive most winters in mild regions, but it is usually treated as an annual since the lustrous foliage becomes coarse in later years. Clusters of groundsellike yellow flowers appear during summer but are best removed, as they are less attractive than the leaves.

Popular species and cultivars
Cultivars offer various leaf forms. '**Cirrhus**' has bright silver, rounded leaves. '**Silverdust**' forms a mound of silvery fernlike foliage.

Cultivation
Sow the seeds indoors in late winter to early spring, taking care not to cover them with soil as they need strong light to germinate. Keep at 64-70°F (18-21°C) until germination. Prick out the seedlings into pots or boxes, and harden off before planting out in late spring — set out 2-3 weeks before the last spring frost. Place the plants 1 ft (30 cm) apart in good soil in sun.
Pests/diseases Birds may attack the leaves, and powdery mildew can be a problem.

SHELLFLOWER —
see *Moluccella*
SHOO-FLY PLANT —
see *Nicandra*

Silene
campion, catchfly

Silene pendula

Silene coeli-rosa 'Red Angel'

- ❏ Height ½-1½ ft (15-45 cm)
- ❏ Planting distance 6 in (15 cm)
- ❏ Flowers late spring to early fall
- ❏ Any well-drained soil
- ❏ Sunny or lightly shaded site
- ❏ Hardy annual

Campion and its many cultivars are easily grown, hardy annuals valued for their prolific flowering through summer's warm weather. The slender stems carry delicate five-petaled cup-shaped flowers in attractive shades of blue, lilac, pink, and white, with contrasting centers. They are suitable as cut flowers.

Their fragile appearance belies their robust growth habit, and they are seen to best advantage in large swaths in cottage-garden beds and borders; the dwarf species and cultivars are ideal for rock gardens and as edging.

Popular species and cultivars
Silene coeli-rosa (now classified as *Lychnis coeli-rosa,* but still commonly listed in catalogs under the older name) grow 1½ ft (45 cm) tall, its slender stems set with oblong gray-green leaves and topped with white-eyed rose-purple flowers in succession from early to late summer.

Several cultivars are popular. 'Angel Hybrids' grows 10 in (25 cm) high and can be purchased in blue, rose-cerise, or as a mixture. 'Fire King,' which grows to 10-15 in (25-38 cm) high, bears vivid red blooms. 'Treasure Island Hybrids,' 1-1½ ft (30-45 cm) high, come in soft shades of blue, purple, pink, crimson, and white. *Silene pendula* is rather different, growing only 6-9 in (15-23 cm) high. It is the most widely grown of the annual species, forming compact plants ideal for edging. The erect stems bear loose clusters of pale pink flowers above mounds of pointed, hairy mid-green leaves.

Several cultivars are available. 'Dwarf Hybrids' (9 in/23 cm) flower in white or shades of pink. 'Peach Blossom' (6 in/15 cm) is of branching and cascading habit and suitable for hanging baskets. Its stems are covered with a profusion of double flowers that open from deep pink buds to become salmon-pink and when mature turn nearly white.

Cultivation
Sow the seeds in the flowering site in early spring to midspring, and thin the seedlings to their required spacings. Seeds of *Silene pendula* and its cultivars can also be sown outdoors in early fall, for flowering in late spring, if protected by a blanket of evergreen boughs during the colder part of winter.

All campions will grow in ordinary garden soil provided it is well drained; they tolerate light shade but perform best in an open, sunny site and flourish in warm weather.

Pests/diseases Trouble free.

Silybum
holy thistle, milk thistle

Silybum marianum

- ❏ Height 4 ft (120 cm)
- ❏ Planting distance 2 ft (60 cm)
- ❏ Flowers midsummer to early fall
- ❏ Any garden soil
- ❏ Open, sunny site
- ❏ Hardy annual

The fast-growing *Silybum marianum* is cultivated mainly for its striking foliage of ovate, glossy dark green and spiny leaves heavily marbled with white veins. They are carried in flat, widespreading rosettes topped from midsummer on with tall stems carrying deep violet-red thistle-like flowers.

Cultivation
Sow seeds in the flowering site in early spring or, in mild-winter regions, in early fall, just covering them with soil. Thin the seedlings to 2 ft (60 cm) apart. Plant in any soil, at the back of a border or in a semiwild garden in full sun.
Pests/diseases Trouble free.

SLIPPER FLOWER —
see *Calceolaria*
SNAPDRAGON —
see *Antirrhinum*
SNOW-ON-THE-MOUNTAIN —
see *Euphorbia*
SPIDER FLOWER — see *Cleome*
STATICE — see *Limonium*
STRAWFLOWER —
see *Helichrysum*
SUNFLOWER — see *Helianthus*
SWEET PEA — see *Lathyrus*
SWEET SULTAN —
see *Centaurea*
SWEET WILLIAM —
see *Dianthus*

Tagetes
marigold

Tagetes patula 'Tiger Eyes'

- ❏ Height ½-3 ft (15-90 cm)
- ❏ Planting distance 1-1½ ft (30-45 cm)
- ❏ Flowers midsummer to fall
- ❏ Ordinary garden soil
- ❏ Open, sunny site
- ❏ Half-hardy annual

Easily cultivated, French and African marigolds have single, semidouble, or double flowers in every shade of orange, yellow, and mahogany-red. They are good for cutting. When crushed, the deeply cut green leaves give off a pungent smell.

Popular species and cultivars
Tagetes erecta (African marigold) has given rise to many cultivars, most of which are F1 hybrids of uniform vigor and flower size. Popular tall types (2-3 ft/60-90 cm) with double flowers up to 6 in (15 cm) wide, are 'Crackerjack Hybrids' (orange, gold, and lemon), 'Doubloon' (primrose-yellow), and the 'Jubilee' series (mixed yellow, orange, and gold).

Dwarf double-flowered cultivars (10-18 in/25-45 cm) include the 'Inca' series (mixed or in gold, bright yellow, and deep orange).

Mule cultivars, so called because they are sterile and cannot seed, are hybrids between African

Tagetes patula 'Honeycomb'

Tagetes patula 'Boy O Boy'

Tagetes erecta 'Inca Gold'

and French marigolds. They bloom throughout the growing season until the first frost. Mule types are dwarf, growing to a height of 12-14 in (30-35 cm), and bear a profusion of frilled, double, 2-in (5-cm) wide blooms in shades of yellow, orange, and red. Popular types are 'Fireworks Hybrids,' whose blooms may grow 3 in (8 cm) wide, and 'Nugget Hybrids,' which tolerate wet weather well.

Tagetes patula (French marigold), a dwarf plant, is excellent for edging and window boxes. Its cultivars range in height from 6 in (15 cm) to 10-12 in (25-30 cm). Most bear double or crested flowers; some have dainty single flowers. Double-flowered ones are 'Boy Hybrids' (a mixture of yellow, gold, orange, or mahogany-red cultivars), 'Happy Days Hybrids' (mahogany-red or golden yellow; very heat tolerant), 'Honeycomb' (red and yellow, crested), 'Queen Bee' (interlaced red and yellow), 'Queen Sophia' (russet petals edged with gold), 'Royal Crested Hybrids' (mixed, crested), and 'Tiger Eyes' (red and deep orange, crested).

Single-flowered French marigolds include 'Disco Hybrids' (red, yellow, orange, or gold and maroon; early blooming; rain tolerant), 'Marietta Hybrids' (golden yellow with maroon blotches), and the 'Mischief' series (mixed or yel-

low, gold, mahogany, or red and gold).

Tagetes tenuifolia pumila (signet marigold), a delicate plant with slender growth, has finely divided, sweet-smelling light green leaves and small yellow flowers. Cultivars include 'Golden Gem' (golden yellow) and 'Lemon Gem' (pale yellow).

Cultivation

Sow seeds directly into the garden 2-3 weeks before the last spring frost, barely covering them with soil. Thin seedlings to a spacing of 1 ft (30 cm) for smaller cultivars and 1½ ft (45 cm) for taller African types. For an early start, sow indoors in early spring

to midspring, and keep at a temperature of 64°F (18°C). When the seedlings are large enough to handle, prick out into flats, and harden off before planting out after all danger of frost is past.

Marigolds will grow in any garden soil — even in poor dry conditions — though a moderately rich soil is best. Give them an open, sunny site, and deadhead often.

Pests/diseases Botrytis may cause browning and stop flowering during wet weather. Slugs and snails eat the plants.

TIDYTIPS — see *Layia*
TOADFLAX — see *Linaria*
TOBACCO — see *Nicotania*

Tagetes tenuifolia pumila 'Golden Gem'

Torenia
wishbone flower

Torenia fournieri

❏ Height 4-12 in (10-30 cm)
❏ Planting distance 6-9 in (15-23 cm)
❏ Flowers midsummer to early fall
❏ Moist garden soil
❏ Partial shade
❏ Tender annual

The wishbone flower *(Torenia fournieri)* is named for the shape of the stamens in the throats of its trumpet-shaped flowers. Carried in profusion all summer, the blooms almost hide the pointed and finely toothed pale green leaves. Gardeners value the exotic flowers, with violet-purple lips and throats of lilac-purple with yellow splashes, and the plant's preference for shade. It is suitable for bedding and makes a fine container plant.

A few seed cultivars are available, including the small 'Pink Panda,' which grows 4-8 in (10-20 cm) high, with flowers in a blend of white and cerise-pink.

Cultivation
Sow the seeds indoors 8-10 weeks before the last spring frost in pots or flats of seed-starting mix, just covering them. Germinate at 64°F (18°C). When large enough to handle, prick seedlings out singly into small pots; harden off before planting out in early summer.

Wishbone flowers thrive in any good, moist soil and need a sheltered, lightly shaded site. For bushy growth, pinch growing tips on young plants.
Pests/diseases Trouble free.

Trachymene
blue laceflower

Trachymene coerulea

❏ Height 1½-2½ ft (45-75 cm)
❏ Planting distance 9 in (23 cm)
❏ Flowers mid- to late summer
❏ Any good garden soil
❏ Sheltered, sunny site
❏ Half-hardy annual

The modest lavender-blue flowers of *Trachymene coerulea* (syn. *Didiscus caeruleus)*, the blue laceflower, make a welcome change from the strong, startling colors characteristic of so many annuals and biennials. Composed of dainty florets arranged in small round umbels, they resemble the cushions of the wild Queen Anne's lace. They have a slight scent and appear from mid- to late summer.

The flowers are carried on 1½-2½ ft (45-75 cm) high bushy plants with light green deeply divided, sticky leaves.

Blue laceflowers look their best when grown in groups with other annuals in a sunny border. Their long, stiff stems make them good for cutting.

Cultivation
Sow the seeds indoors in early spring, and keep at a temperature of 59°F (15°C). As soon as the seedlings are large enough to handle, prick them out into 3 in (7.5 cm) pots or seed flats. Harden off and plant out after all danger of frost is past.

Blue laceflowers grow in any well-drained garden soil in a sheltered, sunny site. The plants may need the support of twiggy sticks and bloom better when somewhat crowded.
Pests/diseases Trouble free.

Tricholaena
Natal grass, ruby grass

Tricholaena rosea

❏ Height 2½ ft (75 cm)
❏ Planting distance 1 ft (30 cm)
❏ Flowers early to late summer
❏ Well-drained fertile soil
❏ Open, sunny site
❏ Tender perennial grown as half-hardy annual

Trichlaena rosea (syn. *Rhynchelytrum repens)* is an ornamental grass grown for its attractive flower heads, which appear from early to late summer. Slender and graceful, these 10-in (25-cm) long reddish-maroon fluffy spikelets fade, becoming silvery pink as they age.

This is a clump-forming species reaching 2½ ft (75 cm) high, excellent for growing at the front of a border or in an isolated patch on its own. A sunny, open site is essential for it to thrive.

Cultivation
Sow the seeds in late winter or early spring in flats of seed-starting mix. Keep at a temperature of 55-61°F (13-16°C). Harden off before transplanting the seedlings to the flowering site in late spring or early summer, when the danger of frost has passed.

Alternatively, sow the seeds in the flowering site in late spring; thin the seedlings to stand 1 ft (30 cm) apart.

Natal grass should be grown in fertile, well-drained soil in an open, sunny site.
Pests/diseases Trouble free.

Tropaeolum
nasturtium

Tropaeolum majus 'Alaska Hybrids'

Tropaeolum majus

- ❑ Height 9-144 in (23-360 cm)
- ❑ Planting distance 15 in (38 cm)
- ❑ Flowers early summer to midfall
- ❑ Poor soil
- ❑ Sunny site
- ❑ Tender annual

This tender annual's spurred, lightly perfumed orange and yellow flowers and trailing stems with round, smooth green leaves are some of the most familiar summer sights in gardens. The blooms appear from early summer until fall and grow on compact, trailing, or climbing plants, depending on the cultivar.

Nasturtiums can be grown in containers and hanging baskets, in bedding displays, or at the front of a border, and they can be trained up a wall or trellis. However, aphids find the smooth green leaves irresistible and will destroy the plants if they are not controlled.

Popular species and cultivars

Tropaeolum majus is the species from which most garden cultivars, including the following climbing, compact, and semitrailing types, have been developed.

Climbing cultivars reach 6 ft (180 cm) or more high and are suitable for training up a trellis or a wall.

'Fordhook Favorites' offer single flowers from gold to red.

Compact cultivars have a compact bushy habit and reach 9 in (23 cm) high.

'Alaska Hybrids' have single red and orange flowers. The pale green leaves are marbled with cream.

'Empress of India' has deep crimson-scarlet flowers and dark green leaves.

'Tom Thumb Hybrids' have single flowers in shades of red, orange, and yellow.

'Whirlybird Hybrids' bear a mass of semidouble blooms in mixed colors. These are held well above the foliage and face upward. Single colors — scarlet, mahogany, cherry, tangerine, orange, gold, and cream — are also available.

Semitrailing cultivars have a trailing habit and reach 12-15 in (30-38 cm) high.

'Double Gleam Hybrids' have fragrant double and semidouble flowers in golden yellow, orange, and scarlet.

'Jewel Hybrids' are an early-flowering mixture with semidouble blooms in mixed colors.

Tropaeolum peregrinum is a short-lived perennial species usually grown as an annual. Rapidly reaching 12 ft (360 cm) high in one season, it bears irregularly shaped yellow flowers with green spurs from midsummer to midfall among blue-green leaves. It will tolerate shade.

Cultivation

Sow the seeds ¾ in (2 cm) deep in poor soil in a sunny site a couple of weeks before the last spring frost. Thin to 15 in (38 cm) apart. With *Tropaeolum peregrinum* sow two seeds where one plant is required, and if both germinate remove one. This species requires ordinary garden soil.

To cultivate plants for hanging baskets, sow the seeds in late winter to early spring in pots of seed-starting mix and germinate at a temperature of 55-61°F (13-16°C). When the seedlings are large enough to handle, prick them out singly into 3-in (7.5-cm) pots of well-drained potting soil and pot on as required. Harden off and plant out in early summer.

Pests/diseases Aphids may infest leaves and stems, and viral diseases may affect leaves.

TWINSPUR — see *Diascia*

Tropaeolum majus 'Whirlybird Hybrids'

Tropaeolum peregrinum

Tropaeolum majus 'Empress of India'

Ursinia
ursinia

Ursinia anethoides

- ❑ Height 1-1½ ft (30-45 cm)
- ❑ Planting distance 10-12 in (25-30 cm)
- ❑ Flowers early summer to early fall
- ❑ Light, even poor soil
- ❑ Open, sunny site
- ❑ Half-hardy annual

This South African daisylike annual is a particularly bright and graceful plant. The pale green finely dissected foliage forms a misty green mass, above which brilliant orange-yellow, purple-centered flowers are borne. The floral display extends from early summer to early fall. When each flower fades, the protective sepals around it become white.

Ursinias look best grown in mixed borders, bedding displays, or containers. They thrive in coastal gardens. The cultivar 'Solar Fire' (1 ft/30 cm high) has bright orange flowers.

Cultivation
Sow the seeds indoors in early spring 6-8 weeks before the last frost, barely covering them with soil; germinate them at a temperature of 59°F (15°C). Prick out the seedlings into flats. Harden off before planting out after the danger of frost is past, setting them 10-12 in (25-30 cm) apart.

For the best results, grow in light, even poor soil in an open, sunny site.

Pests/diseases Trouble free.

VELVET FLOWER —
see *Salpiglossis*

Venidium
Cape daisy

Venidium fastuosum

- ❑ Height 2-3 ft (60-90 cm)
- ❑ Planting distance 1 ft (30 cm)
- ❑ Flowers early summer to midfall
- ❑ Well-drained soil
- ❑ Sunny site
- ❑ Half-hardy annual

Cape daisy (*Venidium fastuosum*), a half-hardy annual from South Africa, deserves more attention from gardeners. Its large sunflowerlike blooms are particularly striking — rich orange with black central disks — and are attractively set off by the silver-white, deeply lobed woolly leaves. The cultivar 'Zulu Prince' has creamy white flowers with black central disks.

Appearing between early summer and midfall, Cape daisies look best planted in bold clusters in beds. They are long-lasting as cut flowers.

Cultivation
In early spring to midspring, sow the seeds indoors at a temperature of 61°F (16°C), just covering them with soil. Prick out the seedlings into pots, potting on as necessary. Harden off before planting outdoors in late spring, 1 ft (30 cm) apart.

For late-flowering plants, sow the seeds directly in the flowering site in late spring. Thin the seedlings once they are established.

Cape daisies will grow reasonably well in most soils, but they require a well-drained, sunny site. Take care not to overwater; usually the plants need staking.

Pests/diseases Trouble free.

Verbascum
mullein

Verbascum bombyciferum

Verbascum phlomoides

- ❑ Height 3-6 ft (90-180 cm)
- ❑ Planting distance 1-2 ft (30-60 cm)
- ❑ Flowers late spring to early fall
- ❑ Ordinary well-drained soil
- ❑ Sunny site
- ❑ Hardy biennial or annual

Mulleins are stately plants, excellent for growing at the back of a border, in groups in island beds, or in a wild garden. The spikes of yellow flowers are carried 3-6 ft (90-180 cm) high above rosettes of white-felted leaves and appear between late spring and early fall.

Popular species and cultivars
Verbascum bombyciferum has silvery branching stems covered with sulfur-yellow flowers from early summer to midsummer. It reaches 4-6 ft (120-180 cm) high,

so space the plants 1½-2 ft (45-60 cm) apart. 'Silver Lining' has pale yellow flowers.
Verbascum phlomoides has spikes of clustered creamy white flowers between late spring and early fall and oblong gray woolly leaves. This 6-ft (180-cm) high species is most suitable for wild gardens, where it self-seeds easily if left alone. Plant 1½ ft (45 cm) apart.
Verbascum phoeniceum bears spikes of flowers in shades of white, pink, and purple from late spring to early fall. Its dark green leaves are arranged in a rosette around the base of the plant. Reaching 3½-4½ ft (105-135 cm) high, this species is usually grown as an annual and planted 15-18 in (38-45 cm) apart. 'Benary's Hybrids' grow only 3 ft (90 cm) high

and bear pale pink, salmon, and purple flowers.
Verbascum thapsus has spikes of yellow flowers from early to late summer and toothed leaves covered with white woolly hairs. It reaches 3 ft (90 cm) high and should be planted 1 ft (30 cm) apart, ideally in a wild garden.

Cultivation
Sow the seeds of biennial species in midspring in pots of seed-starting mix, and set in a cool but protected spot such as a cold frame or unheated glass-enclosed porch. Prick out the seedlings and plant them 6 in (15 cm) apart in nursery rows outdoors, finally moving the plants to their flowering site in early fall.
Verbascum phoeniceum can be grown as an annual. Sow the seeds indoors in late winter to early spring at a temperature of 55°F (13°C). Prick out the seedlings into flats, and harden off before planting out in midspring 15-18 in (38-45 cm) apart.
Grow mulleins in ordinary well-drained soil in full sun. Stake in exposed sites.
Pests/diseases Trouble free.

Verbena
verbena

Verbena × *hybrida* 'Dwarf Jewels'

- ❏ Height ½-1 ft (15-30 cm)
- ❏ Planting distance 10-15 in (25-38 cm)
- ❏ Flowers early summer to first fall frost
- ❏ Fertile, well-drained soil
- ❏ Open, sunny site
- ❏ Tender annual

The many cultivars of *Verbena* × *hybrida* are beautiful plants that, throughout the summer, produce tight clusters of small pale-eyed primroselike flowers in scarlet, crimson, purple, lavender-pink, and white. Providing a foil for these cheerful colors are attractively toothed dark green leaves.

The bushy plants are popular for summer beds and borders, and the dwarf cultivars are ideal for containers, edging, and window boxes.

Popular species and cultivars
The following are readily available as seed strains.

'Amethyst' has cobalt-blue flowers with white eyes and reaches 9-12 in (23-30 cm) high.

'Blaze,' a compact cultivar reaching 9 in (23 cm) high, has scarlet flowers.

'Blue Lagoon' has true blue flowers without eyes; it grows 9 in (23 cm) high.

'Delight' has coral-pink flowers flushed with salmon. It is a small cultivar, just 6 in (15 cm) high.

'Dwarf Jewels' is a mixture of dwarf cultivars, 10-12 in (25-30 cm) high, bearing red, purple, lavender-pink, and white flowers.

'Imagination' bears deep violet-blue flowers and grows up to 1 ft (30 cm) tall.

'Peaches and Cream' is only 8 in (20 cm) high but smothered with blooms in pastel shades of coral, salmon, and cream.

'Showtime Hybrids' come in a range of brilliant colors, some with bold central eyes. They grow to 10 in (25 cm) high.

'Sissinghurst' is 10-12 in (25-30 cm) high with rose-pink flowers.

Cultivation
Sow the seeds indoors in late winter, 12 weeks before the last frost, just covering them with the seed-starting mix, and keep at 64-70°F (18-21°C). Prick out the seedlings into flats, and harden off before planting out during late spring when all danger of frost is past.

Grow verbenas in any light, fertile soil in a sunny, open location. Pinching the tips of young plants will encourage bushy growth. Deadhead to prolong the flowering season.

Pests/diseases Trouble free.

Verbena × *hybrida* 'Sissinghurst'

Viola
pansy

Viola cornuta 'Arkwright Ruby'

- ❏ Height 6-9 in (15-23 cm)
- ❏ Planting distance 10 in (25 cm)
- ❏ Flowers throughout the year
- ❏ Fertile, moist soil
- ❏ Sunny or partially shaded site
- ❏ Hardy biennial, may be treated as an annual

Pansies *(Viola × wittrockiana)* can be grown in the garden for most of the growing season — and in the South and on the Pacific Coast, nearly year-round. Summer-flowering cultivars bloom from late spring to early fall; in mild regions winter-flowering ones begin in fall and carry on until spring.

Pansies make good ground-cover plants or informal edgings. They bring color to a mixed bed and are good for containers and window boxes. The small-flowered cultivars are best in rock gardens.

Popular species and cultivars

Viola cornuta ("horned violet" or "tufted pansy"), a perennial that blooms the first year after seed is sown, may be grown as an annual. There are two popular cultivars. **'Arkwright Ruby'** produces blossoms of a rich red-brown hue.

'Bambini Hybrids' has small pink, apricot, yellow, blue, copper, bronze, and red flowers, all with whiskered faces.

Viola tricolor (heartsease, or wild pansy) has very small bicolored flowers in cream, yellow, purple-red, or blue-black.

Viola × wittrockiana offers numerous cultivars and seed selections, in mixed or single colors. Unless stated otherwise, they flower in spring and summer.

'Azure Blue' has flowers in shades of cool blue.

'Clear Crystal Hybrids' are a mixture of gold, red, orange, violet, and white flowers without any patterns on them.

'Majestic Giants Hybrids' have large red, yellow, and blue flowers with dark central blotches.

'Padparadja' bears flowers of a luminous orange red.

'Paper White' has white flowers with yellow eyes.

'Queen of the Planets' has very large flowers in rich, bright yellow, violet, red, and maroon.

'Rippling Waters' has deep pur-

Viola × *wittrockiana* 'Rippling Waters'

ple-blue flowers with broad cream-white edging.

'Roggli Giant Elite Hybrids' bloom in mixed colors: blues, reds, violets, and yellows.

'Super Chalon Giants Hybrids' are deep blue, mahogany-red, and yellow with dark blotches. Their petals are waved and frilled.

'Ullswater' has gentian-blue flowers with darker blotches.

'Universal Hybrids' bloom in winter and summer in many clear single and blotched colors.

Viola × *wittrockiana* 'Majestic Giant'

Viola tricolor

Cultivation

Pansies may be grown as annuals if seed is sown indoors 10-12 weeks before the last frost and germinated at 64-70°F (18-21°C), then moved to a cool windowsill with a temperature of about 50°F (10°C).

For the best-quality blooms, however, grow pansies as biennials. Sow seeds in an outdoor nursery bed in mid- to late summer, and thin to 4 in (12 cm) apart. Transplant to the flowering site in fall. The soil should be fertile and moist but well drained, and the site should be in sun or partial shade. Deadhead regularly.

Pests/diseases Pansies are susceptible to anthracnose, gray mold, and downy mildew.

VIPER'S BUGLOSS —
see *Echium*
VIRGINIA STOCK —
see *Malcolmia*
WALLFLOWER —
see *Cheiranthus*
WISHBONE FLOWER —
see *Torenia*
WOODRUFF — see *Asperula*

Viola × *wittrockiana* 'Padparadja'

Viola × *wittrockiana* 'Paper White'

Viola tricolor

Viola 'Bambini Hybrids'

Xeranthemum
common immortelle

Xeranthemum annuum

- ❏ Height 2-3 ft (60-90 cm)
- ❏ Planting distance 1½ ft (45 cm)
- ❏ Flowers midsummer to early fall
- ❏ Any well-drained garden soil
- ❏ Sunny site
- ❏ Hardy annual

Common immortelle *(Xeranthemum annuum)* is an attractive daisylike annual, grown for its seemingly everlasting flowers — the petals keep their color for a long time after drying, making the flowers excellent for winter decoration. Coming in a range of pinks, lilacs, purples, and white, the dainty single or double flowers appear between midsummer and early fall, 2 ft (60 cm) above the ground on wiry stems. They are accompanied by small, narrow silver leaves.

'Immortal' bears white, purple, lilac, and rose flowers.

Cultivation
In mild-winter regions sow seeds directly into the garden as soon as the danger of frost is past. Where the growing season is short, start seeds indoors in peat pots 8-10 weeks before the last frost. Immortelles flourish in any well-drained soil, but even poor soil is acceptable. The site must be sunny. Thin to 1½ ft (45 cm) apart.

For indoor decoration, cut the flowers before they are fully open. Tie them in bunches and hang upside down in a cool, dry place.
Pests/diseases Trouble free.

Zea
ornamental corn

Zea mays 'Gracillima Variegata'

- ❏ Height 3-5 ft (90-150 cm)
- ❏ Planting distance 1½ ft (45 cm)
- ❏ Cobs early summer to midsummer
- ❏ Rich soil
- ❏ Open, sunny site
- ❏ Half-hardy annual

Several cultivars of corn *(Zea mays)* have variegated foliage or colored cobs, which make them suitable for garden decoration. Grow them as accent plants in summer bedding displays, or use them to fill gaps in mixed and herbaceous borders.

They are tall plants, reaching up to 5 ft (150 cm) high, so they will have considerable impact wherever you plant them, ideally in an open sunny site that is protected from strong winds.

The cobs appear between early summer and midsummer, but before and after the leaves make an attractive display.

Popular species and cultivars
The following cultivars are grown for garden decoration.
'**Gigantea Quadricolor**' is a robust 5 ft (150 cm) high cultivar with leaves variegated with white, pale yellow, and pink.
'**Gracillima Variegata**' is a dwarf cultivar, 3 ft (90 cm) high, with slender white-striped leaves.

'**Rainbow,**' 5 ft (150 cm) high, has green leaves and colored cobs composed of yellow, red, orange, and purple-blue seeds. When cobs are ripe, dry them for use as winter decoration.
'**Strawberry,**' a green-leaved cultivar reaching 5 ft (150 cm) high, has strawberry-shaped maroon cobs.

Cultivation
Sow the seeds indoors 6 weeks before the last frost, setting them singly ½ in (1 cm) deep in 3-in (7.5-cm) pots of seed-starting mix. Keep at a temperature of 61-64°F (16-18°C). Harden off and plant out as soon as the danger of frost is past. Set seedlings 1½ ft (45 cm) apart in groups of several plants to ensure full pollination later and a better crop of cobs.

Alternatively, sow seeds in the open in late spring. Sow them in groups of three, ½ in (1 cm) deep and 1½ ft (45 cm) apart, later removing two plants from each group to leave the strongest.

An open, sunny site, protected from strong winds, is essential for ornamental corn. Ideally, the soil should have been enriched with well-decayed compost.
Pests/diseases Birds may damage the cobs.

Zinnia
youth-and-old-age, zinnia

Zinnia elegans 'Border Beauty'

- ❑ Height ½-3 ft (15-90 cm)
- ❑ Planting distance ½-1 ft (15-30 cm)
- ❑ Flowers midsummer to early fall
- ❑ Fertile, well-drained soil
- ❑ Sunny site
- ❑ Half-hardy annual

The species name, *elegans*, is not as appropriate for this Mexican annual as it once was, as breeders are producing ever-larger flowers on ever-smaller plants. There are, however, many colors: white, cream, yellow, orange, scarlet, crimson, purple, and even green. The blooms of most cultivars are fully double and resemble solid, drier-petaled ball dahlias. They appear from midsummer to early fall and last well as cut flowers.

Popular species and cultivars
Cultivars developed from *Zinnia elegans* offer dwarf or tall plants.
Dwarf cultivars, usually 1-1½ ft (30-45 cm) high, are good as edging plants or for beds and pots.
'Fairyland' is compact and bears a profusion of small red, orange, yellow, pink, purple, cream, and gold flowers.
'Persian Carpet' has miniature double flowers in yellow, orange, mahogany-red, maroon, chocolate, and cream.
'Thumbelina Hybrids,' 6 in (15 cm) high, bear double and semi-double flowers in mixed colors.
'Border Beauty Hybrids' are

of intermediate height, 22 in (55 cm), producing bushy plants and 3½-in (9-cm) wide dahlia-type flowers in yellow, red, and pink.
Tall cultivars, 2-3 ft (60-90 cm) high, are suitable for bedding or cutting.
'Envy,' with chartreuse blooms, is favored by flower arrangers.
'Peppermint Stick Hybrids' are a dahlia-flowered strain with flowers that are striped or streaked with contrasting colors.
'State Fair Hybrids' are vigorous plants with salmon, orange, lavender, purple, rose, scarlet, and yellow flowers.
'Zenith Hybrids' bloom in white through pink to scarlet. The 6-in (15-cm) wide blooms top 2½-ft

(75-cm) tall plants, which are heat and drought tolerant.

Cultivation
Where summers are short, sow seeds indoors 6 weeks before the last frost. Sow into 3-in (7.5-cm) peat pots (zinnias resent transplanting) and germinate at 70°F (21°C). Harden off and plant out when danger of spring frost has passed. Set tall-flowered cultivars 1 ft (30 cm) apart and dwarf ones 6 in (15 cm) apart. Grow in fertile, well-drained soil in full sun.

If the growing season is long and warm, sow seeds directly in the flowering site in late spring.
Pests/diseases Viruses may cause mottling of the leaves.

Zinnia elegans 'State Fair Hybrids'

111

Cheerful bulbs Dainty snowdrops and brilliant early crocuses announce the end of winter.

A–Z of bulbs and corms

Bulbs, corms, tubers, and rhizomes are perennial plants in which the lower part of the stem has evolved into an underground food store. Compared with other perennials, bulbs are inexpensive to buy, easy to grow, and apart from such notable exceptions as dahlias, demand little attention after planting.

There are bulbs for every garden, whatever its size and soil type, and for every situation. Bulbs can be grown in formal beds or naturalized in grass, set in pockets of rock gardens or used to fill gaps in a herbaceous border. They can be grown in raised beds, pots, tubs, and window boxes. If desired, they can often be used as cut flowers.

Bulbs bloom throughout the year — snowdrops, aconites, and tiny irises appear in late winter, followed in early spring by cheerful crocuses, golden daffodils, and narcissi, muscaris, hyacinths, and tulips in almost every color. Late spring brings fritillaries, bluebells, lilies of the valley, irises, and alliums, and with summer come the glorious lilies, crocosmias, and gladioli. In fall it is the turn of dahlias, autumn crocuses, sternbergias, and exotic nerines.

Many bulbs die down and disappear underground after flowering; others become a mess of untidy leaves. Don't be tempted to remove the foliage until it has withered — it needs exposure to sun and air to replenish the bulbs for the following year. Half-hardy types, such as gladioli, dahlias, and begonias, must be lifted before the first frost, dried, and kept in frost-free storage for next year's colorful display.

SEASONAL BULBS

Coming in all colors, sizes, and shapes, the flowers of bulbs furnish year-round impact in the garden.

Bulbous plants deserve their popularity. Their flowers offer some of the most beautiful and striking colors found in the garden, and they come in a wide variety of shapes. They also come in a range of heights — from miniatures such as crocuses, for the rock garden, to giant 10 ft (30 m) lilies best suited to the back of a border. In addition, there is a choice of bulbs, corms, or tubers to flower throughout the entire growing season.

Such diversity provides plenty of scope for combining different bulbs or pairing them with trees, shrubs, and other plants.

Spring is the time for crocuses, anemones, narcissi, and scillas, which are often planted in informal groupings. Tulips and hyacinths can be bedded out in more formal displays or grown in containers and window boxes.

In summer use bulbous plants in mixed borders. The tall summer hyacinth (*Galtonia candicans*) bears dangling bell-like flowers on 4 ft (120 cm) stems in mid- and late summer; it looks pretty against a background of the crimson flowers and gray-green leaves of *Fuchsia magellanica.* Complete the grouping by setting the silver-gray foliage and magenta blooms of rose campion (*Lychnis coronaria*) in front.

In fall the elegant pink blooms of *Nerine bowdenii* look even lovelier when fronted by the pale blue of *Lobelia erinus* 'Cambridge Blue.' This partnership can be extended with clumps of lilyturf *(Liriope muscari),* which has grassy leaves and spikes of violet blooms reminiscent of grape hyacinths. In addition, the white goblets of *Colchicum autumnale* 'Album' make a fine contrast for the fall-tinted leaves of deciduous shrubs.

Enliven the dull days of late winter by setting snowdrops *(Galanthus nivalis),* cyclamen *(Cyclamen coum),* and winter aconite *(Eranthis hyemalis)* amidst the trees. Their white, pink, and yellow flowers give a foretaste of spring beneath the bare branches and yellow flowers of wintersweet (*Chimonanthus praecox);* for a touch of blue, add *Iris histrioides* 'Major.' The green flowers and fingered evergreen foliage of *Helleborus foetidus* lend height and leafy interest.

▲ **Winter cheer** Undeterred by the weather, glistening white snowdrops and golden aconites *(Eranthis)* are the first to announce the coming of longer and warmer days. The silver-blue flowers of *Scilla mischtschenkoana* soon follow.

▶ **Early-summer bulbs** The ornamental onion (*Allium christophii*) mingles its heads of metallic pink flowers with the velvety color of flag irises. They brighten up borders before perennials come into their own.

▲ Golden trumpets True harbingers of spring, trumpet daffodils *(Narcissus)* are ideal for naturalizing beneath deciduous trees in a meadow, where they can be left to colonize over the years. 'Golden Harvest' is one of the first to flower, bringing life to the gaunt silhouettes of bare-stemmed shrubs and trees, such as this honey locust *(Gleditsia triacanthos)*.

▶ Trouble-free bulbs One of the joys of growing bulbs is the ease with which many appear year after year, making few demands but producing a steadily increasing display of flowers. Here, cyclamineus narcissi, with their long golden trumpets and backswept petals, jostle against hyacinthlike sprays of the pure white form of striped squill *(Puschkinia scilloides)*.

◀ Exotic lilies The magnificent blooms of lilies bring a touch of class and sophistication to gardens. The Asiatic hybrids come in a range of colors and are particularly easy to grow in mixed borders, where they reach a manageable height of about 3 ft (90 cm). The sturdy stems grow unsupported and bear a succession of upward-facing blooms in early summer and midsummer.

◄ **Cyclamen colonies** In the light shade cast by a cascading bridal wreath *(Spiraea × arguta),* a miniature *Cyclamen hederifolium* has spread a carpet of its delicate pink flowers. Only 4 in (10 cm) high, they will stay in bloom for weeks before being replaced by equally handsome white-marbled leaves. Woodland plants by nature, the hardy cyclamens colonize most successfully in shaded soil away from hot sun and searing winds.

◄ **Bedding hyacinths** The deliciously scented hyacinths in shades of blue, pink, white, and yellow are popular winter-flowering indoor bulbs, but they are hardy outdoors to zone 5. Perfect for spring beds, containers, and window boxes, the elegant flower spikes blend happily with other spring flowers, such as short-growing tulips, polyanthus primroses, primulas, and winter pansies.

▲ **Formal bedding** Tulips are traditional in late-spring bedding displays, often lifting their goblets above classic combinations of forget-me-nots and wallflowers. Here, a bed of mixed tulips, including the stunning near-black 'Queen of the Night,' is underplanted with pansies.

▼ **Late-winter scene** Miniature bulbs hold the stage against a backdrop of winter-flowering jasmine *(Jasminum nudiflorum)*. Its yellow starry flowers reflect the blue of tiny *Iris histrioides,* deep pink *Cyclamen coum,* white snowdrops *(Galanthus nivalis),* and the golden goblets of *Crocus flavus.*

▲ **Stately crown imperials** Resentful of disturbance, the spring-flowering crown imperial *(Fritillaria imperialis)* adorns its tall stems with crowns of nodding bells, yellow in the cultivar 'Lutea.' These blooms are accompanied by clumps of trout lily *(Erythronium revolutum* 'White Beauty') with creamy reflexed flowers, which are held above brown-mottled leaves.

Allium
ornamental onion

Allium giganteum

- ❏ Height 1-5 ft (30-150 cm)
- ❏ Planting distance 3-12 in (7.5-30 cm)
- ❏ Flowers summer
- ❏ Any well-drained soil
- ❏ Sunny, open site
- ❏ Bulbs available fall
- ❏ Hardy zones 4 or 5-10

Allium moly

Ornamental onions are becoming increasingly popular because of their easygoing nature, tough constitution, and long-lasting flowers. The flowers appear in summer and, depending on the cultivar, range in color from white, yellow, and blue to deep lilac and rose. Some alliums are ideal for mixed or herbaceous borders, others for rock gardens, window boxes, and even indoor displays. Their onionlike smell is apparent only when the leaves and stems are bruised.

Popular species and cultivars
Allium christophii (syn. *A. albo-pilosum*) is best grown among herbaceous plants that hide its untidy gray-blue leaves without giving too much shade. Plant the bulbs 4-5 in (10-13 cm) apart. In early summer the large heads of striking star-shaped lilac-pink flowers appear on stems that are 2 ft (60 cm) tall. The seed heads that follow in fall and winter are good for cut flower arrangements.
Allium caeruleum (syn. *A. azureum)* has densely packed balls of starlike flax-blue flowers among long, thin midgreen leaves in early summer and midsummer. Set the bulbs 6 in (15 cm) apart. The flowers are carried on 2-3 ft (60-90 cm) high stems and thus are suitable for cutting.

Allium giganteum stands well above most other herbaceous plants, often reaching an impressive height of 5 ft (150 cm). It is grown for its large decorative flower heads: balls of purple star-shaped florets, which appear in early summer. Like many of the ornamental onions, it has long, thin gray-blue leaves. Plant 9-12 in (23-30 cm) apart.
Allium moly forms a vivid display in early summer and midsummer with its bright yellow star-shaped leaves. It reaches only 1 ft (30 cm) high but is particularly invasive, so avoid planting it among small, delicate plants. Space the bulbs 4 in (10 cm) apart.
Allium ostrowskianum (syn. *A. oreophilum),* a popular member of the family, reaches only 1 ft (30 cm) high. When planted 3 in (7.5 cm) apart, it can spread rapidly. The small rose-colored flowers and drooping gray-blue leaves are excellent for livening up a rock garden in early summer.
Allium roseum has elegant rose-pink star-shaped flowers, which come out in early summer. It reaches 2 ft (60 cm) high and has long, broad midgreen leaves. Plant the bulbs 4 in (10 cm) apart in a sunny, sheltered site.

Cultivation
Alliums generally grow best in ordinary well-drained soil in open, sunny sites. Plant the bulbs in early fall to midfall or spring, setting them in groups of six or more so the flowers have impact. Cover

each bulb with soil to twice its depth — if the dormant bulb is 1½ in (4 cm) high, plant it at a depth of 3 in (7.5 cm).

Every spring apply a dressing of general fertilizer or bonemeal. When the flowers have faded, cut off the heads (some make good dried arrangements). In fall remove the dead leaves and stems. Tall alliums growing in a windy site may need staking.
Propagation Detach bulblets from the base of mature bulbs in fall or spring, and replant immediately in moist soil. Or increase from mature home-saved seed.
Pests/diseases Young shoots, leaves, and stems are often eaten by slugs. Bulb rot can stop the flower stem from developing and cause the leaves to turn yellow and die back; the roots will also rot, and the bulbs become covered with a fluffy white fungus.

Allium ostrowskianum

Alstroemeria
Peruvian lily

Alstroeomeria aurea

Amaryllis
amaryllis

Amaryllis belladonna

❏ Height 2-3 ft (60-90 cm)
❏ Planting distance 1 ft (30 cm)
❏ Flowers early to late summer
❏ Well-drained fertile soil
❏ Sheltered, sunny site
❏ Tubers available late winter
   and early spring
❏ Hardy zones 7-10

The beautiful Peruvian lilies provide glorious color both outdoors in the herbaceous border and indoors as long-lasting cut flowers. Their lilylike flowers, ranging in color from light pink to yellow, flame, or orange, appear in summer and are carried on slender stems adorned with silvery twisted leaves. Being delicate plants, they have the greatest impact when grown in clumps.

Popular species and cultivars
Alstroemeria aurea, one of the most flamboyant of the garden Peruvian lilies, is also among the hardiest, commonly overwintering successfully in zone 7 if well mulched. Its fiery orange, trumpet-shaped flowers, splashed with maroon on the upper petals, create a magnificent blaze of color in summer. A popular cultivar is 'Lutea,' which has bright yellow flowers with carmine markings. All types stand 3 ft (90 cm) high. *Alstroemeria ligtu* 'Hybrids' are near-hardy and come in a range of pastel colors: white, cream, pink, rose, flame orange, and yellow. They stand 2-3 ft (60-90 cm) high and flower in summer.

Cultivation
Plant the tubers in early spring in a fertile, well-drained soil; Peruvian lilies dislike root disturbance so give them a sheltered site where they can be left untouched for several years. Arrange the tubers in groups, setting each at a depth of 6 in (15 cm) and about 1 ft (30 cm) apart. Peruvian lilies usually take 2 years to become established, so don't expect top growth the first year. The plants may need sticks for support.

Apply liquid fertilizer during and after flowering. Deadhead the flowers regularly, and cut the stems back to the ground in fall when the leaves have died down. Protect from winter frosts with a deep organic mulch of straw or composted bark.

Propagation Every 3-4 years divide established plants into 4-6 in (10-15 cm) clusters in early spring or midspring. Replant the divisions immediately.

Pests/diseases Slugs may eat the young shoots, leaves, and stems, stopping any early growth. The plants can also be stunted by a viral disease, which appears as yellow mottling on the leaves.

Alstroemeria ligtu 'Hybrids'

❏ Height 2-2½ ft (60-75 cm)
❏ Planting distance 1 ft (30 cm)
❏ Flowers early fall to midfall
❏ Well-drained fertile soil
❏ Sheltered, sunny site
❏ Bulbs available spring to summer
❏ Hardy zones 6-10

Only one species of true amaryllis, *Amaryllis belladonna*, grows outdoors in most of North America. It saves its magnificent display of fragrant satiny pink flowers until early fall, after summer has withered the foliage. Because the long purple stems are leafless at flowering time, surround them with other plant foliage, but don't create too much shade. Cultivars with pure white or purplish blossoms (typically with yellow throats) exist, but they are hard to find.

Cultivation
In the northern part of its range, an ideal site for *A. belladonna* is the foot of a south-facing wall, where it can get maximum benefit from summer sunshine and protection for the young leaves when they appear in late winter and early spring. (In warm climates the foliage appears earlier, in late fall.) Plant from spring to midsummer; in warm climates, plant in fall. Set the bulbs 6-8 in (15-20 cm) deep in good, well-drained soil. Remove faded flowers as well as stems and leaves when they die down.

Propagation Lift mature plants when the leaves turn yellow in summer, detach the offsets, and replant immediately.

Pests/diseases Narcissus fly larvae may tunnel in the bulbs.

Anemone
anemone

Anemone blanda

❏ Height ½-1 ft (15-30 cm)
❏ Planting distance 4-6 in (10-15 cm)
❏ Flowers late winter to midspring
❏ Good, well-drained soil
❏ Sunny or partially shaded site
❏ Tubers available fall and winter
❏ Hardy zone 5-9

Spring-flowering anemones have tuberous roots or corms. They are ideal for naturalizing in a semi-wild shady corner of the garden, for bringing spring color to a rock garden, and for cutting.

Popular species and cultivars
Anemone blanda stands only 6 in (15 cm) high and is enchanting in a seminatural setting. Left undisturbed, it will form a carpet of white, pink, or blue flowers from late winter to early spring. It tolerates dappled shade, so a good site for it is under a deciduous tree. Here the flowers provide ground interest before the tree leaves are fully out. For blue flowers select such cultivars as 'Atrocaerulea' or 'Blue Star.' For white flowers try 'White Splendor,' and for pink flowers 'Pink Star.' Mixtures are also sold.

Anemone coronaria, often called the poppy anemone, is the red, blue, cream, or purple species seen in florists. Two strains are widely available: 'De Caen,' which has up to 20 single saucer-shaped flowers in a season, and 'St. Brigid,' a double or semidouble strain. Mixtures and cultivars of single colors are available. All grow about 1 ft (30 cm) high and are suitable for the front of a bed.

Anemone × fulgens has striking scarlet flowers and stands 1 ft (30 cm) high; it is an eye-catching sight throughout spring.

Anemone coronaria 'De Caen'

Anemone nemorosa (wood anemone) is a woodland wildflower that looks best in a seminatural setting, where its clusters of feathery leaves, 6 in (15 cm) high, make a superb ground cover in early spring and midspring. The flowers are naturally white, tinged pink, but lavender cultivars such as 'Robinsoniana' and blue forms such as 'Royal Blue' are sometimes available.

Cultivation
Plant the corms or tubers 2 in (5 cm) deep and 4-6 in (10-15 cm) apart in any rich, well-drained soil from early fall to midfall. *A. coronaria* and *A. × fulgens* do best in sunny sites, while *A. blanda* and *A. nemorosa* prefer partial shade. In mild climates, protect with mulch in winter. In the North, dig up the tubers, allow them to dry for a couple of days, then store in a cool but frost-free location and replant in spring.

A. coronaria and *A. × fulgens* deteriorate quickly and should be replaced after a couple of years.

Anemone nemorosa

Propagation When the top growth dies down in late summer, lift the tuberous roots or corms; separate and replant the offsets.

Pests/diseases Aphids may attack the leaves of anemones, and watch out for the twisting tracks of leaf miners. Few pests and diseases attack species anemones, but 'De Caen' and 'St. Brigid' can be susceptible to a rust disease.

ANGELS' FISHING RODS — see *Dierama*

Anthericum liliago

Anthericum
St. Bernard's lily

Anthericum liliago

❏ Height 1½-2 ft (45-60 cm)
❏ Planting distance 1 ft (30 cm)
❏ Flowers late spring to early summer
❏ Well-drained, moisture-retentive soil
❏ Partial shade or sun
❏ Tuberous roots available fall
❏ Hardy zones 6-7

The starry white flowers of *Anthericum liliago*, one of two hardy species in this genus, appear in late spring and early summer. With its grasslike leaves and delicate flowers, *A. liliago* is best grown in herbaceous borders in groups of five or more plants.

Cultivation
Choose a lightly shaded or sunny spot with soil that is humus-rich and well-drained but unlikely to dry out in summer. Plant the tuberous roots 4 in (10 cm) deep in fall. In early spring mulch with garden compost or well-composted manure. Cut the stems back to ground level after flowering. St. Bernard's lily does not like hot, dry summers.
Propagation Divide overcrowded plants between midfall and early spring, or raise new plants from seed. Sow the seed in spring in a cold frame.
Pests/diseases Generally trouble free.

AUNT ELIZA — see *Curtonus*

Begonia
begonia

Begonia × *tuberhybrida* (Fimbriata)

❏ Height ½-2 ft (15-60 cm)
❏ Planting distance 15 in (38 cm)
❏ Flowers early summer to early fall
❏ Rich, moist, well-drained soil
❏ Sun or partial shade
❏ Tubers available late winter or spring
❏ Hardy to zone 10

The tuberous begonia *(Begonia* × *tuberhybrida)*, with its vibrant scarlet, orange, yellow, white, or pink blooms borne throughout summer, is often regarded as the queen of bedding plants. It is ideal for adding summer color to pots, window boxes, hanging baskets, and borders, in sun or partial shade. While too tender to tolerate even a light frost, it grows well outdoors in summer, provided it is planted in a rich, moist, but well-drained soil. The cultivars developed from this hybrid are divided into four groups.

Popular species and cultivars
Fimbriata cultivars are vigorous, weather-resistant plants in spite of their fragile appearance. They bear fully double flowers with frilled petals and come in white and shades of pink, orange, and yellow.
Camellia-flowered (large double) cultivars have blooms 3-6 in (7.5-15 cm) wide. The plants reach up to 1-2 ft (30-60 cm) high and grow well in containers. A very

Begonia × *tuberhybrida* (Pendula)

great number of cultivars are sold, offering almost every shade of orange, yellow, red, and pink.
Multiflora nonstop cultivars have clusters of small bright flowers carried well above the foliage. The plants grow 6 in (15 cm) high and have a compact, bushy habit that makes them excellent for bedding and containers. The cultivars come in a wide range of colors — some with unusual foliage colors as well.
Pendula types have a slender, trailing habit, making them particularly well-suited to hanging baskets and window boxes. From early summer to early fall they bear a myriad of semidouble white, yellow, orange, scarlet, salmon, or rose flowers, depending on the cultivar.

Brodiaea
brodiaea, triplet lilies

Brodiaea laxa

- ❏ Height 1½-2 ft (45-60 cm)
- ❏ Planting distance 2-3 in (5-7.5 cm)
- ❏ Flowers late spring to early summer
- ❏ Well-drained soil
- ❏ Sheltered, sunny site
- ❏ Corms available fall
- ❏ Hardy to zone 7 with winter protection

As they have only a few long, narrow green leaves, brodiaeas should be grown in groups. The flowers have a star or trumpet shape, depending on the species. Borne on stems 1½-2 ft (45-60 cm) high, they make good cut flowers.

Popular species and cultivars
Brodiaea coronaria (syn. *B. grandiflora*) reaches 1½ ft (45 cm) high and has starry blue-purple flowers in late spring to early summer. *Brodiaea laxa* (syn. *Triteleia laxa*) has loose clusters of dark blue trumpet-shaped flowers that resemble a tiny *Agapanthus*. The flowers appear in late spring to early summer on 2 ft (60 cm) stems. The cultivar 'Queen Fabiola' is somewhat taller than the species, has sturdier stems, and flowers in June or July.

Cultivation
Plant the corms in early fall in small or large groups, and space them 2-3 in (5-7.5 cm) apart. For the best results choose a sheltered, sunny site and well-drained soil. Where winter temperatures drop to 20°F (-7°C) protect plants with a winter mulch of leaves.
Propagation Remove and replant offsets every 4 years.
Pests/diseases Trouble free.

BUTTERCUP —
see *Ranunculus*

Begonia × tuberhybrida (Camellia-flowered)

Cultivation
Start the tubers in late winter or early spring — hollow side facing up — in 3 in (7.5 cm) deep flats filled with equal parts moist peat and sand. Keep at a temperature of 64°F (18°C). When leafy shoots appear, transfer plants to individual pots of a regular potting soil mixed with sand. When the plants recover from transplanting and resume growth, feed them with a complete liquid fertilizer on a weekly schedule. Plant out in early summer in flower beds or containers, once the risk of frost is over. Fill containers with well-drained peat or compost-rich potting soil. Set plants 15 in (38 cm) apart, and grow them in groups of at least three.

Begonias will grow happily in light shade or sun, provided the soil is enriched with humus. Water them regularly during dry weather — erratic watering will cause the flowers to fall off. Give begonias in containers a dilute liquid foliar fertilizer once a week until the last flowers have faded.

Lift the tubers before the first frosts. Dry the plants off well, remove the stems, and clean any soil off the tubers. Store them in boxes of dry potting soil in a cool but frost-free place over winter. Water lightly now and then to prevent the tubers from shriveling.
Propagation In midspring take 3-4 in (7.5-10 cm) basal cuttings, preferably with a heel of the parent tuber attached. Root the cuttings in a medium composed of peat moss and sand, then keep the medium at a temperature of 64-68°F (18-20°C). When the cuttings have rooted, pot up for planting out in early summer. Alternatively, cut tubers into pieces in midspring when the shoots are small. Make sure that each piece includes a healthy shoot.
Pests/diseases Black vine weevils as well as southern root-knot nematodes may attack tubers.

BLUEBELL — see *Scilla*

Camassia
quamash

Canna
canna, Indian shot

Camassia leichtlinii

Canna × generalis 'Tropical rose'

❑ Height 2-3 ft (60-90 cm)
❑ Planting distance 6 in (15 cm)
❑ Flowers early summer to midsummer
❑ Moist, humus-rich soil
❑ Lightly shaded or sunny site
❑ Bulbs available fall
❑ Hardy to zones 4-5

An ideal site for these spiky-looking plants is a spot where their roots can reach down to water, such as the bank of a pond. They will also grow in herbaceous borders and naturalize well in semi-wild grassy areas, if the soil does not dry out during the growing season. The starlike flowers — large spikes in blue and violet or white on 2-3 ft (60-90 cm) tall stems — arrive in early summer to midsummer. All species are hardy and need very little attention once they have been planted.

Popular species and cultivars
Camassia cusickii has wisteria-blue flowers on stems 2 ft (60 cm) high. Plant the bulbs 3 in (7.5 cm) deep and 6 in (15 cm) apart, and they will spread freely.
Camassia leichtlinii is striking, with creamy white or aster-blue flowers in midsummer. These plants are 3 ft (90 cm) high; set the bulbs 6 in (15 cm) apart.
Camassia quamash is 2½ ft (75 cm) high. Its violet-blue flowers are densely clustered together at the tops of the stems.

Cultivation
Plant the bulbs 3-4 in (7.5-10 cm) deep in early fall or midfall in humus-rich, heavy, moist soil that is unlikely to dry out in the spring and early summer. (Covering the bulbs with plenty of leaf mold will help keep the soil damp.) Arrange the bulbs 6 in (15 cm) apart in large groups in light shade or full sun for the best effect. Deadhead after flowering in early summer and midsummer.
Propagation When the clumps become too dense, lift the bulbs in early fall, remove any offsets, and replant immediately. These offsets take between 1 and 3 years to produce flowers.
Pests/diseases Trouble free.

Camassia leichtlinii

❑ Height 2½-4 ft (75-120 cm)
❑ Planting distance 1½-2 ft (45-60 cm)
❑ Flowers late summer to early fall
❑ Moist, humus-rich soil
❑ Sunny, sheltered site
❑ Rhizomes available fall and winter
❑ Hardy zones 8-10; elsewhere grown as tender annual

The bold tropical leaves of cannas are up to 1½-2 ft (45-60 cm) long and 1 ft (30 cm) wide, and may be green, bronze, purplish, red, or variegated in color. The large blossoms resemble a cross between an orchid and a gladiolus. Cannas are tall and should be planted at the back of a bed.

The cultivars available have all been developed from *Canna × generalis,* or horticultural cannas. Green-leaved cultivars are 'Crimson Beauty' (deep red flowers), 'Cupid' (pearly lavender-pink), 'Gold Mine' (deep gold), 'Honeycomb' (combination of orange, pink, and yellow), 'Los Angeles' (coral pink), 'Orange Beauty' (soft orange), and 'President' (vivid scarlet). Bronze-leaved cultivars are 'Ambassador' (red flowers) and 'Mohawk' (orange). 'Cleopatra' bears yellow- and red-striped flowers and green leaves variegated with red; 'Intrigue' has orange flowers and purple leaves.

Cultivation
In the South, plant cannas direct-

Cardiocrinum
giolly

Cardiocrinum giganteum

Canna × generalis

ly into the garden as soon as the soil has warmed, setting rhizomes 3 in (7.5 cm) deep into soil that is rich in organic matter. In the North, plant rhizomes 1 in (2 cm) deep in pots of moist potting soil in early spring. Place them in a sunny window where the temperature won't drop below 61° F (16° C). If more than one shoot appears, divide the rhizome into sections, each with a shoot and some roots, and repot. Plant out from early summer on in rich soil in a sheltered, sunny spot. Alternatively, transfer young plants to tubs in midspring and move these outside after risk of frost has passed. Bring the plants inside again before fall frosts.

Partially dry plants lifted from beds, cut off the leaves and roots, and store them in moist potting soil or leaf mold in a frost-free place for winter. Don't let them become either too dry or too wet.
Propagation Divide cannas in early spring to midspring. In the South, dig up established clumps as they begin to show growth and cut into pieces. Each piece should include an "eye" (a bud) or shoot and some roots. Replant at once. In the North, divide recently potted rhizomes with more than one shoot and pot in moist potting soil. Plant out in early summer.
Pests/diseases Slugs and Japanese beetles may attack leaves; bud rot may cause black spotting on leaves and blackening and abortion of flower buds.

❏ Height 6-10 ft (180-300 cm)
❏ Planting distance 3-4 ft (90-120 cm)
❏ Flowers mid- to late summer
❏ Deep rich, moist soil
❏ Partial shade
❏ Bulbs available late fall
❏ Hardy to zone 7, to zone 5 with winter protection

There are few more majestic sights than the giant lily (*Cardiocrinum giganteum*) raising its robust 6-10 ft (180-300 cm) tall flower stems topped with clusters of long trumpet flowers in mid- and late summer. The fragrant blossoms are creamy white, streaked with purple or crimson inside their trumpets, and up to 6 in (15 cm) long. The dark green heart-shaped leaves are equally impressive — as much as 20 in (50 cm) long and arranged in a spiral along the flower stem.

Giant lily is monocarpic, which means that it dies after flowering. However it leaves behind two or more offset bulbs, which reach flowering size after about 3 years.

Cultivation
Giant lilies thrive at the edge of woodland or planted among low-growing shrubs, which offer protection against spring frost and excessive summer heat. They will also grow in any cool, lightly shad-

ed spot where the soil is deep and moist but well-drained and rich in organic matter. Set the bulbs shallowly, with their tops just level with the surrounding soil; space them 3 ft (90 cm) apart.
Propagation Lift the flowered bulbs in midfall, discard the old collapsed bulbs, and replant the offsets immediately. Leave them undisturbed until they reach flowering size.
Pests/diseases Trouble free.

Cardiocrinum giganteum (growth habit)

Chionodoxa
glory of the snow

Chionodoxa sardensis

Chionodoxa luciliae

Chionodoxa luciliae 'Pink Giant'

❏ Height 4-8 in (10-20 cm)
❏ Planting distance 2-4 in (5-10 cm)
❏ Flowers late winter to late spring
❏ Ordinary well-drained garden soil
❏ Sunny or lightly shaded site
❏ Bulbs available late summer
  and fall
❏ Hardy zones 3-10

Glory of the snow casts swaths of brilliant starlike flowers over the ground from late winter throughout spring. In northern gardens, the blue stars rise above the melting snow. These little plants are among the easiest bulbs to grow, and left to their own devices, they will spread and colonize readily. They are ideal for brightening a rock garden in early spring, planting at the front of a border, or naturalizing in short grass.

Chionodoxas grow equally well in full sun and light shade. They look stunning as a carpet below deciduous shrubs and trees.

Popular species and cultivars
Chionodoxa luciliae, the most popular species, has porcelain-blue flowers with white centers, and a pure white form, 'Alba,' is also available. The cultivar 'Pink Giant' is outstanding, with robust flower spikes of rosy pink.

These flower from late winter to midspring on stems 6 in (15 cm) high. *C. luciliae* 'Gigantea,' sometimes listed in catalogs as *C. gigantea,* is taller, reaching a height of 8 in (20 cm). The flower spikes are violet-blue with white centers and appear from late winter to midspring. A related cultivar, 'Blue Giant,' is 6 in (15 cm) tall and bears bright blue flowers with large white centers. Plant *C. luciliae* bulbs 2-4 in (5-10 cm) apart, except for 'Gigantea' and 'Blue Giant,' which should be set 3-4 in (7.5-10 cm) apart.
Chionodoxa sardensis is the smallest species, 4-6 in (10-15 cm) high. Its nodding sky-blue flowers

with tiny white centers appear slightly later than the other chionodoxas, from early spring to late spring.

Cultivation
Plant the bulbs as soon as they are available in fall, setting them 2-3 in (5-7.5 cm) deep and 2-4 in (5-10 cm) apart in large groups. They do well in any ordinary well-drained garden soil in a sunny or lightly shaded site. They need little attention apart from removing the foliage as it dies down and lifting and dividing the clumps as they become crowded. Replant these divisions immediately, 2-4 in (5-10 cm) apart.
Propagation The easiest method of propagation is division in late spring, when the leaves are turning yellow. Many chionodoxas also spread rapidly by self-sown seed; the round seedpods can be gathered in late spring when they mature and the seeds sown in an outdoor nursery bed. Transplant the seedlings to their flowering sites during the second summer. Cultivars do not breed true to type from seed and should be propagated from divisions.
Pests/diseases Slugs sometimes eat the leaves and flowers.

Colchicum
autumn crocus

Colchicum 'Waterlily'

- ❏ Height 6-16 in (15-40 cm)
- ❏ Planting distance 6-9 in (15-23 cm)
- ❏ Flowers early to late fall
- ❏ Well-drained soil
- ❏ Sunny or partially shaded site
- ❏ Corms available mid- and late summer
- ❏ Hardy zones 4-8

Despite their name, do not confuse these flowers with genuine crocuses. Colchicums are renowned for the lovely colors they add to the garden in fall — muted lilacs, purples, and pinks, which seem to blend perfectly with fallen leaves covering the ground. An ideal site is among tall grass, which supports the 6-8 in (15-20 cm) high leafless stems during flowering time and hides the mass of untidy leaves in spring. All colchicums are hardy, so they can be left in the ground undisturbed for years.

Popular species and cultivars
Colchicum autumnale has lilac-pink goblet-shaped flowers that appear in early fall and midfall. The stems are particularly fragile,

so ideally this species should be grown in rough grass, which can be left uncut in spring and fall. Plant 4 in (10 cm) deep and 8 in (20 cm) apart. A double-flowered white form, 'Alboplenum,' and a single white form, 'Album,' are also available.

Colchicum speciosum has flowers in varying shades of purple and appears from early to late fall. It is a more robust species than *C. autumnale,* with a stronger stem, so it can be grown in a shrub border where the 16 in (40 cm) high leaves that appear in spring won't smother other plants. Plant in a group of at least 10 corms in dappled shade. Set them 4 in (10 cm) deep and 6 in (15 cm) apart. Cultivars include 'Album,' a pure white form.

Dutch hybrids have stronger-colored flowers, arriving in early and late fall. They are more robust and easier to grow. Popular cultivars are 'The Giant' (rosy lilac), 'Lilac Wonder' (lilac-rose), and 'Waterlily' (purple with double flowers).

Cultivation
Colchicums grow in any soil, pro-

Colchicum autumnale

vided it is well drained, but they are more likely to spread in fertile soil. A site in sun or partial shade is suitable. Plant in mid- to late summer or as soon as they're available, setting them in small clumps. Remove dead foliage.

Propagation Every third year, when the leaves die down in summer, dig up the corms, separate any small cormels, and then replant them.

Pests/diseases Slugs may eat the leaves and corms.

Convallaria
lily of the valley

Convallaria majalis

- ❏ Height 6-8 in (15-20 cm)
- ❏ Planting distance 6 in (15 cm)
- ❏ Flowers mid- to late spring
- ❏ Good, moist soil
- ❏ Shady site
- ❏ Rhizomes available mid- and late fall
- ❏ Hardy zones 3-9

Convallaria majalis is the only species in this genus. It has delicate white bell-shaped flowers that are arranged in loose spikes. These blooms appear in mid- and late spring and have a magnificent heady scent that makes them popular as cut flowers. The berries that appear in fall and the roots are poisonous.

Lily of the valley is best planted in large clumps in a cool, shady corner or in a wild garden; it spreads rapidly, so avoid confined borders or spaces where it can overcome more delicate plants. When you choose the site, bear in mind that the broad green leaves, which provide deceptively good ground cover in late spring and early summer, become an untidy decaying yellow and brown mass toward fall. This problem becomes worse if the plants are growing in a bright, sunny site.

Cultivation
Grow lily of the valley in ordinary garden soil containing plenty of leaf mold or compost. The site should be shady. Plant the crowns singly in early fall and midfall at least 6 in (15 cm) apart, pointed end upward, just below the soil surface. When the leaves die down in summer, topdress with leaf mold, compost, or shredded bark — this encourages continuous flowering the following year. Avoid disturbing the roots except for propagation.

Propagation Lift and divide the rhizomes in mid- to late fall or early spring. Replant 6 in (15 cm) apart just below the surface, then apply a topdressing of compost and leaf mold, and water well.

Pests/diseases A fungal stem rot sometimes appears as small grayish spots on stalks and leaves, and these develop into sunken brown spots. The stem rot stunts growth and may cause the flowers to decay.

CORN LILY, AFRICAN —
see *Ixia*

Crinum
crinum

Crinum × powellii

- ❏ Height 1½-2 ft (45-60 cm)
- ❏ Planting distance 1-1½ ft (30-45 cm)
- ❏ Flowers late summer to early fall
- ❏ Rich, well-drained soil
- ❏ Sunny, sheltered site
- ❏ Bulbs available year round
- ❏ Hardy zones 8 or 9-10, with winter protection into zone 7

If you'd like to bring a subtropical feeling to your garden, consider planting *Crinum × powellii,* the hardiest member of the *Crinum* genus. It is not an easy bulb to grow, needing sun, mild conditions, and frequent tidying up, but you'll be rewarded with exotic white or pink lilylike blooms.

Cultivation
In the South, crinums succeed in any good, moist garden soil in a sunny spot. In the North, grow crinums in clumps in a sunny site protected from north and east winds. They also thrive in containers on sunny patios in summer. Plant in spring in the North (spring or fall in the South) in rich, moisture-retentive, but well-drained soil. Set them 1-1½ ft (30-45 cm) apart with their necks just below soil level. Water well during the summer, then ease off in fall. Keep those in containers almost dry in winter. Protect young shoots from frost with a light mulch of coarse sand or straw. Move container-grown crinums indoors during winter into a cool but frost-free place.

Propagation Crinums prefer not to be disturbed. You can propagate them by removing offsets in early spring and replanting. However, these will take 3 years to develop into flowering plants.

Pests/diseases Trouble free.

Crocosmia
crocosmia

Crocosmia × crocosmiiflora

Crocosmia × crocosmiiflora 'Citronella'

❏ Height 3-4 ft (90-120 cm)
❏ Planting distance 4-6 in (10-15 cm)
❏ Flowers midsummer to early fall
❏ Well-drained soil
❏ Sunny, sheltered site
❏ Corms available early to late spring
❏ Hardy zones 7-10

A clump of crocosmias presents a cheerful sight in summer and early fall with their sword-shaped green leaves and profuse sprays of orange flowers. They like well-drained soil and sun, and spread rapidly, so give them plenty of room — sunny banks are a favorite spot, but the flowers also look attractive planted in clumps among shrubs or herbaceous perennials. The tubular flowers are held on wiry stems 4 ft (120 cm) tall. They come in varying shades of orange or yellow, depending on the cultivar, and are excellent for flower arranging.

Popular species and cultivars
Crocosmia × crocosmiiflora, (montebretia) has orange flowers opening from midsummer to late fall. In milder parts of the country this race of hybrids will naturalize; up through zone 7 they

Crocosmia masoniorum

will overwinter reliably if given a warm, sheltered site. Montebretias spread rapidly, so allow plenty of room. Several cultivars, which are less rampant, have been developed from *C. × crocosmiiflora.* They offer the gardener almost every shade of orange, as well as yellow and red: 'Bressingham Blaze' and 'Emberglow' are orange-red; 'Emily McKenzie' is deep orange with crimson-brown markings; 'Jenny Bloom' is deep

yellow; 'Lucifer' (3 ft/90 cm) is brilliant flame-red and early flowering; 'Solfatare' is apricot-yellow with bronze-flushed leaves; and 'Spitfire' is fiery orange. Mixed collections of these cultivars are available from some nurseries.
Crocosmia masoniorum has bright orange blooms that appear in succession in mid- and late summer. Smaller than the hybrids' flowers, they are also more densely packed together on their arching stems.

Cultivation
Plant the corms about 4-6 in (10-15 cm) apart and 3 in (7.5 cm) deep in clumps in early spring. These plants need full sun and well-drained soil that has been deeply dug. *C. masoniorum* prefers a site where it can be left undisturbed. Water regularly in the summer. In the northern part of these plants' range, cover the root area in mid-fall with a winter mulch of dry leaves. If your garden is in a frost pocket, lift the corms, dry them off, and store in a frost-free place. Remove dead leaves of plants left in the ground in early spring, before the new foliage appears.
Propagation Divide clumps every 3 years, either just after flowering or before the new growth starts in spring.
Pests/diseases Trouble free.

Crocus
crocus

Crocus chrysanthus 'E. A. Bowles'

Crocus medius

- ❏ Height 2-5 in (5-13 cm)
- ❏ Planting distance 3-4 in (7.5-10 cm)
- ❏ Flowers late winter to early spring; also fall
- ❏ Any well-drained soil
- ❏ Full sun or dappled shade
- ❏ Corms available midsummer for fall flowering and fall for spring flowering
- ❏ Hardy zones 3-8

Crocuses come from the mountainous regions of southern and eastern Europe, so they are remarkably hardy. In gardens they provide some of the earliest spring color, though there are also several fall-flowering species. Most species stand about 3 in (7.5 cm) high — the Dutch hybrids are slightly taller at 4-5 in (10-13 cm). The flower colors vary greatly, with shades of yellow, blue, purple, lilac, and white. Some are only one color; others are bicolored or striped. All have thin green leaves, each with a faint white stripe. The leaves of spring-flowering crocuses appear with the flowers.

Crocuses are able to thrive well in both sun and dappled shade. They make a fine addition to rock gardens and also look attractive when used as edging for flower or shrub borders. The more robust species of crocus are suitable for naturalizing in short grass, provided the grass is not mowed before the crocus leaves turn yellow in late spring. Try planting fall-flowering crocuses among low ground covers.

Crocus chrysanthus 'Lady Killer'

Popular species and cultivars
Crocus ancyrensis, often listed as 'Golden Bunch,' is 2 in (5 cm) high with rich yellow flowers in late winter and early spring.
Crocus angustifolius stands 2-3 in (5-7.5 cm) high and has star-shaped flowers that are bronze outside and yellow inside. They appear in February where winters are not too harsh. It is one of the oldest crocuses cultivated.
Crocus chrysanthus is 3 in (7.5 cm) high with golden yellow flowers in late winter. It is suitable for rock gardens, borders, and containers. Popular cultivars are 'Advance' (yellow and violet), 'Blue Bird' (violet and white), 'Blue Pearl' (blue and white), 'Cream Beauty' (cream), 'E. A. Bowles' (yellow with bronze base), 'Lady Killer' (purple and lilac-white), 'Princess Beatrix' (clear blue with yellow base), 'Prince Claus' (deep violet-blue flushed with

white), 'Snowbunting' (white), and 'Zwanenburg Bronze' (garnet-brown and yellow).
Crocus imperati, 3-4 in (7.5-10 cm) high, has flowers with buff outer petals, streaked purple, and bright purple satiny inner petals. It is an early-flowering species, appearing from late winter to very early spring.
Crocus medius, 3 in (7.5 cm) high, has lightly scented lilac blooms with deep orange stigmas. Grow this fall-flowering species in a sunny spot.
Crocus sieberi, 3 in (7.5 cm) high, has pale purple flowers with yellow bases in late winter and early spring. Two garden hybrids are 'Firefly' (vivid lilac-pink with orange stamens) and 'Violet Queen' (violet-blue).
Crocus speciosus, 4-5 in (10-13 cm) high, has bright lilac-blue flowers with yellow anthers and red stigmas, opening in midfall. This species multiplies freely, making it the most popular fall-flowering crocus. *C. speciosus aitchisonii* (pale lavender-blue) is a popular variety. A white form, 'Albus,' is sometimes available.
Crocus tomasinianus has lilac flowers that appear in late winter, 3 in (7.5 cm) above ground. For a deeper purple, try 'Whitewell Purple.' It is one of the best crocuses for naturalizing in grass.
Dutch hybrids, developed from the species *Crocus vernus,* have large robust flowers in an enormous range of colors. The goblet-

Dutch crocus 'Pickwick'

Crocus tomasinianus 'Whitewell Purple'

Crocus vernus

Crocus speciosus

shaped flowers stand about 4-5 in (10-13 cm) high and open in early spring. Plant them in rough grass or a border, where they will develop into dense clumps if left undisturbed. Cultivars are 'Enchantress' (pale blue), 'Jeanne d'Arc' (white), 'Pickwick' (light lilac), 'Purpureus Grandiflorus' (purple-blue), 'Remembrance' (soft violet-blue), 'Striped Beauty' (white striped violet), 'Yellow Mammoth,' (golden yellow), and 'Queen of the Blues' (blue).

Cultivation

Plant spring-flowering crocuses when the corms are available in early fall, although the Dutch hybrids can wait until late fall. Choose a sunny or partially shaded site with well-drained soil. Set the corms 2-3 in (5-7.5 cm) deep and 3-4 in (7.5-10cm) apart in small clumps. After the flowers die, don't deadhead them or remove the leaves until they turn yellow, at which time they are easy to pull off without disturbing the corms.

Propagation When the leaves die down, lift the corms, remove any small cormels, and replant. Under good conditions *C. tomasinianus* and the Dutch hybrids multiply naturally.

Pests/diseases Mice and squirrels may eat corms in the soil. Watch for birds pecking at young flower buds — especially yellow cultivars.

CROWN IMPERIAL —
see *Fritillaria*

Curtonus
Aunt Eliza, pleated leaves

Curtonus paniculatus

❏ Height 4 ft (120 cm)
❏ Planting distance 9 in (23 cm)
❏ Flowers late summer to early fall
❏ Rich, well-drained soil
❏ Sunny site
❏ Corms available fall
❏ Hardy zones 7-10

Curtonus paniculatus (syn. *Antholyza paniculata*) is the only species in this South African genus. It is closely related to *Crocosmia* species, but is taller, up to 4 ft (120 cm), and is distinguished by its pleated, sword-shaped midgreen leaves and its zigzagging flower stems carrying orange-red trumpets during late summer and fall. The flowers are good for cutting.

Once established, curtonus naturalizes well from New York City south; farther north, treat it like gladiolus. Grow curtonus in sunny mixed borders, among low shrubs, or at the foot of a south-facing wall.

Cultivation
Plant the corms in early fall, setting them 6 in (15 cm) deep in groups of three to five spaced 9 in (23 cm) apart. They will grow in any well-drained soil but thrive on plenty of organic matter and in full sun, with some shelter. After flowering, trim the faded stems back, but leave the foliage as protection during winter. Cut it back to the ground in spring.

Propagation Where winter hardy, lift crowded clumps in midfall, separate, and replant the corms, taking care that each division is complete with corm, roots, and leaf cluster. In the North, divide corms when lifted in fall and replant separately in spring.

Pests/diseases Trouble free.

Curtonus paniculatus (growth habit)

Cyclamen
cyclamen

Cyclamen hederifolium 'Album'

❏ Height 3-6 in (7.5-15 cm)
❏ Planting distance 6 in (15 cm)
❏ Flowers midsummer to midspring
❏ Well-drained, humus-rich soil
❏ Shaded, sheltered site
❏ Corms available midsummer for fall flowering and fall for winter and spring flowering
❏ Hardy zones 5-9

The pretty pink or white flowers of cyclamen present a charming sight in a shaded area of a rock garden, beneath a tree, or around the base of a shrub — it is one of the few bulbous plants to flourish under conifers.

Closely related to the florist's cyclamen, several species are hardy enough to be grown outdoors throughout most of the United States, in well-drained but moisture-retentive soil. As natural woodland plants, they prefer a soil rich in leaf mold or well-decayed garden compost and need a site shaded from hot summer sun and protected from cold winds. Although sometimes slow to establish themselves, cyclamens may colonize to form carpets of color from midsummer through to midspring.

Popular species and cultivars
Cyclamen cilicium, 4 in (10 cm) high and hardy in most winters, produces its honey-scented flowers in early fall and midfall, usually before the silver-speckled leaves have appeared. Flower color varies from near-white to a deep rose-pink.

Cyclamen coum has purplish-pink, rose-pink, or more rarely, pure white flowers ('Album'), usually appearing in midwinter. The 'Pewter' selection ranges from pale to deep pink. In the southern part of their range, they

Cyclamen coum

Cyclamen hederifolium

may just come out in time for Christmas. The plants are only 3 in (7.5 cm) high, with round green leaves marbled with silver. This species does best under trees and self-seeds freely.

Cyclamen europaeum (syn. *C. purpurascens)* has strongly scented rose-pink to purple flowers standing 4 in (10 cm) high. These begin to appear in mid- and late summer and continue in succession until Christmas. The rounded to kidney-shaped green leaves have faint silver markings. This is one of the hardiest cyclamens.

Cyclamen hederifolium (syn. *C. neapolitanum)* has delicate pink or white flowers on stalks 4 in (10 cm) high. The blooms open in early fall and midfall. The deep green leaves are variegated with silver and form an attractive car-pet through the winter (in the South) and spring months, until they die down in late spring. Plant in a rock garden or beneath shrubs, where the soil is rarely disturbed. The cultivar 'Album' is pure white, sometimes with a hint of pink around the mouth.

Cyclamen libanoticum grows in mild regions only, producing its scented pale pink flowers in early spring. The ivy-shaped, toothed leaves are dark green and white-marbled above, red on the undersides. The plant grows to 6 in (15 cm) tall.

Cultivation

Cyclamens do best in woodland conditions — in shady sites, sheltered from the wind, with well-drained, humus-rich soil. Choose a spot where the plants can be left undisturbed. Plant the corms in late summer and early fall, setting them 6 in (15 cm) apart in clusters. Place *C. coum* and *C. europaeum* 1-2 in (2.5-5 cm) or more deep in light soil. With *C. hederifolium* barely cover the corms, but add a 1 in (2.5 cm) mulch of leaf mold annually after it has finished flowering.

Propagation The corms do not divide or produce offsets, and seed propagation is the only means of increase. Many cyclamens will seed themselves, and commercially purchased seed can also be sown in late summer or early fall in pans or pots of sterilized seed-starting mix. Leave the seeds to germinate in a cold frame or on a cool windowsill, or place the pots outdoors against a north wall for sturdier seedlings.

Prick off the seedlings singly into 2½ in (6 cm) pots of potting soil, and grow them on in a cold frame or other cool but frost-free spot before planting them out in their flowering sites in late spring or summer. They will usually flower in their second year.

Pests/diseases Mice sometimes eat the corms in the ground. The nearly microscopic cyclamen mite attacks foliage and buds, stunting and deforming new growth.

DAFFODIL — see *Narcissus*

Dahlia
dahlia

Single-flowered

Giant decorative

- ❏ Height 10-60 in (25-150 cm)
- ❏ Planting distance 1-4 ft (30-120 cm)
- ❏ Flowers midsummer to first severe frost
- ❏ Any well-drained garden soil
- ❏ Sunny or lightly shaded site
- ❏ Tubers available midwinter to late spring
- ❏ Hardy to zone 9; farther north lift and overwinter tubers indoors

Dahlias come in a range of forms, sizes, and colors unmatched by any other garden plant. Their glorious flower heads appear from midsummer until midfall or the first severe frosts, filling the garden with color when most other plants are past their best.

Garden dahlias are grown from tubers or cuttings, but dwarf bedding dahlias are grown from seed and are treated as true annuals. (For bedding dahlias, see page 42.)

The bold flower heads and strong colors of dahlias make them outstanding plants for garden decoration and cutting. Depending on their size, they can be grown in beds of their own, in perennial borders, in open shrubberies, or along walls. They prefer a sunny site but will tolerate shade. As they are only half-hardy, the tubers should be lifted in fall north of zone 9 and stored in a frost-free place over winter.

Anemone-flowered 'Comet'

They are easy to grow if you just want bright splashes of color in late summer and fall. If you're aiming for the perfect exhibition flower head, however, there's a host of refining techniques that specialist growers use.

Popular species and cultivars
Border dahlias are divided into nine groups, determined by the shape of the flower heads.

Anemone-flowered dahlias have blooms up to 4 in (10 cm) wide that resemble anemones: their double flowers have flat outer florets that surround a dense group of shorter tubular florets, often of a different color. The plants reach 10-18 in (25-45 cm)

high and should be grown 1-1½ ft (30-45 cm) apart in beds, borders, tubs, or deep window boxes. This is one of the rarer groups; it includes several cultivars in pastel shades. Cultivars available are 'Comet' (maroon), 'Honey' (apricot-pink), and 'Sweden' (yellow).

Cactus dahlias have fully double blooms with pointed ray florets. This group is divided into sections, determined by the size of the blooms. *Giant* cultivars reach 4-5 ft (120-150 cm) high with blooms over 10 in (25 cm) wide; plant 4 ft (120 cm) apart. Their flowers don't appear until early fall. *Large* cultivars are also 4-5 ft (120-150 cm) high with slightly smaller blooms at 8-10 in (20-25 cm) wide; plant 4 ft (120 cm) apart. *Medium* cultivars are 3½-4½ ft (105-135 cm) high with blooms 6-8 in (15-20 cm) wide; plant 3 ft (90 cm) apart. *Small* cultivars are 3½-4 ft (105-120 cm) high with blooms 4-6 in (10-15 cm) wide; plant 2½ ft (75 cm) apart. *Dwarf* cultivars are 3-4 ft (90-120 cm) high with blooms up to 4 in (10 cm) wide; plant 2½ ft (75 cm) apart. All cactus cultivars are easy to grow and make impressive cut flowers. Popular cultivars are 'Apple Blossom' (rose with lighter center), 'Doris Day' (bright red), and 'Orchid Lace' (white with purple tips).

Collarette dahlias have blooms 4 in (10 cm) wide, each single-flowered with an inner ring or collar (often of another color) and a central disk. This group includes cultivars reaching 30-40 in (75-100 cm) high. Set the plants 2-2½ ft (60-75 cm) apart. Collarette dahlias have especially strong stems, which make them

Collarette

Peony-flowered 'Bishop of Llandaff'

Small decorative 'Heidiland'

favorites among flower arrangers. Popular cultivars are 'Awaikoe' (mahogany-red with white collar), 'Jack O'Lantern' (orange with yellow), and 'Kaiserwalzer' (fiery red and yellow).

Decorative dahlias have double blooms consisting of broad, flat ray florets without central disks. This large group is subdivided into sections according to flower form and size. *Formal* decorative cultivars are fully double with all the florets regularly arranged with slightly incurved edges and flattened tips. *Informal* decorative dahlias are also fully double but with looser, less regular inflorescences; the petallike rays are not regularly arranged. Decorative dahlias may be *giant, large, medium, small,* or even *miniature,* and can range in height from 3-5 ft (90-150 cm), depending on the type. Blooms may be spectacular — 10 in (25 cm) wide or more. Space tubers according to the expected stature of the cultivar: giants should be planted 4 ft (120 cm) apart, miniatures just 2½ ft (75 cm). Decorative dahlias have an extensive color range and are good for both exhibiting and cutting. Popular cultivars are 'Daniel Edward' (formal, fuchsia-purple), 'Duet' (formal, red and white), 'Edinburgh' (formal, maroon and white), 'Envy' (informal, red), 'Heidiland' (formal, fuchsia), 'Playboy' (informal, yellow), and 'Purple Taiheijo' (informal, purple).

Peony-flowered dahlias have blooms up to 5 in (13 cm) wide, each consisting of two or more rings of flat ray florets and a central disk. The plants reach 40 in

Show or Ball

(100 cm) high and should be grown 2-2½ ft (60-75 cm) apart. Only a few cultivars are available. They include 'Bishop of Llandaff' (scarlet), 'Gerrie Hoek' (pink), and 'Japanese Bishop' (dark orange with blackish foliage).

Pompon dahlias have fully double globular-shaped flowers, 2 in (5 cm) wide. The free-flowering plants reach 3-4 ft (90-120 cm) high and should be planted 2 ft (60 cm) apart. Their selling point is their long-lasting cut flowers. Popular cultivars include 'Andrew Lockwood' (lilac), 'Moorplace' (purple), and 'Stoneleigh Cherry' (red).

Semicactus dahlias have flow-

ers similar to the cactus cultivars, but the ray florets are wider. They are divided into the same sections as the cactus group, determined by flower size. Semicactus dahlias are excellent for exhibiting. Popular cultivars are 'Andriana' (white) and 'Reginald Keene' (orange and flame).

Show or Ball dahlias have blooms similar to those of pompon dahlias, but these flowers are larger and more ball-shaped and are sometimes flattened on top. Reaching 3-4 ft (90-120 cm) high, they are suitable for growing in mixed borders, cutting, and exhibiting. Plant the tubers 2½ ft (75 cm) apart. The cultivars are

Pompon 'Stoneleigh Cherry'

Large semicactus 'Reginald Keene'

Dwarf cactus

subdivided into two groups: small ball with blooms 4-6 in (10-15 cm) wide and miniature ball with blooms up to 4 in (10 cm) wide.

Single-flowered dahlias have blooms up to 4 in (10 cm) wide, each with a single outer ring of florets and a central disk. The plants are 12-20 in (30-50 cm) tall and should be grown 1-1½ ft (30-45 cm) apart. Cultivars in this group can be grown in beds or mixed borders, as they don't require support. Their flowers are abundant and will last a long time if deadheaded regularly. Popular cultivars include 'G. F. Hemerick' (soft orange), 'Irene van der Zwet' (soft yellow), 'Nellie Geerlings' (red), and 'Sneezy' (white).

Cultivation

Dahlias will grow in any well-drained soil enriched with compost, composted manure, or other organic material. Rake in some bonemeal at planting time. Plant the tubers in midspring, or as soon as all danger of frost is past; leave any that have sprouted until late spring. If it is cold and wet, delay planting until the weather improves. Dig holes 4-6 in (10-15 cm) deep for the tubers, insert stout supporting stakes 1 ft (30 cm) shorter than the final height of the dahlia, and then place the tuber in the hole and cover with soil. Water well after planting. As the stems grow, tie them loosely to the stakes.

About 3-4 weeks after planting, pinch back the tips on the main stems to encourage strong side growths. To grow large flowers on long stems suitable for cutting or exhibiting, disbud regularly and deadhead as necessary.

A week after frosts have blackened the leaves in fall, cut down the stems to 6 in (15 cm) above ground. Using a spade, make a cut one spade's depth around each plant, 1 ft (30 cm) from the main stem. Holding the stems, gently ease the tubers from the soil with a fork. Be careful not to damage the point at which the stem joins the tuber — this is the crown, where new growth begins. Discard any broken or rotting tubers. Place the rest upside down and under cover for a week to drain off water that has accumulated in the hollow stems.

Put tubers (right side up) in shallow boxes of dry potting soil or sand. Store in a frost-free place at 41-46°F (5-8°C). Inspect the tubers every few weeks for signs of disease or shriveling. Place any shriveled tubers in a bucket of water overnight, then dry thoroughly before storing them again.

Propagation Division is the simplest method for propagating dahlias. In early spring, begin watering stored dahlia tubers, but avoid watering the crowns. After 2-3 weeks the eyes on the crowns of the tubers should swell. Divide the tubers with a sharp knife, making sure each division has an undamaged eye. Dust the cut parts of the tubers with sulfur to prevent fungal attack. Then plant out when weather permits.

If planting outdoors is delayed, pot up the tubers individually in potting soil and keep in a cool but frost-free spot (a cold frame is ideal) until conditions improve.

Pests/diseases Aphids and tarnished plant bugs may attack foliage, and European corn borers may begin feeding on new growth and buds in late summer, causing the death of shoot tips. Gray mold (botrytis blight) may be troublesome on flower stalks and tubers in a wet summer.

Dierama
angels' fishing rods, wandflower

Dierama pulcherrimum

Eranthis
winter aconite

Eranthis hyemalis

❏ Height 4 in (10 cm)
❏ Planting distance 3 in (7.5 cm)
❏ Flowers midwinter to midspring
❏ Well-drained, moisture-retentive soil
❏ Sun or partial shade
❏ Tubers available in early fall and midfall
❏ Hardy zones 4-9

These small hardy perennials are some of the earliest plants in the garden, sometimes appearing in mid- and late winter in the South. Their enchanting buttercuplike flowers stand 4 in (10 cm) above ground, surrounded by deep green ruffs. For greatest impact, plant them in large groups to form a carpet. A sunny or partially shaded site with plenty of humus-rich soil is best.

Popular species and cultivars
Eranthis hyemalis has lemon-yellow flowers that appear in late winter, or even earlier in mild areas. It stands 4 in (10 cm) high, and its tubers should be planted 3 in (7.5 cm) apart. As a woodland species thriving in dappled shade, it is best grown in a semiwild setting below deciduous trees or in between shrubs.
Eranthis × *tubergenii* has robust, slightly larger rich golden yellow flowers that emerge in early spring. It tolerates sunnier conditions than *E. hyemalis* and can be grown in a rock garden or at the front of a border, provided there is plenty of humus in the soil. Two cultivars are available: 'Guinea Gold,' with bronze leaves and

❏ Height 3-6 ft (90-180 cm)
❏ Planting distance 9-24 in (23-60 cm)
❏ Flowers late summer to midfall
❏ Well-drained fertile soil
❏ Sunny, sheltered site
❏ Corms available early spring or fall
❏ Hardy to zone 8 in a protected site

Dieramas look superb grown in gaps in paving surrounding a garden pond. While only winter hardy in nearly frost-free regions such as southern California, they will survive farther north in a sheltered, south-facing site. Two species, *Dierama pulcherrimum* and the smaller *D. pendulum* are available. They have long, narrow grasslike leaves that are joined in late summer and fall by drooping heads of purple-red flowers on curving stems.

Cultivation
Grow in well-drained soil enriched with organic matter. Pick a sunny, sheltered site, although partial shade is tolerated. Plant the corms in early spring, or midspring (at the north end of their range), or in fall, 3-4 in (7.5-

Dierama pendulum

10 cm) deep and 9-24 in (23-60 cm) apart. After flowering, remove the stems and cut back damaged leaves. In zone 8 cover the plants with a winter mulch.
Propagation Plants may be increased by lifting and separating the offsets in midspring. Plant them in a nursery bed, and grow on until they reach flowering size.
Pests/diseases Trouble free.

DOG-TOOTH VIOLET —
see *Erythronium*

137

Erythronium
erythronium

Eranthis × *tubergenii*

stems and large deep yellow fragrant flowers that appear in early spring and midspring, and 'Glory,' with slightly less fragrant flowers that appear in late winter and early spring, and bronze-tinted young foliage.

Cultivation
Plant the tubers as soon as they are available in early fall, setting them 2 in (5 cm) deep and 3 in (7.5 cm) apart in groups. You may be able to buy these plants in leaf at a local nursery in midspring; these establish themselves more quickly than dormant tubers. They grow best in well-drained, moisture-retentive soil, preferably a heavy loam. Incorporating leaf mold into the soil at planting time is often a good idea. An ideal site for winter aconites is below deciduous trees or between shrubs where the ground is cool and moist in summer, but where the sun reaches the plants in winter and spring. Avoid too much disturbance after planting. Water, if necessary, during the growing season, until the leaves die down.
Propagation When the plants die down, lift the tubers, divide the large knobby ones into several pieces, and replant them immediately. Tubers straight from the supplier should not be propagated for 3-4 years to allow them to swell in size. Winter aconites will also spread rapidly to form colonies by self-seeding.
Pests/diseases Mice and chipmunks may eat tubers.

Erythronium revolutum

❏ Height 4-12 in (10-30 cm)
❏ Planting distance 4-6 in (10-15 cm)
❏ Flowers early to late spring
❏ Moist, humus-rich soil
❏ Shady site
❏ Corms available early fall and midfall
❏ Hardy zones 3-9

Erythroniums are among the most attractive spring-flowering plants with delicate white, yellow, or purple-pink flowers that resemble little Turk's cap lilies and broadly lance-shaped marble-patterned leaves. All four common species are natives of woodland, requiring some shade and moist, humus-rich soil. The best place for them in the garden is a semiwild wooded corner or a cool, shady patch among shrubs. If you have a peat garden or a border full of rhododendrons, erythroniums are the ideal flowers for providing ground interest in spring.

Popular species and cultivars
Erythronium americanum (dogtooth violet) bears fragrant yellow flowers that are on stems 4-8 in (10-20 cm) tall. Native to eastern North America, it blooms in early spring and is well adapted for planting in the rock garden or in a woodland garden. The

Erythronium dens-canis

leaves, with their purple and white spots, are attractive even when the plant is not in flower.
Erythronium dens-canis (dogtooth violet of Europe) has pink-purple flowers carried on 4-6 in (10-15 cm) high stems and green leaves blotched gray or brown. Cultivars include 'Lilac Wonder' (pale purple with brown blotches at the base of the flowers), 'Pink Perfection' (clear pink with yellow centers), and 'Snowflake' (white). These cultivars are often sold as a mixed selection.
Erythronium revolutum (Pacific Coast fawn lily) is the parent of a number of garden cultivars with yellow or white flowers. 'White

Erythronium tuolumnense

Beauty' (white flowers with yellow centers) is the free-flowering form most often found in gardens. It has two beautiful brown-and-white mottled leaves and 1 ft (30 cm) high stems carrying one or two flowers. Other garden forms range in color from pink to purple with deeper markings. The yellow 'Kondo' is a hybrid of *E. revolutum* and *E. tuolumnense*.

Erythronium tuolumnense has bright yellow drooping flowers and pale green leaves on 9-12 in (23-30 cm) high stems. It is named after California's Tuolumne River, on whose banks it grows wild. The plants have taken readily to garden cultivation and quickly form clumps.

Cultivation

Erythroniums should be planted in moist, but not water-logged, soil that is rich in organic matter. A shady site or north-facing slope is best, as the soil there is less likely to dry out. Avoid any site that will become hot and dry in summer. Plant the corms in early fall, immediately after purchase. Arrange them 4-6 in (10-15 cm) deep and 4-6 in (10-15 cm) apart, in groups of at least 12. Top-dress annually in late summer with composted bark or leaf-mold. Once in the ground, erythroniums are best left undisturbed. If you have to move them, do so after flowering, when the leaves die down.

Propagation As the plants dislike disturbance, it's best to buy fresh corms to increase stock. Left undisturbed and grown under suitable conditions, erythroniums will sometimes seed themselves.

Pests/diseases Trouble free.

Eucomis
pineapple lily

Eucomis comosa

❑ Height 1½- 2 ft (45-60 cm)
❑ Planting distance 1 ft (30 cm)
❑ Flowers late summer to early fall
❑ Any good, well-drained soil
❑ Sunny, sheltered site
❑ Bulbs available spring
❑ Hardy zones 9-10, to zone 8 with winter protection

The South African pineapple lily is named for the small tuft of pineapplelike leaf bracts found on top of the robust flower stem. This rises as a dense spike of starry flowers above a basal rosette of arching, bright green strap-shaped leaves.

The species are reliably hardy only in the lower South and southern Pacific Coast. Here, they make unusual and exotic additions to late-summer beds. In the North they are suitable for growing in deep pots or tubs on a sunny patio.

Popular species and cultivars

Eucomis autumnalis grows 1½ ft (45 cm) tall and has wavy edges to the leaves. The flower spikes, in early fall, are white, sometimes tinged green. The individual flowers expand to form wide stars.

Eucomis bicolor is of similar height, with crimped leaf edges and very pale green flower spikes with petals edged in purple

Eucomis comosa, the tallest species, 2 ft (60 cm) or more high, has purple-spotted leaves and stems. Its scented flower spikes are greenish-yellow with lilac throats.

Cultivation

Plant the bulbs in midspring, 4-6 in (10-15 cm) deep in fertile and very well-drained soil. In zone 8, provide a sheltered site, such as the foot of a warm wall, in full sun. Farther north, grow the bulbs singly in 6 in (15 cm) pots of potting soil, overwintering them on a cool windowsill or in a greenhouse. Alternatively, grow them like gladioli, planting the bulbs out in the garden only when the soil warms in spring. Lift the bulbs in midfall after the foliage has died down, and store them in a frost-free place during the winter.

Propagation Detach offset bulbs when the plants are lifted, and grow on in 3 in (7.5 cm) pots of potting soil. They should reach flowering size in a couple of years.

Pests/diseases Slugs and snails eat holes in the leaves.

Freesia
freesia

Freesia × hybrida (single)

- ❑ Height 8-18 in (20-45 cm)
- ❑ Planting distance 4 in (10 cm)
- ❑ Flowers midsummer to early fall
- ❑ Well-drained good soil
- ❑ Sunny, sheltered site
- ❑ Corms available late winter to midspring
- ❑ Hardy zones 9-10

Freesias may be grown outdoors in the lower South, but are so vulnerable to wind or rain that they are best grown indoors. The single or double flowers (white, pink, yellow, orange, red, mauve, purple, and blue) are carried on 8-18 in (20-45 cm) high wiry stems. They appear in late summer outdoors, but may be forced indoors in winter. Their wonderful scent enhances a cut flower display.

Cultivation
In the South, plant corms in any well-drained good soil in early spring. Freesias thrive in sandy soils in a sunny, sheltered site; as freesias are mostly grown for cutting, a spot in a vegetable patch would be ideal. Set the corms 2-3 in (5-7.5 cm) deep and 4 in (10 cm) apart, and support each one with a twiggy stick. Water often during the growing period.

In the North, plant six corms

Freesia × hybrida (double)

to a 5 in (13 cm) pot filled with light, well-drained potting soil in late fall or early winter. Set the tops 1 in (2.5 cm) below the soil's surface; keep pots on a well-lighted cool windowsill (45-50°F/7-10°C at night). Each corm flowers for about 6 weeks.
Propagation Corms may produce offsets, which can be separated from the parent (after flowering is over and foliage yellows) and replanted. For the best bloom, buy new corms each year.
Pests/diseases Aphids sometimes infest the stems and leaves.

Fritillaria
fritillary

Fritillaria imperialis 'Lutea'

- ❑ Height 8-36 in (20-90 cm)
- ❑ Planting distance 4-8 in (10-20 cm) unless otherwise stated
- ❑ Flowers spring to early summer
- ❑ Fertile, well-drained soil
- ❑ Sun or partial shade
- ❑ Bulbs available early fall and midfall
- ❑ Hardy zones 3-9

Fritillaries are a large group of mainly spring-flowering bulbous plants, whose exquisite flowers add charm to any garden. Bell-shaped and nodding, the blooms are borne either in clusters atop robust stems or singly at intervals along thin but wiry stalks. Fritillaries range from the majestic crown imperial to the beguiling little snake's-head fritillary and more than repay the extra care they require. Sometimes difficult to establish and maintain, the species and cultivars described here are among the easiest to grow.

Popular species and cultivars
Fritillaria imperialis (crown imperial) carries clusters of large red, orange, or yellow flowers. These appear in midspring on 2-3 ft (60-90 cm) high stems. Each cluster of flowers has a crowning tuft of leaves to complete the beauty of a plant that has only one fault — an unpleasant foxlike smell when the new growth appears in spring. Crown imperial looks best grown in groups among other herbaceous plants in a border, or in clumps on its own at focal points in the

Fritillaria meleagris

Fritillaria imperialis

garden. Popular cultivars include 'Aurea-marginata' (orange-red flowers; green leaves with distinct yellow edges), 'Aurora' (orange-yellow), 'Lutea' (golden yellow), and 'Rubra' (deep red). Plant the bulbs 10-12 in (20-25 cm) apart.

Fritillaria meleagris (snake's-head fritillary) has pairs of flowers resembling large drooping white bells that are heavily overlaid with purple checkering. They come out in late spring on 10-12 in (25-30 cm) high stems, accompanied by a few narrow gray-green leaves, which contribute to the plants' particularly delicate appearance.

Snake's-head fritillary inhabits moist meadows in the wild, so in the garden it looks at home growing in rough grass. Other possible planting sites would be an undisturbed border, a peat garden, or around a garden pond. A white form ('Alba') with green or pink checkering is also available and excellent for naturalizing. The two frequently cross-breed.

Fritillaria michailovskyi grows about 8 in (20 cm) tall and is ideal for a cool, shady spot in the rock garden. In early spring to mid-

spring, it has solitary bell-shaped maroon-purple flowers with striking golden yellow rims.

Fritillaria pallidiflora flowers in mid- to late spring, bearing a cluster of creamy to greenish-yellow flowers atop 14 in (35 cm) high stems. The bell-shaped blossoms are marked with red or brown spots on the inside.

Fritillaria persica has loose spikes of small reddish or purple bells that appear in late spring. It has gray leaves and a twisted stem that reaches up to 2 ft (60 cm) high.

Fritillaria pontica thrives in most gardens. It is 1 ft (30 cm) tall and in late spring and early summer this plant produces single lemon-green flowers that are suffused with brownish purple.

Cultivation

Plant all fritillaries immediately after purchase; handle the fleshy bulbs carefully as they deteriorate if bruised or damaged. Plant them 4-6 in (10-15 cm) deep, except for *F. imperialis,* whose large bulbs should be planted 8 in (20 cm) deep. Place the bulbs on their sides so that the hollow

crowns do not collect water — a layer of coarse sand beneath the bulbs will improve drainage.

Fritillaries are best grown in fertile, well-drained soil in a sunny or lightly shaded spot where they can be left undisturbed for several years. *F. meleagris* prefers moist soil. Cut all stems back to the ground as they die back in early summer.

Propagation Although propagation can be done from seed, it takes 6 years to produce flowers, so it is better to increase stock with purchases of new bulbs. Left undisturbed, snake's-head fritillary seeds itself.

Pests/diseases Trouble free.

Galanthus
snowdrop

Galanthus nivalis

❏ Height 4-7 in (10-18 cm)
❏ Planting distance 2-8 in (5-20 cm)
❏ Flowers midwinter to early spring
❏ Moist, heavy soil
❏ Partial shade
❏ Bulbs available early fall and midfall
❏ Hardy zones 3-9

The delicate drooping white flowers of the snowdrop are always a welcome sight in spring. As natural plants of mountains and woods, they thrive under cool, moist conditions. They look most effective planted in clusters under deciduous trees to flower among the fallen brown leaves.

Popular species and cultivars
Galanthus elwesii has larger flowers than the common snowdrop, with deep green on the inner petals. The flowers appear in late winter and early spring on stems 4-7 in (10-18 cm) high. *Galanthus nivalis,* the common snowdrop, flowers from midwinter on. Its height varies from 4-6 in (10-15 cm), depending on the growing conditions; it will grow tallest in rich soil in partial shade. Single- and double-flowered forms are available, as well as the cultivar 'Flore Pleno,' which has large, scented double flowers.

Cultivation
Plant in early fall, 2-4 in (5-10 cm) deep. Set 2-3 in (5-7.5 cm) apart for *G. nivalis* and 4-8 in (10-20 cm) apart for *G. elwesii*. Snowdrops do best in a heavy, moist loam in a shady site with a northerly aspect. They can be difficult to establish, but once started they need little attention.
Propagation Divide clustered plants at, or just after, flowering time. Lift and divide carefully so that each bulb is separated, with its roots and leaves intact. Then replant immediately at the same depth.
Pests/diseases Stem and bulb nematodes may invade the bulbs. Gray mold can affect the leaves and stalks, destroying them as the growth spreads.

Galtonia
summer hyacinth

Galtonia candicans

❏ Height 4 ft (12 m)
❏ Planting distance 8-10 in (20-25 cm)
❏ Flowers midsummer to early fall
❏ Any well-drained soil
❏ Full sun
❏ Bulbs available late winter to midspring
❏ Hardy zones 8-10, to zone 7 with winter protection

Pure white hanging bell-shaped flowers, tinged green at the base, make the summer hyacinth a particularly beautiful plant for a border. Its slightly scented flowers appear from midsummer to early fall, in clusters of 10-30 at the top of a single leafless stem, up to 4 ft (12 m) high. *Galtonia candicans* is the only widely available species. It looks best at the back of a herbaceous bed, with shrubs, or in large outdoor containers.

Cultivation
In early spring or midspring, set the bulbs 8-10 in (20-25 cm) apart, covering them with 6 in (15 cm) of soil. Group three or five bulbs, or scatter them among early-flowering herbaceous plants or annuals. Do not disturb once established. Remove the stems in fall, and mulch with 2 in (5 cm) of compost.
Propagation Every 4 years, divide offsets in early fall and replant. They will flower after 2-3 years.
Pests/diseases Generally trouble free, though gray mold may affect newly planted bulbs.

GIANT LILY —
see *Cardiocrinum*

Gladiolus
gladiolus, sword lily

Large-flowered hybrid

South, gladioli are often planted in the fall for winter bloom. The species gladioli are less spectacular than the hybrids but they are hardier and will overwinter in the ground as far north as zone 7 or rarely to zone 5.

Popular species and cultivars
Catalogs may identify cultivars by the blooming time: early, early midseason, midseason, or late.
Gladiolus byzantinus, the hardiest species, overwinters in protected spots in zone 5. It bears 15 in (38 cm) long spikes of wine-red blooms in early summer. 'The Bride' is pure white.
Gladiolus × colvillei hybrids have white florets. Only 1-1½ ft (30-50 cm) high, these delicate gladioli flower in mid- and late summer. They are hardy to zone 7.
Gladiolus nanus (syn. *Babiana nana*) hybrids — which have been developed from species gladioli — come in pink, rose, or scarlet with violet to purple blotches. They stand 1½-2 ft (45-60 cm) high and flower in mid- and late summer.
Half-hardy hybrids (often listed under *Gladiolus × hortulanus*) are divided into four groups by the size of the "floret," or the flower spikes' individual blossoms.

Each group has different virtues and applications. The *giants* tend to be stiff but impressive flowers that are suitable as cut flowers. *Large* and *decorative* gladioli, though smaller, are still impressive and more graceful in appearance, better adapted to use in borders or beds. *Small* gladioli are less spectacular, but also less vulnerable to rain and weather, while "miniatures" have a unique delicacy and tend to be early bloomers.

Mixed large-flowered hybrids

❏ Height 1-5½ ft (30-165 cm)
❏ Planting distance 4-8 in (10-20 cm)
❏ Flowers midsummer to midfall
❏ Humus-rich, well-drained soil
❏ Sunny, sheltered site
❏ Corms available late winter to midspring
❏ Hardy typically zones 8-10, with hardy types overwintering with protection to zone 7 or even farther

The showy flower heads of gladioli are popular for cutting and exhibiting. They are less frequently used as bedding plants, as the flower spikes last only 2 weeks and the plants often need staking.

Half-hardy hybrids have mostly replaced the original gladiolus species. These hybrids are planted in spring in the North, then lifted in fall, and stored in a frost-free place over winter. In the

Miniature hybrid

Butterfly hybrid

Gladiolus byzantinus 'Robinetta'

Decorative hybrids bear florets 3½-4½ in (9-11 cm) wide. Choose 'Norseman' (rich red; very early), 'Queen's Lace' (lightly ruffled, soft rose; midseason), or 'Tango' (deep pink tinted orange, white throat; early midseason).

Small hybrids bear flowers 2½-3½ in (6-9 cm) wide, while the florets of the "miniature" gladioli are less than 2½ in (6 cm)wide. Small-flowered types are 'Pierre' (blackish red; early midseason) and 'Sonnet' (yellow with an orange edging to the petals; midseason). Good miniatures are 'Carolee' (salmon with dark pink throat; early) and 'Whiskers' (red with white throat streaked red; early).

In addition to the formal classification system, many growers identify hybrids by their form and the coloration of the flowers. One popular type is the so-called "primulinus" hybrids, which bear hooded florets, typically in shades of orange-yellow. A Dutch strain, the "butterfly" hybrids bear 18-in (45-cm) spikes of ruffled florets that are commonly blotted with a contrasted color at the throat.

Cultivation

Gladioli grow best in well-drained soil in a sunny spot. In the North, prepare soil as soon as the ground is workable in the spring; in zones 9-10, planting may be continued from fall into winter. Dig in well-composted manure, rake in some

Large-flowered hybrid

Giant hybrids bear florets over 5½ in (14 cm) wide. Superior giants are 'Ivory Tower' (ivory-cream flowers with light yellow lip petals; midseason), 'Jungle Flower' (huge carmine florets on 5½ ft/165 cm tall spikes; midseason), and 'Mother's Day' (lavender; midseason).

Large, or standard florets are 4½-5½ in (11-14 cm) wide. Popular types are 'Candy Cane' (red with white striping; midseason), 'Fairy Dancer' (medium pink with light yellow throat; early midseason), 'Golden Wave' (golden yellow; midseason), and 'Plum Tart' (velvety purple; early).

Hermodactylus
snake's-head iris

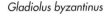

Gladiolus byzantinus

"*Primulinus*" hybrid

Hermodactylus tuberosus

❏ Height 10-12 in (25-30 cm)
❏ Planting distance 6 in (15 cm)
❏ Flowers mid- to late spring
❏ Well-drained alkaline soil
❏ Sheltered, sunny site
❏ Tubers available early fall
❏ Hardy zones 6-9

bonemeal, and if the soil is too heavy or too light, work in plenty of organic material, such as compost. For spring planting in the North, wait until the soil has warmed and the danger of frost is past before setting out corms. For continuous flowering in summer, make three or four plantings at 2-week intervals.

Planting depth is determined by the size of the corm: the smallest should be set no more than ½ in (1 cm) deep, while the largest ones — those 1¼ in (3 cm) wide — are set 6-8 in (15-20 cm) deep. The plants will be sturdier if you set corms below the bottom of a 2 in (5 cm) deep trench and refill this with soil as the foliage shoots up.

Gladioli used as garden plants should be grown in clumps; set the corms 4-6 in (10-15 cm) apart. Gladioli grown for cutting are best planted in single or double rows, 12-15 in (30-38 cm) apart.

About 8-10 weeks after planting (once the flower spikes appear), begin to water well, particularly in dry periods, and regularly apply a liquid fertilizer. Stake giant and large-flowered hybrids, and those grown in an exposed site. Put the stake on the side away from the developing flowers. Secure the stem with soft twine.

In cold-winter areas (zone 7 and north), the foliage turns yellow-brown in fall. Before the first frost, lift the corms with a fork. (There is no need to lift *G. byzantinus*, *G.* × *colvillei* hybrids, and *G. nanus* hybrids.) Clean the soil off and cut off the main stem ½ in (1 cm) above the corm. Do not bruise. Discard old, shriveled corms at the base of the new corm as soon as they will come away easily. Pull off the

tough outer skin on large corms, but save small cormels for propagation. Allow all corms and cormels to dry for 7 to 10 days, then store them in shallow boxes or labelled paper bags in a cool, frost-free place. Check the corms and cormels during the winter, and discard any that seem to have become diseased.

Propagation Plant the pea-sized cormels in early spring in an outdoor nursery bed, setting them close together in drills 2-3 in (5-7.5 cm) deep, with a layer of sand below and above to help growth and make lifting easier in fall. Keep the young plants weed free and well watered.

When the leaves become discolored in fall, lift the cormels and store them in the same way as adult corms. The following spring plant out and tend as before. Most cormels reach flowering size in the second year; if they don't, repeat storing and growing cycle for another year.

Pests/diseases In stored corms, thrips and aphids may cause rough brown patches. When plants are flowering thrips can make the blooms mottled. A fungal "yellows" disease causes growing plants to yellow and die before flowering.

Hermodactylus tuberosus (syn. *Iris tuberosa*) is the only species in this genus of iris look-alikes. It is an interesting plant to have in the garden, with its greenish-yellow flowers turning dark brown at the tips of the drooping lower petals. To ensure that the delicately scented flowers appear in mid- and late spring, give the plants a warm, sunny site.

Cultivation
Plant the tubers in early fall, 2-3 in (5-7.5 cm) deep and 6 in (15 cm) apart. They grow particularly well in alkaline soil but tolerate other soil, provided it is warm, well drained, and doesn't dry out in summer.

Propagation Lift and divide established clumps in fall.

Pests/diseases Slugs may attack emerging flower buds.

Hyacinthus
hyacinth

Hyacinthus orientalis

❏ Height 9-12 in (23-30 cm)
❏ Planting distance 3-8 in (7.5-20 cm)
❏ Flowers late winter to late spring
❏ Any light, well-drained soil
❏ Full sun
❏ Bulbs available early to late fall
❏ Hardy zones 4-8

The large-flowered Dutch hyacinths have mostly replaced the wild species, *Hyacinthus orientalis*. They have deliciously scented spikes of flowers, making them popular for window boxes and containers in late winter and early spring, or for beds in sunny formal borders in late spring. The compact flowers, on stems 9-12 in (23-30 cm) high, bloom from late winter until late spring.

A substantial number of Dutch hyacinth cultivars are available. Early-flowering garden cultivars include 'Jan Bos' (red) and 'Pink Pearl' (pink). Popular midseason cultivars include 'Blue Jacket,' 'Delft Blue,' 'Lady Derby' (pink), and 'Ostara' (blue). Late-season cultivars are 'Carnegie' (white) and 'City of Haarlem' (yellow).

Cultivation
Plant bulbs 5-6 in (13-15 cm)

Dutch hyacinth 'City of Haarlem'

deep in fall in any light, well-drained soil; a sunny location is best. Set bulbs 3-6 in (7.5-15 cm) apart if they are being grown alone in a group, and an inch or two farther apart if they are among other plants. Deadhead after flowering. Allow leaves and stems to die down. In the North cover bulbs with a mulch of leaves or bark over winter.
Propagation Propagation by division is rarely successful, and stock is best increased by planting new bulbs or leaving the hybrids to increase naturally.
Pests/diseases Bacterial soft rot may attack bulbs that have been planted in wet soil.

Ipheion
ipheion

Ipheion uniflorum

❏ Height 4-6 in (10-15 cm)
❏ Planting distance 2-3 in (5-7.5 cm)
❏ Flowers mid- to late spring
❏ Well-drained soil
❏ Sheltered, sunny or partially shaded site
❏ Bulbs available early fall and midfall
❏ Hardy zones 6-10

This pretty native of South America has one disconcerting characteristic: when crushed, the foliage smells like garlic. Still, the narrow pale green leaves make an attractive ground cover, clothing the earth from fall through winter. The perfumed lilac-blue blooms appear in mid- and late spring. Only one starlike flower is carried on each 4-6 in (10-15 cm) high stem, but a bulb produces several stems, so a noticeable clump is soon formed.

Ipheion looks most effective planted in groups in a rock garden or arranged at the front of a border. It tolerates full sun or partial shade, and it is a useful addition to any seaside garden. *Ipheion uniflorum* (also known as *Brodiaea uniflora* and *Triteleia uniflora*) is the only species available. The cultivar 'Wisley Blue' is violet-blue.

Cultivation
In early fall to midfall, choose a sheltered spot in sun or shade. The soil should be well-drained. Plant bulbs 2-3 in (5-7.5 cm) deep and 2-3 in (5-7.5 cm) apart. Keep the site free of weeds. In late summer, after the plants are dormant, remove the dead leaves and flower stems.
Propagation Divide in fall and replant immediately.
Pests/diseases Trouble free.

Iris (bearded)
iris

Tall bearded

Iris Sibirica 'Little White'

- ❑ Height 4-60 in (7.5-150 cm)
- ❑ Planting distance 6-15 in (15-38 cm)
- ❑ Flowers midspring to midsummer
- ❑ Any good garden soil
- ❑ Open, sunny site
- ❑ Rhizomes available early to late summer
- ❑ Hardy zones 5-9

Bearded irises are a large group of irises that spread underground by means of rhizomes. Above ground, they are characterized by thick leaves arranged in a flat fan shape and flowers with tufts of hair (beards) on the three outer petals (falls). The flowers, some of which are scented, come in a wide range of colors. They are carried on strong stems above the spears of foliage between midspring and midsummer.

Nearly every kind of bearded iris will flourish in zones 6 and 7. But because of a diverse heritage that includes ancestors from the Alps and the warm shores of the Mediterranean, there are cultivars that will flourish up to two zones farther north and a zone farther south. Bearded irises grow in most garden soils, but must be given an open, sunny site. The most widely grown bearded irises belong to the Eupogon group, recognized by their gray-green leaves, which die down to small fans in winter.

Popular species and cultivars
Bearded irises have been divided into several groups, according to their height.

Dwarf bearded irises flower in mid- and late spring. This group is often further subdivided into *miniature* dwarfs, which grow only 4-10 in (10-25 cm) high and bear flowers no more than 3 in (7.5 cm) wide, and *standard* dwarfs, which may grow from 10-15 in (25-38 cm) tall, with flowers from 3-4 in (7.5-10 cm) wide. Plant the rhizomes in small clumps 6-8 in (15-20 cm) apart in well-drained soil in a rock garden or at the edge of a raised border. Replant every 2-3 years.

Iris pumila, an outstanding miniature dwarf, has flowers in shades of purple, white, yellow, and yellow with brown tints in midspring. It is stemless and stands only 4 in (10 cm) high. As it grows naturally on mountains, well-drained soil in a rock garden provides an ideal site. It is advisable to divide the rhizomes every 2 years after flowering.

Hybrids come in similar colors to *I. pumila* but tend to be taller — some reaching 10 in (25 cm) high. Popular cultivars include 'Bee Wings' (yellow with brown spots on the falls), 'Blue Denim' (lilac-blue), and 'Bright White' (white).

Intermediate bearded irises, sometimes called border irises, flower in late spring. They reach 15-28 in (38-70 cm) high. Plant 1 ft (30 cm) apart at the front of a herbaceous border or in a large pocket in a rock garden. Divide and replant every third year.

Iris × germanica (London flag, or purple flag) has rich blue-purple falls with a white beard and light purple standards (upright inner petals). The sweetly scented flowers appear in early summer, 2-3 ft (60-90 cm) above ground. The foliage is evergreen.

Hybrids have well-shaped flaring flowers throughout late spring. These vigorous, free-flowering irises come in a range of yellows, creams, whites, purples, and blues. Popular hybrids include 'Am I Blue' (light blue with darker blue beard), 'Arctic Fancy' (purple and white), 'Golden Fair' (deep yellow), and 'Red Rooster'(deep red-brown).

Tall bearded irises flower in early summer on stalks 28 in (70 cm) or more tall. The tallest

147

Tall bearded

Tall bearded

Dwarf bearded 'Blue Denim'

Intermediate bearded

Tall bearded

Iris (*beardless Pacific Coast*)
iris

Intermediate bearded 'Arctic Fancy'

Pacific Coast hybrid

cultivars sometimes need staking. Plant the rhizomes 15 in (38 cm) apart. An enormous variety of hybrids are available in a range of colors. Some outstanding cultivars are 'Amethyst Flame' (amethyst), 'Black Dragon' (dark blue-black), 'Bride's Halo' (white edged with gold band), 'Christmas Rubies' (white with red beard), 'Gold Galore' (deep golden yellow with golden beard), 'Mulled Wine' (deep burgundy with red beard), and 'Ragtime' (yellow and violet-blue with yellow beard).

Cultivation
Plant the rhizomes from early to late summer (early fall in the South) in beds prepared with composted manure, compost, bonemeal, and a little lime. Arrange the rhizomes so they all face the same way — leaf-shoot end away from the sun. Plant so that the top of the rhizome is just visible above ground. Make sure the soil doesn't dry out for the first 2-3 weeks after planting. Keep the weeds down and peel off any dead leaves. In winter cut back foliage to discourage slugs. In early spring apply a dressing of general fertilizer. Deadhead during the flowering season.
Propagation Every 3 years after flowering, divide the rhizomes by cutting off pieces from the outer part of the clump and discarding the center. Make sure each piece has one or two strong foliage fans; replant immediately
Pests/diseases See Iris (bulbous).

❏ Height ½-1½ ft (15-45 cm)
❏ Planting distance 9-24 in (23-60 cm)
❏ Flowers late spring to early summer
❏ Neutral or acid soil
❏ Sun or partial shade
❏ Rhizomes available fall
❏ Hardy zones 7-9

The plants in this rhizomatous group of Western natives have no beards. Their evergreen foliage is narrow, tough, and dark green. All are moderately hardy, and all flower in late spring to early summer and make good cut flowers. Invaluable for the West Coast garden, they are less reliable on the East Coast and generally poorly adapted to the central regions of the country. They do best in neutral to acid soils and so may be grown with rhododendrons.

Popular species and cultivars
Iris douglasiana has flowers of blue-purple or lavender with veining on the falls. Each stem carries four or five blooms, 1-1½ ft (30-45 cm) above ground. Plant the rhizomes 2 ft (60 cm) apart. This species tolerates alkalinity.
Iris innominata has cream, buff, yellow, or orange flowers with rich brown veins; others are pink and blue-purple. Each 6 in (15 cm) stem bears one or two flowers, and grasslike evergreen leaves. In humus-rich soil, it forms small

Iris innominata

clumps. Plant 9 in (23 cm) apart.
Iris tenax bears lovely blooms shading from cream and white to lavender and orchid on ½-1 ft (15-30 cm) stems. It is the most easily cultivated Pacific Coast species.
Hybrids, resembling *I. douglasiana* and *I. innominata,* are 9-18 in (23-45 cm) high. This free-flowering plant bears blooms that shade from white to yellow and orange to pale blue and purple. Plant 1 ft (30 cm) apart.

Cultivation
Plant the rhizomes in late fall in sun or partial shade. *I. douglasiana* tolerates alkaline soil; *I. innominata* and the hybrids require neutral or acid soil.
Propagation In early fall, when new roots start to grow, divide and replant rhizomes. Water well; do not let the soil dry out.
Pests/diseases See Iris (bulbous).

Iris *(beardless laevigata)*
bog iris

Iris pseudacorus

❏ Height 1½-5 ft (45-150 cm)
❏ Planting distance 9-36 in (23-90 cm)
❏ Flowers late spring to summer
❏ Humus-rich soil at water's edge
❏ Full sun
❏ Rhizomes available fall
❏ Hardy zones 4-9

Bog irises are often seen growing around the edges of ponds and in ornamental bog gardens. They form another section in the group of beardless rhizomatous irises. All prefer moist growing conditions and should be planted in full sun.

Popular species and cultivars
Iris laevigata has three blooms per stem — deep royal blue flowers with white streaks on the falls. The deciduous leaves are pale green. This iris flowers in

Iris kaempferi

early summer and is a true water plant, growing best in water up to 6 in (15 cm) deep. Each plant reaches 1½-2 ft (45-60 cm) high and they should be set 9-18 in (23-45 cm) apart.
Iris kaempferi (bog iris) may have white, blue, or purple flowers with yellow streaks on the falls. The flowers appear in early summer and midsummer — three to four single or double, flat or peony-shaped blooms on each stem. The plants stand 2-3 ft (60-90 cm) high; set the rhizomes 1-1½ ft (30-45 cm) apart in moist soil. This species and its cultivars will not tolerate alkaline soil.
Iris pseudacorus (yellow flag, or flag iris) has five or more yellow flowers — sometimes pale orange with brown veins — and attractive yellow and green leaves. The flowers appear in late spring and early summer. This is another true water iris, thriving in water 1½ ft (45 cm) deep, where it can reach 3-5 ft (90-150 cm) high.

Cultivation
Plant the rhizomes from midsummer to early fall in full sun beside streams and in ponds.
Propagation Divide the rhizomes after flowering every 3 years, and replant at once.
Pests/diseases See Iris (bulbous).

Iris *(beardless sibirica)*
iris

Iris sibirica hybrid

❏ Height 24-44 in (60-110 cm)
❏ Planting distance 1½-2 ft (45-60 cm)
❏ Flowers early summer
❏ Good, moisture-retentive soil
❏ Sun or partial shade
❏ Rhizomes available late spring to early summer
❏ Hardy zones 3-9

The species and hybrids in this section of the rhizomatous beardless iris group are hardy and easy to cultivate, provided the soil is moisture retentive. Grow them in herbaceous borders for garden decoration and cutting, or along the edges of garden ponds. A sunny site is preferable, but these summer-flowering irises will tolerate very light shade as well.

Popular species and cultivars
Iris sibirica flowers in shades of blue with white veins on the falls. It is 24-44 in (60-110 cm) high, with a well-branched stem. Plant the rhizomes 2 ft (60 cm) apart.
Hybrids come in shades of blue or white and have larger flowers. The plants reach 3 ft (90 cm) high and have a less branching habit. Set the rhizomes 1½-2 ft (45-60 cm) apart.

Cultivation
Plant from midsummer to fall or in midspring in good, moist soil in a sunny or slightly shaded site. Set 1 in (2.5 cm) deep in groups. Near water, make sure the rhizomes are at least 6 in (15 cm) above water level. Avoid hoeing or cultivating around plants.
Propagation Divide large clumps every 5 years. Replant 1 in (2.5 cm) deep, after flowering, in fall, or in spring when growth restarts.
Pests/diseases See Iris (bulbous).

Iris (miscellaneous beardless)
iris

Iris unguicularis

Iris foetidissima

❏ Height 9-30 in (23-75 cm)
❏ Planting distance 1-1½ ft (30-45 cm)
❏ Flowers early summer or midfall to midspring
❏ Moist, humus-rich or well-drained soil
❏ Shady or sunny site
❏ Rhizomes available spring
❏ Hardy zones 5-9

Some other beardless rhizomatous irises have a distinctive character, which makes them well worth considering.

Popular species and cultivars
Iris foetidissima (stinking iris, or gladwin) is renowned for its seedpods, which split open and peel back to reveal striking scarlet seeds in fall. These are far more attractive than the insignificant pale purple flowers that appear in early summer. The plants stand 2½ ft (75 cm) high and give off a rank smell when bruised. Several forms are available: *I. foetidissima lutea* has yellow flowers with brown veining and orange-red seeds, and 'Variegata' has attractive variegated leaves.
Iris unguicularis (syn. *I. stylosa*), sometimes called the Algerian iris, may bloom in November and flower through the winter in zone 9; elsewhere it blooms in early spring. The flowers are soft lavender or lilac, marked by a yel-low blaze on the falls. The plants are 9 in (23 cm) high with dark green evergreen foliage.

Cultivation
Plant *I. foetidissima* rhizomes in late summer to early fall in a moist, humus-rich soil. Set the rhizomes 1-1½ ft (30-45 cm) apart in clumps and 1½ in (3 cm) deep. This species likes partial shade.

Plant *I. unguicularis* rhizomes in late summer to early fall, too, setting the plants 15 in (38 cm) apart and 1 in (2.5 cm) deep, in small clumps. The site must be sunny with well-drained, even poor, soil. This species is not winter hardy north of zone 7.
Propagation Divide and replant rhizomes in early fall and midfall.
Pests/diseases See Iris (bulbous).

Iris (bulbous)
iris

Iris danfordiae

❏ Height 4-27 in (10-67 cm)
❏ Planting distance 2-8 in (5-20 cm)
❏ Flowers early winter to late spring or early summer to midsummer
❏ Well-drained soil
❏ Sheltered, sunny site
❏ Bulbs available early fall to midfall
❏ Hardiness varies with species; generally reliable zones 5-9

The irises in this group all grow from bulbs, unlike bearded and beardless irises, which are rhizomatous. The species bulbous irises, which flower in winter and spring, are the smallest and ideal for pockets of soil in a rock garden, the front of a border, or bare ground under deciduous shrubs. The hybrids, which appear in early summer and midsummer, make good cut flowers, as they are taller and have larger flowers. Most bulbous irises prefer light, well-drained soil (ideally alkaline) and a sheltered, sunny site.

Popular species and cultivars
Iris bucharica has up to seven sweetly scented cream and yellow flowers on 1½ ft (45 cm) high stems. These appear in mid- and late spring. This iris grows best in light, well-drained soil containing humus and some lime. An ideal site is below deciduous shrubs or trees, which will shelter the plants and keep them dry in summer. Plant the bulbs 6 in (15 cm) apart in early fall.
Iris danfordiae has vivid lemon-yellow flowers, which appear in mid- and late winter in the southern part of its range and in early spring in the North. The plants stand only 4 in (10 cm) high, and the flowers have an attractive

Spanish hybrid

Dutch hybrid

Iris histrioides 'Major'

honeylike scent. Hardly any leaves are evident at flowering time. Plant the bulbs 2-4 in (5-10 cm) apart in light, well-drained chalky soil and full sun.

Iris histrioides 'Major' has bright royal blue flowers, each with a yellow central ridge on the falls. It is one of the earliest bulbous irises to appear, flowering in early winter to midwinter in the South and early spring in the North. The plant is extremely hardy, with blooms that can remain unscathed through frosts and snow. At flowering time the leaves are only 1 in (2.5 cm) high, but by spring they may have reached 1½ ft (45 cm). As the flower stems are just 5 in (13 cm) high, they look most effective grown as a mass in a rock garden. This is a

useful species for the garden, since it is one of the few small bulbous irises to tolerate dappled shade. Set the bulbs 2-4 in (5-10 cm) apart in light, well-drained alkaline soil.

Iris reticulata has deep violet-blue flowers with a gold spot in the center of each fall. The flowers appear in late winter and early spring (depending on the climate) and are accompanied by taller leaves. This species and its cultivars are 6 in (15 cm) high and should be planted 2-4 in (5-10 cm) apart. 'Joyce' (sky-blue), 'Katharine Hodgkin' (large, pale blue and yellow), 'Natascha' (white and blue, yellow markings), and 'Pauline' (violet, white and blue variegated blotches) are popular cultivars.

Iris xiphium, a tender Mediterranean plant, is the main species from which three types of hybrids have been developed.

Dutch hybrids flower in late spring. Their colors range from white, yellow, and blue to purple. The plants reach 15-24 in (38-60 cm) high. Set the bulbs 4-6 in (10-15 cm) apart in light, fertile soil in a sunny site.

English hybrids are the last of the bulbous irises to flower, coming out in early summer. They have the largest flowers, but the smallest color range: whites, blues, pinks, and purples that are often flecked. The plants reach 15-27 in (38-67 cm) high and should be set 6-8 in (15-20 cm) apart in rich soil.

Spanish hybrids flower between the Dutch hybrids and English hybrids in late spring to early summer. The fragrant blossoms come in a good color range, including smoky shades: whites, browns, blues, purples, and mauves. The plants stand 1-1½ ft (30-45 cm) high. Set the bulbs 6-8 in (15-20 cm) apart in light soil in a sunny spot.

Cultivation
Plant the species and hybrid bulbs in early fall and midfall. Set species bulbs 2-3 in (5-7.5 cm) deep and set hybrids 4-6 in (10-15 cm) deep. The soil should be well drained; enrich with compost at planting time. In the northern part of their range, these irises will benefit from a winter mulch of leaves or straw.

Propagation After the foliage dies down in summer, lift, divide, and store the bulbs until planting time in fall. The large bulbs will flower the following year; small offsets may take 2 years.

Pests/diseases Aphids and stem and bulb nematodes may attack stored bulbs. Slugs and snails may eat foliage. Iris borers attack leaves of bearded and *kaempferi* irises in spring, tunnelling down to eat roots. Rust may occur on rhizomatous irises. Blue mold may cause the bulbs of Spanish, English, and Dutch hybrids to rot; iris mosaic virus may cause yellow striping or mottling of the leaves and a decline in vigor.

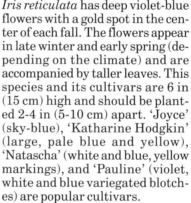

Ixia
African corn lily

Ixia hybrid

❑ Height 1-1½ ft (30-45 cm)
❑ Planting distance 4 in (10 cm)
❑ Flowers spring to midsummer
❑ Full sun
❑ Well-drained soil
❑ Corms available fall
❑ Hardy zones 7-9

The species in this South African genus grow outdoors only in the mild parts of North America. Hybrids can be planted in midfall in warmer areas and in spring in the cooler part of their range for flowering from spring to midsummer. Their starry flowers gather in dense clusters on wiry stems, 1-1½ ft (30-45 cm) high. Blooms come in orange, yellow, pink, red, purple, and white — and are usually sold mixed. The flowers open only in bright sunlight, so a sunny site is best, though where the weather is truly hot the plants like light shade. Water well during the growing season, but stop as the corms become dormant.

Cultivation
Plant the corms in fall or spring, depending on the local climate. Set them 4 in (10 cm) apart and 3 in (7.5 cm) deep in well-drained sandy soil in full sun.
Propagation Plants naturalize in the Southwest. Elsewhere, buy fresh corms as necessary.
Pests/diseases Trouble free.

KAFFIR LILY — see *Schizostylis*

Leucojum
snowflake

Leucojum aestivum 'Gravetye Giant'

❑ Height 8-18 in (20-45 cm)
❑ Planting distance 3-4 in (7.5-10 cm)
❑ Flowers winter to spring
❑ Moisture-retentive, fertile soil
❑ Full sun or partial shade
❑ Bulbs available late summer, fall
❑ Hardy zones 4-8

The delicate white bell-shaped flowers of snowflakes are similar to those of snowdrops, except that they are more rounded and are carried on taller stems. The foliage is daffodillike: long, narrow, and green. Two species are hardy and grow outdoors throughout most of the United States. They thrive in full sun or partial shade.

Popular species and cultivars
Leucojum aestivum, commonly known as the summer snowflake, has nodding white, green-tipped bell-shaped flowers that appear in clusters at the top of 1½ ft (45 cm) high stems. They bloom in late spring among clumps of spiky fresh green leaves. Summer snowflakes thrive in moist conditions — the ground around a garden pond is a good site for them. 'Gravetye Giant' is a large, robust form suitable for a shady site.
Leucojum vernum has similar flowers to *L. aestivum*, but they appear in late winter or early spring, depending on the local climate. These 8 in (20 cm) high plants naturalize well in damp grassy places; they're also useful for brightening a rock garden when little else is in flower. Bear in mind that they tolerate partial shade as well as full sun.

Cultivation
Plant the bulbs as soon as they are available in late summer or early fall. Set 3-4 in (7.5-10 cm) deep in moisture-retentive, humus-rich soil. Leave undisturbed for several years.
Propagation When the groups become overcrowded, producing too many leaves and too few flowers, lift and divide as the leaves die down. Replant at once, giving the offsets the same spacing and depth as you would new bulbs.
Pests/diseases Trouble free.

Lilium
lily

Lilium auratum

❏ Height 1½-7 ft (45-210 cm)
❏ Planting distance 4-12 in (10-30 cm)
❏ Flowers early summer to early fall
❏ Well-drained, humus-rich soil
❏ Heads in sun, roots in partial shade
❏ Bulbs available early to late fall and late winter to spring
❏ Hardy zones 4-8

Some lilies thrive in acid soil and some in alkaline soil; some like sun and some like partial shade. This means that nearly every garden, provided the soil is well drained and fertile (and the climate neither too hot nor excessively cold), can grow a clump of these striking plants. Their stately habit, elegant flowers in every color except blue, and lush green foliage covering most of the stem combine to form a magnificent sight in summer. Plant lilies so they'll be seen — massed together in a mixed border, among shrubs, or in tubs on a patio. The lily genus has many species and hybrids. Those listed here are readily available and suitable for growing outdoors.

Popular species and cultivars
Lilium amabile has nodding Turk's cap flowers (recurved or rolled-back petals), which are bright red spotted with black. These appear in early summer to midsummer on 3 ft (90 cm) high stems. This is a particularly hardy species, thriving in light shade, and it will tolerate alkaline soils as long as they are well drained. Plant the bulbs 5 in (13 cm) deep.
Lilium auratum, also known as the golden-rayed lily, has large, fragrant bowl-shaped flowers. These appear in late summer and early fall — a brilliant waxy white

Lilium candidum

with golden yellow rays and crimson-purple spots inside. The plant stands 5-6 ft (1.5-1.8 m) high. Although easy to grow, it is a short-lived species requiring neutral to acid soil. A sunny, sheltered spot where the lower part of the stem is kept in shade is best. Plant 4-5 in (10-13 cm) deep. It is excellent grown in pots.
Lilium bulbiferum croceum (orange lily) has trumpet-shaped flowers of tangerine spotted with purple. The blooms appear in early summer and midsummer. The plants are 3 ft (90 cm) high and should be set 6-8 in (15-20 cm) apart. They are vigorous but need replanting every 5-6 years in ordinary soil in a sunny or shaded site. Alkaline soil is tolerated.
Lilium candidum (Madonna lily) has pure white trumpet-shaped flowers with yellow pollen. These appear in early summer and are renowned for their fragrance. The plants reach 4-5 ft (1.2-1.5 m) high. Plant the base-rooting bulbs 9 in (23 cm) apart and 2 in (5 cm)

deep, preferably during warm, damp weather in midfall to late fall. They need a warm, sunny site and will tolerate an alkaline soil. Although hardy, Madonna lily can be difficult to establish and dislikes disturbance. So plant it in a bed where it can be left alone.
Lilium davidii bears profuse orange-red Turk's cap flowers in mid- to late summer. The petals are covered with black spots, and the pollen is red. This lily reaches 4-6 ft (1.2-1.8 m) high. Plant the bulbs 9 in (23 cm) apart in ordinary soil in sun or light shade. Although short-lived, the species is easily raised from seed.
Lilium hansonii has pale orange-yellow Turk's cap flowers with brown spots and a waxy sheen. They come in late spring and early summer, crowded together at the top of 3 ft (90 cm) high stems, and have a pleasant fragrance. Plant the bulbs 10 in (25 cm) apart in lime-free soil enriched with leaf mold, in light shade.
Lilium henryi has large apricot-

Lilium martagon

Lilium regale

Lilium speciosum

yellow and recurved Turk's cap flowers in mid-to late summer. It is a tall species, reaching 7 ft (210 cm) high and usually needs staking. Plant the bulbs 1 ft (30 cm) apart in a lightly shaded site in any ordinary soil; alkaline soil is tolerated.

Lilium lancifolium (tiger lily) has strongly recurved Turk's cap flowers, which are orange-red spotted purple-black. These are carried on 3-6 ft (90-180 cm) high stems in mid-to late summer. Plant the bulbs 9 in (23 cm) apart in neutral to acid soil in full sun.

Lilium martagon (Martagon or Turk's cap lily) has nodding rose-purple Turk's cap flowers, which open in late spring and early summer. Despite the unpleasant smell of the flowers, it is a particularly popular and easy-to-grow species. The 4 ft (120 cm) high plants grow well in the semishade of a shrub border. They tolerate alkaline soils and are slow growing. Set the bulbs 9 in (23 cm) apart.

Lilium pumilum (syn. *L. tenuifolium)* has small nodding red Turk's cap flowers, which come in late spring to early summer. It is one of the smaller lilies, only 1½-2 ft (45-60 cm) high. Plant the bulbs 4-6 in (10-15 cm) apart in ordinary garden soil in a sunny spot.

Lilium pyrenaicum has tightly recurved Turk's cap flowers in loose clusters in late spring or early summer. They are bright green-yellow with purple-black spots, orange-red pollen, and an unpleasant scent. This lily is only 2-3 ft (60-90 cm) high. Plant the bulbs 9 in (23 cm) apart in a sunny site; it tolerates alkaline soil.

Lilium regale has fragrant white funnel-shaped flowers carried in loose clusters in midsummer. The centers of the flowers are yellow, and the backs of the petals are shaded rose-purple. These popular lilies stand 4-6 ft (120-180 cm) high. Planted 1 ft (30 cm) apart in ordinary soil and full sun, the bulbs will increase quickly. There is also a pure white form, 'Album.'

Lilium speciosum has fragrant bowl-shaped white flowers heavily shaded crimson. These appear in late summer and early fall on 4-5 ft (120-150 cm) high stems. Plant the bulbs 1 ft (30 cm) apart in neutral to acid soil.

Hybrids of many types have been developed from the species, offering more robust plants in a wider range of colors. The hybrids are organized into groups according to flower shape.

Asiatic hybrids have upright flowers, carried singly or in clusters, which appear in early summer and midsummer. These hardy plants are suitable for growing in any ordinary well-drained soil in sun or partial shade. The plants reach 3-5 ft (90-150 cm) high, and the bulbs should be set 6-9 in (15-23 cm) apart. Popular hybrids are 'Chinook' (salmon), 'Connecticut King' (golden yellow), 'Electric' (orange-rose with white bands), 'Enchantment' (warm orange-red), 'Red Lion' (red tipped with white), 'Rose Fire' (red-tipped petals, golden center, orange-red

Asiatic 'Chinook'

Asiatic 'Red Lion'

throat), 'Sterling Star' (white), 'Syndicate' (peach, yellow throat), and 'Uncle Sam' (yellow spotted with brown).

Martagon hybrids have small pendent Turk's cap flowers in early and late summer. They reach 4-6 ft (1.2-1.8 m) high, and the bulbs should be set 9-12 in (23-30 cm) apart. These hybrids are easy to grow in light shade and well-drained soil — they tolerate alkaline soils. Popular hybrids are 'Backhouse Hybrids' (cream, buff, yellow, or pink), 'Marhan' (orange), and 'Paisley Hybrids' (white, yellow, orange, lilac, tangerine, or mahogany).

Candidum hybrids have long, pendent trumpet-shaped flowers carried singly along the 4-6 ft (1.2-1.8 m) high stems. The blooms appear in early summer and midsummer and have an attractive scent. Plant the bulbs 9 in (23 cm) apart in rich soil in full sun. The most popular hybrid is *L. × testaceum* (apricot), also called the Nankeen lily.

American and Bellingham hybrids have brightly colored Turk's cap flowers in midsummer. These tall hybrids, reaching 5-6 ft

Asiatic 'Uncle Sam'

(1.5-1.8 m) high, give the best results in light shade in well-drained, lime-free soil enriched with leaf mold. Plant the bulbs 9 in (23 cm) apart. These lilies make excellent long-lasting cut flowers. A popular hybrid is 'Shuksan' (orange).

Trumpet and Aurelian hybrids have large, fragrant trumpet-shaped flowers in a wide range of colors on 4-7 ft (1.2-2.1 m) high stems. They're vigorous plants, flowering in mid- and late summer. All the hybrids in this group tolerate alkaline soils, but their site requirements differ

slightly: the white- and yellow-flowered cultivars grow in sun or partial shade, but the pink-flowered ones must have shade or their colors fade. Some popular hybrids include 'African Queen' (gold-orange), 'Black Dragon' (white and purple-brown), 'Golden Clarion' (yellow), 'Golden Splendor' (golden yellow; fragrant), 'Pink Perfection' (pink), and 'Sunburst' (yellow).

Oriental hybrids have large flowers strikingly colored in crimsons and pinks. The flowers appear in mid- and late summer on 3-7 ft (90-210 cm) high stems. Plant the large bulbs 1 ft (30 cm) apart and 4-6 in (10-15 cm) deep in well-drained acid soil enriched with leaf mold. A site in dappled shade is best. Popular hybrids include the 'Elegance' strain (white, pink, gold, crimson, or silver), 'Jamboree' (crimson with silver edges), 'Imperial Silver' (white and maroon), 'Kyoto' (pure white, spotted pink), and 'Treasure' (rose-pink, edged with white).

Asiatic 'Enchantment'

Oriental 'Casa Blanca'

Cultivation

Plant lily bulbs in fall or spring; as nurseries generally harvest bulbs in late summer, fall planting is less stressful for the bulbs. Put them in the ground immediately after purchase to reduce the chance they will dry out. If the bulbs are slightly shriveled, place them in a tray of moist potting soil for a week before planting.

All lilies require well-drained soil. With heavy soils this can be achieved by digging in leaf mold and sharp sand. Poor sandy soils may need enriching with humus to make them moisture retentive. Some lilies tolerate alkaline soils, but typically a neutral to slightly acid soil is best. If you want to grow lilies that don't suit the soil in the garden, grow them in containers on the patio.

Lilies prefer their heads in the sun and roots in partial shade. They grow best with plenty of light and space around them, though they must be sheltered from strong winds.

For the best effect, plant in groups of at least three. Cover

Asiatic 'Connecticut King'

species bulbs and hybrids with small bulbs with 2½-3½ in (6-8 cm) of soil, and large-bulbed hybrids with 4-8 in (10-20 cm) of soil. *Lilium candidum* is an exception, requiring the bulb tips to be only just below soil level. Mulch all lilies after planting, and renew mulch annually in spring.

During the growing season, water often. Every spring, mulch with compost or leaf mold. Stake species that are tall, are heavily flowered, or have arching stems.

To grow lilies in containers,

Trumpet and Aurelian 'Pink Perfection'

plant in pots 10 in (25 cm) deep and 8 in (20 cm) wide, putting one bulb in each pot. Alternatively, use pots 1 ft (30 cm) deep and 1 ft (30 cm) wide, and plant three bulbs in each. Place gravel over the drainage holes and add a layer of leaf mold. Fill the container halfway up with a well-drained, organic-enriched potting soil; position the bulbs; and cover with another 2 in (5 cm) of compost. Water well. Keep in a cool but protected frost-free place, or plunge the pot in an outdoor bed for the

Muscari
grape hyacinth

Trumpet and Aurelian 'Sunburst'

winter. When the lilies start to grow in spring, water them to keep the potting soil moist. Place in their flowering site when the weather improves. Stake, if needed, and feed monthly with a balanced fertilizer. Deadhead spent blooms and, when the leaves and stems die back in fall, cut them down and return the pots to a frost-free place. Repot them every 2 years in mid- or late fall. In the years you don't repot, give a topdressing of compost in early spring. Only grow cultivars that are under 3-4 ft (90-120 cm) high in containers.

Propagation Division is the easiest way to increase stock. Separate and replant overcrowded clumps every 3-4 years between midfall and early spring, as weather and climate permit.

Species lilies can also be increased from seed or leaf bulblets sown in early fall and left to germinate in a cold frame or other protected spot. Grow the seedlings on in an outdoor nursery bed; they will flower in 1-3 years.

Pests/diseases Mice may feed on bulbs. Slugs may damage the plants themselves. Aphids can transmit viral diseases, such as the mosaic virus that streaks leaves with yellow. Botrytis can be a problem in humid weather.

LILY OF THE VALLEY —
see *Convallaria*
MONTEBRETIA —
see *Crocosmia*

Muscari armeniacum

❑ Height 6-16 in (15-40 cm)
❑ Planting distance 3-4 in (7.5-10 cm)
❑ Flowers early spring to early summer
❑ Well-drained soil
❑ Full sun
❑ Bulbs available fall
❑ Hardy zones 3-8

The individual flower spikes of grape hyacinths may seem a little insignificant, but *en masse* these plants are always useful for introducing splashes of blue to rock gardens, window boxes, border edges, and woodland corners in spring. They also make good long-lasting cut flowers. All the species look fairly similar, with just slight variations in height, flower color, and flowering time. They are easy to grow and colonize readily.

Popular species and cultivars
Muscari armeniacum has scented cobalt-blue flowers rimmed white, appearing in early spring and midspring. The plant rises 8-10 in (20-25 cm) high. It is a popular species to grow as it increases rapidly.
Muscari aucheri (syn. *M. tubergenianum*) has dark blue and pale blue flowers on the same spike. The blooms appear in early spring, 8 in (20 cm) above ground.
Muscari botryoides 'Album' has scented white flowers appearing from mid- to late spring. It stands 6-10 in (15-25 cm) high.
Muscari comosum has olive-green and purple flowers on the same spike. It flowers later than other *Muscari*, appearing in late spring to early summer, and it is also taller, standing 16 in (40 cm) high. A pretty violet-blue form, 'Plumosum,' popularly called the feather or tassel hyacinth because of its feathery appearance, can also be obtained.

Cultivation
Plant the bulbs in fall, setting them 3 in (7.5 cm) deep and 3-4 in (7.5-10 cm) apart in groups. They grow in any ordinary well-drained soil, but should be planted in full sun — in shade *Muscari* produce excessive leaf growth and fewer flowers.

Propagation Every 3-4 years, divide overcrowded clumps. Lift and divide the clumps when the leaves start to turn yellow; replant the divisions immediately.

Pests/diseases The flowers can be affected by smut fungus.

Narcissus

daffodil, narcissus

❑ Height 2-18 in (5-45 cm)
❑ Planting distance 2-8 in (5-20 cm)
❑ Flowers late winter to early summer
❑ Well-drained, moist, humus-rich soil
❑ Full sun or partial shade
❑ Bulbs available late summer to late fall
❑ Hardy zones 4-10

It's not surprising that narcissi are popular with gardeners: they're inexpensive, easy to grow, spread with little encouragement once in the ground, and offer an eye-catching display throughout spring. The first flowers open as early as late winter in the South, the last in early summer. Depending on the region, with a selection of different cultivars, a colorful display is possible for almost 5 months.

All but the very short stemmed cultivars do well in rough grass or a meadow, where they can be left undisturbed to colonize over the years. The large cultivars grow well in groups in shrub and flower borders, while the flowers of the dwarf cultivars look enchanting in a rock garden or window box. All make excellent cut flowers.

Narcissi thrive in acid and neutral soils, but they will tolerate an alkaline soil. Ideally the soil should be well drained but moist, with plenty of humus in it.

Popular species and cultivars
The botanical name for all mem-

Trumpet 'Mount Hood'

bers of the genus is narcissus; those in the trumpet group are commonly called daffodils. The many narcissus hybrids developed from the species are divided in groups according to the size of the cup or trumpet (corolla) and outer petals, and the species from which they have been developed. There are 11 divisions.

Trumpet daffodils (division 1) have cups that are as long as or longer than the petals. The 8-18 in (20-45 cm) high stem carries only one flower, which appears in late winter or early spring. Daffodils look particularly effective planted in clusters in long grass beneath trees. A vast number of cultivars have been developed, offering sev-

Trumpet 'Trousseau'

Large-cupped 'Romance'

eral color combinations: 'Golden Harvest' and 'King Alfred' (yellow), 'Mount Hood' (white), 'Spellbinder' (greenish-yellow petals, white trumpet), and 'Trousseau' (white and yellow).

Large-cupped narcissi (division 2) have cup-shaped corollas a little more than one-third the length of the petals. Only one flower is held on each 13-18 in (32-45 cm) high stem. The flowers appear between mid- and late spring, depending on the cultivar, in a range of colors. These narcissi are good for naturalizing in grass. Popular cultivars include 'Carlton' and 'St. Keverne' (yellow), 'Romance' (white petals), 'Ice Follies' (pure white), and 'Peaches and Cream' (silvery petals, apricot-pink cup).

Small-cupped narcissi (division 3) have small cups — less than one-third the length of the petals. One flower is held on each 14-18 in (35-45 cm) high stem. The flowers appear in early spring to midspring in several color variations. They are suitable for growing in borders

Large-cupped 'Duke of Windsor'

159

Large-cupped 'Carlton'

Small-cupped 'Barrett Browning'

or for naturalizing in grass. Popular cultivars are 'Barrett Browning' (pure white petals, orange-red cup) and 'Birma' (yellow petals, deep orange cup).

Double-flowered narcissi (division 4) have double flowers. These are scented and stand 1-1½ ft (30-45 cm) above ground in early spring and midspring. Plant in borders. Cultivars are 'Cheerfulness' (cream-white), 'Flower Drift' (white petals, orange-yellow cup), and 'Texas' (yellow).

Triandrus narcissi (division 5) have pendent flowers with funnel-shaped cups and backswept petals. The 6-15 in (15-38 cm) high stems

each carry two or three flowers in midspring. Plant in a sunny spot at the front of a border. Popular cultivars include 'Liberty Bells' (yellow), 'Thalia' (pure white), and 'Tresamble' (white).

Cyclamineus narcissi (division 6) have pendent flowers with long, narrow, frilled trumpet-shaped cups and backswept petals. They stand 6-15 in (15-38 cm) high and appear in late winter or early spring. Grow in fine grass or with dwarf plants in a rock garden. Cultivars include 'Charity May' (soft yellow), 'Peeping Tom,' and 'February Gold' (golden yellow).

Jonquilla narcissi (division 7) have several small sweetly scented flowers, sometimes with backswept petals, on stems 11-17 in (28-42 cm) high. These appear in mid- and late spring. They grow best in a sheltered, sunny spot. Popular cultivars include 'Suzy' (up to four flowers per stem; bright yellow petals, orange cup), the tall 'Trevithian' (two or three lemon-yellow flowers per stem), and 'Waterperry' (ivory-white petals, pink-orange cup).

Tazetta, or Poetaz, narcissi (division 8) have short cups and petals that are often frilled. In late spring, several sweetly scented flowers appear on each 1½ ft (45

cm) high stem. They grow outdoors only to zone 7; elsewhere they can be forced to flower indoors in winter. Cultivars are 'Cragford' (white petals, orange cup) and 'Paper White' (white).

Poeticus narcissi (division 9) have white petals with yellow or red frilly-edged cups. Only one scented flower is held on each 14-17 in (35-42 cm) high stem in late spring. These narcissi are best grown in borders and beds, but they can be naturalized in grass. Popular cultivars include 'Actaea' (white petals, red-rimmed yellow cup) and 'Old Pheasant Eye' (white petals, red cup).

Species narcissi (division 10) have flowers in a variety of shapes and sizes. Most are dwarf plants, suitable for growing in a rock garden or naturalizing in short grass. The most popular is *Narcissus bulbocodium,* also called 'Yellow Hoop Petticoat,' with a wide funnel-shaped cup and narrow insignificant petals. Its yellow flowers appear in late winter and early

Small-cupped 'Birma'

Double-flowered 'Flower Drift'

Double-flowered 'Texas'

Triandrus 'Tresamble'

Jonquilla 'Trevithian'

Narcissus cyclamineus

Tazetta 'Paper White'

Tazetta 'Cragford'

spring only 2-6 in (5-15 cm) above ground. Plant in short grass.

Narcissus pseudonarcissus, the Lent lily, is the true wild daffodil, native to Europe. The flowers, with near-white petals and long lemon-yellow trumpets, appear in midspring ½-1 ft (15-30 cm) above ground. It is best grown in moist soil. An all-white form and an all-yellow form are also available.

Split-cup, or Butterfly, narcissi (division 11) have central cups that are split and spread out against the surrounding petals. 'Tricollet' (orange-yellow cup against cream petals) is a fine example.

Cultivation
Narcissi thrive in rich, well-drained soil in full sun or partial shade — under trees or in the shade of a hedge or taller plants. Scatter a general fertilizer over the ground before planting. Plant as soon as the bulbs are available in late summer and early fall; in the South wait until the soil temperature drops below 70°F (21°C).

Aim for a natural look, setting narcissi in irregular groups rather than precise circles or rows. Scatter the bulbs on their planting site at random to determine their positions, but leave adequate space between them when planting. For most bulbs 4-8 in (10-20 cm) is sufficient; the shorter triandrus and cyclamineus cultivars and *N. bul-*

bocodium should be planted 2-3 in (5-7.5 cm) apart. A trowel works fine for planting a few bulbs, but when planting in bulk, a special bulb planter will help prevent blisters. Make sure the bottoms of the holes are flat, so that the bulbs rest on the soil. Make the holes three times the depth of the bulb, set them an inch or so deeper in borders that will be forked or hoed after the bulbs are planted.

After flowering, always let the leaves die down completely, or at least become yellow. This allows the foliage to feed the bulbs, ensuring flowering the following year. Tying leaves up in a knot, a common practice, is not a good idea. It reduces the leaf surface exposed to the sun and prevents the bulbs' food reserves from building up for next year.

Propagation Lift overcrowded clumps between midsummer and early fall, remove bulb offsets, and plant out in a nursery bed. They reach flowering size in 2-3 years.

Pests/diseases Root rot may decay the bulbs or stunt their growth. Yellow streaks in the leaves are a symptom of mosaic virus.

Poeticus 'Actaea'

Narcissus bulbocodium

Nerine
Guernsey lily

Nerine bowdenii

❑ Height 16-24 in (40-60 cm)
❑ Planting distance 4-6 in (10-15 cm)
❑ Flowers late summer to late fall
❑ Well-drained soil
❑ Sheltered, sunny site
❑ Bulbs available late spring to summer
❑ Hardy zones 8-10

From late summer to fall, when other plants are finishing their display, the beautiful *Nerine bowdenii* from South Africa produces large heads of up to eight flowers, which are long-lasting as cut flowers. Each has six elegant, narrow, backward-arching petals of bright glowing pink. The 16-24 in (40-60 cm) high stems rise from tufts of unexciting strap-shaped leaves. These start to fade in fall, so avoid planting nerines at the front of a border.

Nerine sarniensis (Guernsey lily) produces clusters of up to 10 crimson-pink or scarlet flowers.

Even in a mild climate such as that of southern California, these bulbs must be given full sun and shelter. A protected bed at the bottom of a south-facing wall or fence is ideal.

Cultivation
Plant in spring in any ordinary well-drained garden soil. Set the bulbs with their long necks just covered, 4-6 in (10-15 cm) apart. Do not disturb for 4-5 years. Water regularly through the plant's season of growth, then withhold moisture as it begins to fade to encourage dormancy.
Propagation Lift, divide, and replant overcrowded plants every 4-5 years.
Pests/diseases Trouble free.

ORNAMENTAL ONION —
see *Allium*

Ornithogalum
star-of-Bethlehem

Ornithogalum umbellatum

❑ Height ½-1 ft (15-30 cm)
❑ Planting distance 4 in (10 cm)
❑ Flowers mid- to late spring
❑ Fertile, well-drained soil
❑ Sun or partial shade
❑ Bulbs available fall
❑ Hardy zones 4-10

Ornithogalum umbellatum is hardy and free flowering. It is a small plant, up to 1 ft (30 cm) high, with glistening white star-shaped flowers, which produce a fine display in mid- and late spring. Its one disadvantage is that the flowers open flat only when the sun is out. Any fertile, well-drained soil is suitable, and the plant tolerates partial shade, although a sunny site is preferable. Narrow borders, sod, and rock gardens all make good sites.

Cultivation
Plant in midfall, setting the bulbs 2 in (5 cm) deep and 4 in (10 cm) apart in irregular groups. Deadhead regularly.
Propagation Left alone, star-of-Bethlehem self-seeds and colonizes readily. Crowded clumps can be lifted, divided, and replanted in late summer or fall.
Pests/diseases Trouble free.

Oxalis
wood sorrel

Oxalis

- ❏ Height 2-12 in (5-30 cm)
- ❏ Planting distance ½-1 ft (15-30 cm)
- ❏ Flowers spring, summer, or fall
- ❏ Well-drained, humus-rich soil
- ❏ Sun or light shade
- ❏ Bulbs available early fall and spring
- ❏ Hardy zones 5-9

Many members of the wood sorrel genus are invasive weeds, but a few of these hardy low-growing plants make graceful additions to a rock garden or serve as low edging for a border. All have neat clumps of handsome foliage comprised of several leaflets; the funnel-shaped flowers, with five petals, open wide in full sun.

Popular species and cultivars

Oxalis acetosella, often called Irish Shamrock, is a European native. In fact, it is not a true bulbous species but it spreads to 12 in (30 cm) from a creeping rhizome. It has neat tufts of pale green leaves and pearl-white flowers faintly veined with pink. It grows only 2 in (5 cm) high and is suited to a woodland setting where it will naturalize freely.

Oxalis adenophylla grows 3-4 in (7.5-10 cm) high from a bulbous rhizome and produces compact rosettes of crinkly gray foliage. The long-stemmed lilac-pink flowers are borne above the leaves from late spring to midsummer. It is hardy to zone 7.

Oxalis bowiei grows to a height of 1 ft (30 cm), bearing purple to rose flowers that are 1-1½ in (2.5-4 cm) across. Although not winter hardy north of zone 8, it may be grown as an annual in the North. *Oxalis deppei*, known as the good-luck plant, has foliage resembling a four-leaf clover. Growing to a height of 1 ft (30 cm), it bears red or purplish flowers ½-1 in (1.3-2.5 cm) wide from July through September. It is hardy to zone 8. 'Alba' is a white cultivar.

Oxalis pes-caprae is called the Bermuda buttercup because this South African wildflower has naturalized well on that island. Growing 1 ft (30 cm) high with three notched leaflets as foliage, it bears many yellow flowers in early spring. It is hardy to zone 9. *Oxalis violacea*, a 10 in (25 cm) tall wildflower hardy to zone 5, thrives in most of the eastern half of the United States, with small rose-purple blooms in late spring.

Cultivation

Naturalize *O. violacea* in rich woodland soils, setting bulbs 2 in (5 cm) deep in areas of partial shade. Plant summer-blooming types in early spring in sun or partial shade, then lift and store bulbs during fall. Plant spring bloomers in early fall. Most types die back after flowering — mark their sites to avoid damaging the rootstocks during cultivation.

Propagation Lift, divide, and replant bulbs and rhizomes in late summer, before the leaves die.

Pests/diseases Trouble free.

PACIFIC COAST FAWN LILY —
see *Erythronium*
PERUVIAN LILY —
see *Alstroemeria*
PINEAPPLE LILY —
see *Eucomis*
PLEATED LEAVES —
see *Curtonus*
POPPY ANEMONE —
see *Anemone*

Oxalis

Puschkinia
striped squill

Puschkinia scilloides

- ❏ Height 4-6 in (10-15 cm)
- ❏ Planting distance 2-3 in (5-7.5 cm)
- ❏ Flowers early to late spring
- ❏ Well-drained, humus-rich soil
- ❏ Sun or light shade
- ❏ Bulbs available fall
- ❏ Hardy zones 4-10

Puschkinia scilloides (syn. *P. libanotica*) is the only available member of this hardy genus from the mountains of eastern Turkey and Iran. It is a fine spring-flowering bulb, which deserves to be seen more often.

Its clusters of bell-shaped hyacinthlike flowers are an unusual pale icy blue with creamy centers and a dark blue stripe on the inside of each petal. Two leaves, midgreen and strap-shaped, appear at flowering time.

As the plants are only 4-6 in (10-15 cm) high, they look most effective at the front of a border, in a rock garden, or in an outdoor container.

Cultivation
Plant in fall in sandy but humus-rich soil in an open site in sun or light shade. Set the bulbs 2-3 in (5-7.5 cm) deep and 2-3 in (5-7.5 cm) apart. Do not water after leaves die back in early summer as the bulbs need a period of rest. Leave undisturbed for several years. Striped squill is useful for naturalizing in a lawn.

Propagation When the foliage dies down in summer, lift, divide, and replant overcrowded clumps.

Pests/diseases Slugs sometimes eat the stems and leaves. Disease is not usually a problem.

QUAMASH — see *Camassia*

Ranunculus
buttercup

Ranunculus asiaticus

- ❏ Height 12-15 in (30-38 cm)
- ❏ Planting distance 4-6 in (10-15 cm)
- ❏ Flowers early summer and midsummer
- ❏ Humus-rich, well-drained soil
- ❏ Sunny site
- ❏ Tubers available late winter to midspring
- ❏ Hardy zones 8-10; elsewhere grow in pots or as annuals

Most *Ranunculus* species are herbaceous annuals or aquatic plants, but the turban buttercup *R. asiaticus* is bulbous with tuberous roots. Where it is hardy, plant in fall for flowers the following summer; in colder regions plant the tubers in spring.

Each stem bears a semidouble or double peonylike flower in white, pink, apricot, orange, red, or yellow. The bulbs are usually sold mixed and provide color in borders. When cut, the flowers last a long time.

Cultivation
Plant the tubers with their claw-like roots pointing down, placing them 2 in (5 cm) deep and 4-6 in (10-15 cm) apart. Well-drained soil should be enriched with well-decayed material or garden compost, and the site should be in full sun, except in the Deep South, where light shade is preferable. To overwinter tubers in cold-weather regions, lift them when the foliage yellows in the fall and store them in dry sand in a frost-free place until spring.

Propagation Separate clusters of tubers in fall.

Pests/diseases Trouble free.

ST. BERNARD'S LILY — see *Anthericum*

Schizostylis
kaffir lily

Schizostylis coccinea 'Major'

- ❏ Height 2-3 ft (60-90 cm)
- ❏ Planting distance 6 in (15 cm)
- ❏ Flowers late summer or early fall
- ❏ Moist, fertile soil
- ❏ Sunny, sheltered site
- ❏ Rhizomes available spring
- ❏ Hardy zones 8-10

This splendid genus comes from South Africa. One species, *Schizostylis coccinea,* is garden hardy in the South and makes a fine subject for cultivation in a cool greenhouse or frost-free porch farther north. Kaffir lily's flower spikes stand above the erect swordlike leaves. They bear up to 10 bright scarlet flowers, which are crocus-shaped at first but open into stars in bright sun.

Kaffir lilies are valuable for flower borders, as they bloom from late summer to early fall, when most other herbaceous plants are coming to the end of their display. They also make excellent long-lasting cut flowers. Cultivars are 'Major' (deep pink), 'Mrs. Hegarty' (pale pink), and 'November Cheer' (shell-pink).

Cultivation
Plant in early spring in moist, fertile soil in a sheltered, sunny spot. Set the rhizomes 4 in (10 cm) deep and 6 in (15 cm) apart. Mulch every mid- or late spring with bark or compost to keep the soil moist and encourage new growth. In summer water well. In winter cut down untidy growth and in zone 8 protect the roots with a layer of straw or leaves.

Propagation Every 2-3 years, lift and divide the clumps into clusters of five or six shoots; replant in early spring to midspring.

Pests/diseases Botrytis may infect the leaves and buds.

Schizostylis coccinea

Scilla
bluebell, squill

Scilla nutans

- ❏ Height 4-18 in (10-45 cm)
- ❏ Planting distance 3-4 in (7.5-10 cm)
- ❏ Flowers early spring to early summer
- ❏ Moist but well-drained soil
- ❏ Sun or partial shade
- ❏ Bulbs available late summer to late fall
- ❏ Hardy zones 4-8

This genus includes the bluebells that form such magnificent blue carpets in woodlands from midspring to early summer. In the garden these colonize rapidly, so they are ideal for naturalizing beneath shrubs, in a wooded corner, or in grass that can be left uncut until after the leaves have died down in summer.

The other common species in this group (now reclassified into two genera, *Scilla* and *Hyacinthoides)* are smaller with similarly colored blue flowers. They are ideal for rock gardens and the fronts of borders. All scillas require moist but well-drained soil and therefore a site that is not too dry, in sun or partial shade.

Popular species and cultivars
Scilla campanulata (now *Hyacinthoides hispanica),* the Spanish bluebell, is a robust plant with large flowers and wide glossy green leaves. It stands 1-1½ ft (30-45 cm) high. Blue, pink, and white forms have been developed from this species, and it is hardy to zone 5.

Scilla mischtschenkoana has small, drooping cup-shaped flowers in pale blue or sometimes white.

167

Scilla campanulata

Scilla siberica 'Spring Beauty'

It bears these on 5 in (13 cm) stems in early spring. It is hardy to zone 5. *Scilla nutans* (now *Hyacinthoides non-scripta)*, the English bluebell, is hardy to zone 6. It is distinguished from the Spanish bluebell by its more delicate form, narrower leaves, and the curved tips of its flowering stems. It stands 10-12 in (25-30 cm) high. *Scilla siberica* appears in early spring, bearing nodding bell-shaped blooms of intense blue just 6 in (15 cm) above the ground. Each bulb produces several stems, so only a few bulbs are needed to make quite an impact in a rock garden or at the base of a shrub. A white form, 'Alba,' and an early-flowering sky-blue form, 'Spring Beauty,' are available. The hardiest species of scilla, *S. siberica,* overwinters reliably to zone 4.

Cultivation

Any moist but well-drained soil will suit scilla bulbs. Plant as soon as they are available in fall. Scatter the bulbs so they are approximately 3-4 in (7.5-10 cm) apart, and use a bulb planter or trowel. Bulbs vary in size and should be planted at a depth of three times their size.

Propagation Bluebells increase rapidly if left alone. Lift and divide established clumps in summer or fall and replant them immediately. The smaller scillas produce few offsets, but vigorous leaf growth indicates their presence. Lift and divide them as bluebells, or buy fresh stock.

Pests/diseases Tulip bulb aphids may infest foliage.

SNAKE'S-HEAD FRITILLARY— see *Fritillaria*
SNAKE'S-HEAD IRIS — see *Hermodactylus*
SNOWDROP — see *Galanthus*
SNOWFLAKE — see *Leucojum*

Sparaxis
harlequin flower

Sparaxis tricolor

❑ Height 1-1½ ft (30-45 cm)
❑ Planting distance 4 in (10 cm)
❑ Flowers late spring to early summer
❑ Rich, well-drained soil
❑ Sheltered, sunny site
❑ Corms available fall
❑ Hardy zones 9-10

The South African *Sparaxis tricolor* likes the climates of southern California and the Southwest. Because it requires dry soil when it is dormant, harlequin flower aids water conservation. Excellent for cutting, the flowers come in bright reds, purples, yellows, and white, and the corms are usually sold mixed.

Cultivation

Plant the corms 3-4 in (7.5-10 cm) deep and 4 in (10 cm) apart in fall in frost-free areas and in mid-spring where winters are too cold for corms to overwinter successfully. *Sparaxis* prefers rich, well-drained soil in a sheltered, sunny site. Mulch with shredded bark after planting, and weed the area.

North of zone 9, you can lift the corms for storing when the leaves die down in midsummer. However, corms frequently sprout before they can be replanted; buying fresh corms each year is easier.

Propagation Buy new corms.
Pests/diseases Trouble free.

SQUILL — see *Scilla*
STAR-OF-BETHLEHEM — see *Ornithogalum*

Sternbergia
winter daffodil

Sternbergia lutea

❏ Height 4-6 in (10-15 cm)
❏ Planting distance 4-6 in (10-15 cm)
❏ Flowers fall
❏ Well-drained soil
❏ Sunny, sheltered site
❏ Bulbs available summer
❏ Hardy zones 6-10

This genus of crocus look-alikes produces brilliant yellow goblet-shaped flowers in fall. In the wild these small plants grow in sunny rock crevices and scorched scrubland. In the garden they need a sheltered, sunny spot such as the foot of a south-facing wall.

Sternbergia lutea is the only widely available species grown outdoors. It has golden yellow flowers on short stems in early fall and midfall.

Cultivation
Plant the bulbs 4-6 in (10-15 cm) deep and 4-6 in (10-15 cm) apart in late summer or fall in any well-drained soil in full sun. Disturb only if they become overcrowded.
Propagation In late summer lift, remove any offsets, and replant separately at once.
Pests/diseases Slugs may eat flowers; mice may disturb bulbs.

STRIPED SQUILL —
see *Puschkinia*
SUMMER HYACINTH —
see *Galtonia*
SWORD LILY — see *Gladiolus*
TIGER FLOWER —
see *Tigridia*

Tigridia
tiger flower

Tigridia pavonia

❏ Height 16-18 in (40-45 cm)
❏ Planting distance 6 in (15 cm)
❏ Flowers midsummer to early fall
❏ Rich, well-drained soil
❏ Warm, sheltered site
❏ Corms available spring and fall
❏ Hardy zones 7-10

The flowers of *Tigridia pavonia*, a bulbous plant native to Central America, last only a few hours in the morning, but they look so exotic that it's worth finding a space for them in the garden.

They come out in succession from midsummer to early fall — brilliant yellows, crimsons, oranges, and whites, plain or speckled, usually sold as a mixture. Several butterflylike flowers are carried on a central flower stem 16-18 in (40-45 cm) high. They are accompanied by an elegant fan of upright pleated leaves.

Even in zone 7 the tiger flower must be placed in a sheltered, sunny spot if it is to overwinter successfully. In general, cultivate it as you would gladiolus. As their colors are so strong, tiger flowers are best when grown on their own in a small group.

Cultivation
Plant the corms in rich, well-drained soil in late spring, when the soil begins to warm up in the North, and also from fall into winter in the South. Set each corm 3-4 in (8-10 cm) deep and 6 in (15 cm) apart. During the growing season water the corms well and apply a liquid fertilizer every 2 weeks.

In the North, lift the corms in fall when the leaves are dying back, before the first severe frosts, and store them in dry sand or potting soil in a frost-free place. Keep the storage medium just moist enough to prevent the corms from shriveling. Replant in late spring. From zone 7 south, the corms can be left in the ground, where they will slowly multiply and flower in greater profusion.
Propagation Stock is best increased by planting new corms.
Pests/diseases Because they are relatives of the gladiolus, tiger flowers are subject to many of the same diseases, especially storage rot, mosaic virus, and stem and bulb nematodes.

Trillium
trillium

Tulipa
tulip

Trillium grandiflorum

Triumph 'Paul Richter'

- ❏ Height 3-32 in (7.5-80 cm)
- ❏ Planting distance 3-8 in (7.5-20 cm)
- ❏ Flowers early to late spring
- ❏ Any well-drained soil
- ❏ Sunny site
- ❏ Bulbs available fall
- ❏ Hardy zones 4-8

- ❏ Height 1-1½ ft (30-45 cm)
- ❏ Planting distance 6-8 in (15-20 cm)
- ❏ Flowers midspring to early summer
- ❏ Rich, moist, well-drained soil
- ❏ Partial shade
- ❏ Rhizomes available late summer and early fall
- ❏ Hardy zones 3-7

Trilliums like woodland conditions, so they should be given a shaded spot with humus-rich soil. Most are very hardy. All species have three broad midgreen leaves and blooms with three petals and three stamens. They flower in midspring to early summer. Plant in large clumps for best effect.

Popular species and cultivars
Trillium erectum has small wine-colored flowers, which face outward. The plants may reach up to 1 ft (30 cm) high. Set the rhizomes 8 in (20 cm) apart. A yellow form, 'Luteum,' also exists. *Trillium grandiflorum*, commonly known as wake-robin, is the most popular species. It has large outward-facing flowers, which are snow-white at first but gradually turn pale pink with age. The plants grow 16-18 in (40-45 cm) high, and the rhizomes should be set 8 in (20 cm) apart.

Trillium sessile has erect, narrow pointed flowers with a slight scent. Ranging from red and maroon to a greenish yellow, they are stemless and accompanied by marbled gray and deep green leaves. The plants stand 12-16 in (30-40 cm) high. Plant the rhizomes 6-8 in (15-20 cm) apart. Less hardy than the other species, *T. sessile* overwinters in zone 6 only in protected spots.

Cultivation
Plant the rhizomes as soon as they are available in late summer to early fall, or at any time during the winter in mild, dry weather. Trilliums must be planted in moist but well-drained soil with plenty of humus. Ideally the site should be in partial shade, though trilliums tolerate sun if the soil is always kept moist. The rhizomes of all species should be set 3-4 in (7.5-10 cm) deep.
Propagation Lift and divide the rhizomes after the foliage has died down in fall. Make sure each piece has a growing point. Only divide plants that are at least 5 years old. After division they may take a year or more to recover.
Pests/diseases Slugs attack young shoots and flower buds.

Almost every garden outside the subtropical South boasts at least a few tulips in springtime — a fact that's not surprising, given this bulb's availability, cheapness, and the huge choice of colors and forms. The popular large-flowered garden tulips are ideal for bedding displays — a classic combination being with forget-me-nots and wallflowers. For less formal plantings, however, grow them in scattered clumps among perennials or other bulbs.

The smaller species tulips come in fewer colors than the garden tulips, but their more delicate form gives them a charm of their own. Rock gardens or the front of beds, tubs, and containers are suitable places to grow them.

Tulips have specific growing requirements. During the growing season they need plenty of light, and in the summer the bulbs must be kept warm and dry so they can ripen. Garden tulips should be lifted and stored in a warm, dry place until the fall, when they can be planted out. Species tulips and their hybrids can be left in the ground if they are grown in very well drained soil.

Popular species and cultivars
The vast number of garden hy-

Single early 'Bellona'

Double early 'Electra'

brids are organized into 10 groups, according to flowering time, plant shape, flower size, and form. Most have lance-shaped leaves. Species and species hybrids make up four other groups. Most garden centers and some bulb catalogs sell the large-flowered garden tulips in packets of mixed colors according to group (a selection of Single early tulips, for example) or in packets of individual cultivars.

Single early tulips (division 1) have rounded petals forming small, deep cup-shaped single flowers, which sometimes open up flat in full sun. They are among the earliest garden tulips to flower, appearing in midspring. The plants reach 8-15 in (20-38 cm) high, and the stems are thick, so they stand up well to wind and rain. They are excellent for beds (plant the bulbs 4-6 in/10-15 cm apart), though some cultivars are also suitable for forcing indoors. Popular hybrids include 'Apricot Beauty' (apricot-pink), 'Bellona' (golden yellow), 'General de Wet' (golden orange), and 'Keizerskroon' (scarlet and yellow).

Double early tulips (division 2) have large double flowers resembling peonies — not to be confused with Peony-flowered tulips, which flower later (see *Double late tulips*). The long-lasting flowers appear in midspring, soon after the Single early tulips. They are carried on short, stout stems 10-12 in (25-30 cm) high, and are suitable for growing in mass bed-ding displays or containers. Ideally the site should be sheltered. Plant the bulbs 4-6 in (10-15 cm) apart. Popular cultivars include 'Electra' (cherry-red), 'Mr. Van der Hoeff' (golden yellow), 'Orange Nassau' (deep red), 'Peach Blossom' (rose-pink), and 'Schoonoord' (white).

Triumph tulips (division 3), sometimes called Midseason tulips in bulb catalogs, have large, angular single flowers in midspring. These are long-lasting and carried on sturdy stems 16-20 in (40-50 cm) high. They stand up well to wind and rain, and can be used for bedding in exposed sites. Plant the bulbs 6-8 in (15-20 cm) apart. Popular cultivars include 'Attila' (violet-purple), 'Dreaming Maid' (violet edged white), 'Garden Party' (white and carmine-pink), 'Kees Nelis' (pink and yellow), and 'New Design' (pink, white, and yellow).

Darwin hybrids (division 4) form one of the most popular groups with their large, round brilliantly colored flowers. They appear in late spring on strong stems 22-28 in (55-70 cm) high. Their bold flowers make them useful for focal planting. Set the bulbs 6-8 in (15-20 cm) apart. Popular hybrids include 'Apel-doorn' (orange-red), 'Big Chief' (old rose), 'Elizabeth Arden' (salmon-pink), 'Holland's Glory' (carmine-red), and 'Olympic Flame' (yellow and red).

Single late tulips (division 5) have squared-off oval or egg-shaped flowers in late spring (in catalogs they are sometimes called May-flowering tulips). The blooms are borne on stems 18-36 in (45-90 cm) high. These sturdy tulips are often planted in beds or border displays; place the bulbs 5-7 in (13-18 cm) apart. Popular cultivars include

Darwin 'Olympic Flame'

Fringed 'Fringed Beauty'

Single late 'Avignon' and 'Golden Harvest'

'Avignon' (red), 'Clara Butt' (soft pink), 'Golden Harvest' (lemon-yellow), 'Queen of Bartigon' (salmon-pink), 'Queen of the Night' (maroon-black), and 'Sorbet' (white and red). 'Georgette' (clear yellow, edged red) has several flowers on each stem.

Lily-flowered tulips (division 6), another group of favorites, have long single flowers with pointed petals, often curving out at the tips. These appear in mid-spring. The graceful plants have strong, wiry stems 20-24 in (50-60 cm) high. Set the bulbs 4-6 in (10-15 cm) apart in a sunny site. Among the popular cultivars are 'Aladdin' (crimson and yellow), 'China Pink' (soft pink), 'Red Shine' (deep red), 'West Point' (yellow), and 'White Triumphator' (white).

Fringed tulips (division 7) have flowers similar to those of the Single late group but with fringed petals; these make the flowers attractive when cut. The blooms appear on stems that are 20-26 in (50-65 cm) high. Plant the bulbs 6-8 in (15-20 cm) apart. Popular cultivars are 'Burgundy Lace' (wine-red) and 'Fringed Beauty' (red and yellow).

Viridiflora, or Green, tulips (division 8) are quite similar to

the Single late tulips, but the petals are partly green — a feature that particularly appeals to flower arrangers. The flowers appear in late spring on stems that are 10-20 in (25-50 cm) tall. Plant the bulbs 6-8 in (15-20 cm) apart. Some popular cultivars are 'Angel' (ivory-white and green), 'Artist' (apricot-pink and green), 'Greenland' (green, edged with

rose), and 'Spring Green' (lemon-yellow and green).

Parrot tulips (division 9) have large flowers with frilled and/or twisted petals. The often bicolored flowers open in mid- and late spring. The plants reach only 1½-2 ft (45-60 cm) high, but staking may be necessary as the stems are too weak to support the flowers. Plant the bulbs in a sheltered site 6-8 in (15-20 cm) apart. Popular cultivars are 'Black Parrot' (purple-black), 'Fantasy' (pink), 'Flaming Parrot' (yellow, flamed red), and 'Texas Flame' (buttercup-yellow, striped rose).

Double late tulips (division 10), sometimes called peony-flowered tulips, have large showy flowers, resembling peonies, in late spring. The plants reach 16-24 in (40-60 cm) high. They don't stand up well to wind and rain, so if the

Triumph 'Kees Nelis'

Lily-flowered 'China Pink'

Fosteriana 'Mme. Lefeber'

Kaufmanniana 'Heart's Delight'

Parrot 'Flaming Parrot'

Viridiflora 'Spring Green'

flowers are to complete their full course, they need a sheltered site. Plant these bulbs 6 in (15 cm) apart. Popular hybrids include 'Angelique' (pale pink), 'Gold Medal' (golden yellow), and 'Mount Tacoma' (white).

Kaufmanniana hybrids (division 11), also called water-lily tulips, have long, often bicolored flowers. They are the first species hybrids to flower, appearing in early spring. Only 4-10 in (10-25 cm) high, these tulips look best in rock gardens, in containers, or along the edges of borders. Plant the bulbs 4-6 in (10-15 cm) apart. Popular hybrids are 'Ancilla' (pink flamed with red outside; white with red throat inside), 'Heart's Delight' (carmine, white, and yellow), 'Johann Strauss' (red and white), and 'The First' (white tinted carmine).

Fosteriana hybrids (division 12) have large, long flowers from early spring to midspring. They stand 8-16 in (20-40 cm) high and, with their brilliant colors, make good tulips for focal points. Set these bulbs about 6 in (15 cm) apart. Popular hybrids include 'Cantata' (deep scarlet), Mme. Lefeber (red), 'Orange Emperor' (pure orange), 'Sweetheart' (lemon-yellow edged with white),

Double late 'Angelique'

'White Emperor' (white).

Greigii hybrids (division 13) have particularly colorful flowers in early spring to midspring, accompanied by maroon or purple-brown veined or spotted foliage. They may stand 6-18 in (15-45 cm) tall, but tend to be short, so they look best in rock gardens and containers. 'Cape Cod' (bronze-yellow and apricot), 'Corsage' (rose with yellow edging), 'Plaisir' (creamy white with red stripes), 'Red Riding Hood' (scarlet), and 'Toronto' (salmon-orange) are all popular.

Species tulips (division 14) tend to be smaller and more delicate in form than the garden tulips,

ranging from 4-18 in (10-45 cm) in height. Those listed are the most readily available species, though others are sometimes sold by specialist bulb growers.

Tulipa clusiana (lady tulip) has white, pointed petals flushed red in midspring. Its gray-green leaves are upright and very narrow. The plants reach 9-12 in (23-30 cm) high, and the bulbs should be planted 3 in (7.5 cm) apart. 'Cynthia' is red, tipped green.

Tulipa praestans has long red flowers with blunt petals in early spring and midspring. The plants reach 1-1½ ft (30-45 cm) high. Each stem carries between two and five flowers accompanied by broad gray-green leaves. Plant these bulbs 5-6 in (12-15 cm) apart. 'Fusilier' is a popular multiflowered cultivar; and 'Unicum' grows yellow-variegated leaves.

Tulipa tarda has white narrow-petaled flowers with yellow bases

Single late 'Sorbet'

174

Tulipa clusiana

in midspring. Up to five flowers
are carried in a cluster on each
stem, 4 in (10 cm) above ground.
The narrow midgreen leaves form
a rosette at flowering time. Plant
these bulbs 3 in (7.5 cm) apart.

Cultivation
Do not plant the bulbs of garden
tulips for bedding or informal
group plantings in borders in late
fall, as frost may damage early
growth. The soil should be well
drained and alkaline; if it's acid,
apply lime just before planting.
Set the bulbs 4-8 in (10-20 cm)
deep, depending on the type of
soil and the height of the cultivar.
Taller flowers must be planted
more deeply.

Deadhead as the first petals
fall, leaving the stems and leaves
intact to feed the bulb. Remove
any fallen petals from the ground,
as they may harbor disease.

It's best to lift the bulbs when
the leaves start turning yellow,
but if the site is needed for summer beds, lift the tulips earlier,
replant them in a spare corner,

Kaufmanniana 'Stresa'

and lift again when the leaves
have died down. Place the dormant bulbs in shallow boxes and
store in a dry shed.

Plant the bulbs of species and
Kaufmanniana tulips in early
winter, in well-drained soil in a
south-facing position, sheltered
from strong winds. Set the bulbs
4 in (10 cm) deep.

After flowering, remove the
leaves and stems as they die.
Leave the bulbs in the ground.

South of zone 8, tulips must be
grown as annuals. So-called pre-
cooled bulbs (bulbs that have
been kept in cold storage to fulfill
the bulbs' requirement for dormancy) should be purchased. Or
keep bulbs in the crisper drawer
of the refrigerator (do not let
bulbs freeze!) for 4-6 weeks before planting. Plant in early winter, toward the end of November,
for a late-winter bloom.

Propagation Remove offsets
when the bulbs are lifted. Store
the largest ones in a dry place at
61-65°F (16-18°C). Plant them in

late fall 4-6 in (10-15 cm) deep
and with a gap twice the width of
the offsets in between. They
should flower the next season.

Pests/diseases Stored bulbs may
be eaten by mice or infected with
bulb mites, which set the stage
for a fungal infection called blue
mold. Tulips are also susceptible
to cucumber mosaic virus, which
manifests itself as a yellow streak-
ing or spotting on the foliage. Fire
blight can cause scorched areas
on leaves and flowers, as well as
dwarfing of the whole plant.

Greigii 'Toronto'

ACKNOWLEDGMENTS

Photo credits
A-Z Botanical Collection 15(l), 78(tr), 83(bl), 110(r), 122(tl), 123(r), 128(r), 130(tr); Bernard Alfiera 91(b); Heather Angel 133(r); Pat Brindley 23(l), 37(r), 38, 40(br), 43(tl), 45(tr,br), 53(br), 54(r), 55(tr), 60, 160(bl), 161(cl), 166(r), 167(b), 169(r), 171(tr), 174(b), 175(tl,b); Brian Carter 18(tr), 20(l), 23(c), 27(r), 28(b), 30(b), 31(tl), 34(tr), 37(c), 40(tr), 48(r), 52(l), 53(tr), 66(l), 71(l,r), 72(l), 74(b), 75(tl), 85(t,bl), 87(l,c), 88(c), 108(tr), 110(l), 131(c), 133(l), 140(bl), 155(tl), 168(b), back cover; Michael Chinery 70(tl), 102(r); Eric Crichton, 14(l), 17(l), 21(l), 27(l), 46(r), 49(tr,br), 50(t), 51(l), 57(r), 61(br), 63(tl,tr), 64(l), 69(r), 72(r), 73(l), 78(b), 80(tr), 81(c,r), 89, 90, 91(tl,tr), 92(c), 97(r), 101(c), 103(br), 104(r), 105(r), 106, 107(t), 114, 116–18, 125(br), 132(b); Arnaud Descat 11(b), 36(r), 37(l), 131(tr), 140(tl), 141(r), 167(tr); EWA (Jerry Harpur), 13; Derek Fell 28(tr), 29(tl), 43(tr), 63(b), 84(tr), 108(tl), 124(tr), 125(tl), 127(t), 131(b), 144(tl), 156(tl), 173(bl), 175(tr); Philippe Ferret 15(c), 18(b), 52(r), 53(l), 59(l), 61(l), 169(l); Garden Picture Library (Lyn Brotchie) 8, (Brian Carter) 93(tl), 116, 140(tr), (Marijke Heuff) 115(t); John Glover front cover, 112; Derek Gould 33(r), 43(bl), 56, 86(tl), 87(r), 95(b), 99(br); Diane Grenfell 124(b); Rob Herwig 155(b), 156(tr), 160(tl,tr), 161(t), 168(tr), 171(b), 172(tr), 174(c); Neil Holmes 34(tl), 100(b); Jacqui Hurst 137(tr), 142(l); Lamontagne 18(tl), 31(tr,b), 44(t,b), 61(tr), 62(tl,tr), 68(b), 80(tl), 84(tl), 94(r), 107(b), 118(tl,tr), 119, 120(tl,tr), 121, 122(tr), 126(tl,bl), 128(l), 130(b), 134(tr), 142(r), 148(tr), 150(tl,b), 152(tl,tr), 153, 154(r), 155(tr), 156(c,b), 157(br), 158(l), 162(tr), 167(tl), 168(tl), 172(b), 173(t), 174(tr); Andrew Lawson 82(l), 83(t), 86(b), 172(tl), 173(br); George Leveque 67(r), 129(tr); S. and O. Mathews 11(t), 24, 34(b), 98(l), 148(tl), 159(tr), 164(l); Peter McHoy 26(r), 48(l), 72(c); Tania Midgley 10, 12–13, 16(br), 19(r), 20(r), 36(l), 41(br), 50(b), 58(l), 74(t), 79(t), 82(r), 92(r), 96(l), 103(bl), 109(tl,tr), 111(b), 120(b), 170(l); Clive Nichols 2–5; Philippe Perdereau/Brigitte Thomas 129(b); Photo Nats (Robert E. Lyons) 88(tl), 147(l); (Ann Reilly) 14(tr), 88(tr), 100(tl), 108(b), 111(t); Photos Horticultural, 6–7, 16(l), 21(r), 23(r), 25(b), 26(l), 28(tl), 30(l), 32, 33(l), 46(l), 47, 49(l), 51(r), 54(l), 55(l), 58(c,r), 59(r), 62(b), 64(r), 65, 66(r), 67(l), 68(t), 69(l), 75(b), 77(tl,tr), 78(tl), 79(b), 81(l), 84(b), 86(tr), 88(b), 97(l), 99(l,tr), 100(r), 102(l), 109(b), 115(b), 118(b), 126(r), 132(tr), 134(tl,b), 135, 136, 137(tl,b), 138, 139(r), 143(tl), 145(r), 146(tl,tr), 148(b), 149(tr,br), 150(r), 151(r), 152(b), 159(tl), 161(bl,br), 162(b), 163, 164(r), 165(tl,b), 166(l), 174(tl); Positive Images (Jerry Howard) 157(t), (Michael Miller) 157(bl); Annette Schreiner 129(tl), 141(l); Harry Smith Collection 15(r), 16(tr), 17(r), 19(l), 22, 25(tl,tr), 26(c), 29(r), 30(r), 35(r), 39, 40(tl), 41(tl,tr), 42, 43(br), 45(l), 55(br), 70(tr,b), 73(r), 75(tr), 76, 77(b), 80(b), 83(br), 85(br), 92(l), 93(tr,b), 94(l), 95(tl,tr), 96(r), 98(r), 101(l,r), 103(t), 104(l), 105(l), 122(b), 124(tl), 125(tr), 127(b), 130(tl), 132(tl), 139(l), 143(tr,b), 144(tr,b), 145(l,c), 146(b), 147(r), 148(c), 149(l), 151(tl,b), 154(l), 170(r), 171(tl); Thompson and Morgan 131(tl); D. Woodland 123(r)

Illustrations
All illustrations are © Reader's Digest.